The Spanish Armada

A Campaign in Context

THE SPANISH ARMADA

A CAMPAIGN IN CONTEXT

by

Rupert Matthews

SPELLMOUNT

First published 2009
Spellmount
The History Press
The Mill, Brimscombe Port
Stroud, Gloucestershire, GL5 2QG
www.thehistorypress.co.uk

British Library Cataloguing in Publication Data.
A catalogue record for this book is available from the British Library.

ISBN 978 0 7524 5365 1

Printed in Great Britain

Contents

Introduction: The Armada Legend

The Spanish Armada of 1588 was passing into legend even before the last ships of the ill-fated fleet struggled back to Spain. It suited the propaganda purposes of England's Queen Elizabeth to claim divine assistance, so it was put about that 'God blew, and they were scattered'.

Thereafter the myth makers and balladeers got to work with a will. Incidents were romanticised, invented or forgotten. Individuals were raised to the status of hero by storytellers and historians, while those less lucky were written off as cowards or blamed for the faults of others. Within just a few years, the general public across Europe had been presented with dozens of written versions of the story of the campaign, most of which had been written with a clear political motive which pushed truth and accuracy out of the way.

In the decades that followed other myths and legends grew up. Among the more persistent of these was the idea that the English ships had been smaller and less well armed than the vast Spanish galleons of the Armada. In fact, the largest ship in the campaign had been English, while it was the guns of the English ships that were the more effective and which did much to win the campaign for England. Yet there was an underlying truth in the myth – the English ships had generally been smaller and were certainly less impressive to look at.

Another legend that began early was the story of Drake playing a game of bowls. According to the story as it was most often told, Drake and Lord Howard of Effingham were in Plymouth with the English fleet awaiting news of the Spanish Armada in July. With nothing much to do but kick their heels, the senior officers went up to Plymouth Hoe, a broad grassy hill just outside the town, to play a game of bowls. As they were playing, a messenger raced up to announce that the dreaded Armada had been sighted, and that it was closer than expected. The ships' captains, senior commanders and even Lord Howard began to dash about in a panic, sending out orders and then countermanding them in their haste to get to sea. Drake's voice then boomed out calling on them for silence. The agitated mob turned about to see Drake calmly taking up his stance to bowl his ball; 'There is time to finish our game and beat the Spaniards too', said Drake. Instantly the hubbub was calmed and the game went on even as the Spanish masts came up over the horizon. As we shall see, this particular legend did have a basis in fact.

Then there was the story of Drake's Drum. Sir Francis Drake was the great English naval hero of the age. Like all sea captains of the time his ship had a drum which was used to beat out alerts, dismissals and orders to the ship's crew; each order having its own distinctive combination of beats, rolls and silences that were known to all on board. According to legend, as Drake lay dying in the Caribbean he ordered that his drum should be taken back to England. If ever the Spanish ships came up over the horizon the drum should be beaten with the call to battle, said Drake, and then he would come down from Heaven to join the battle against the hated invaders. There has never been the occasion to beat it, so nobody knows if Drake really would come back to save the kingdom.

The drum, painted with Drake's coat of arms, is now kept in a glass case at his old home of Buckland Abbey where anyone who pays the entrance fee can see it. A variant on the legend has it that the drum will beat itself if danger ever threatens England.

In the nineteenth century, when Britain's Royal Navy was the largest and most powerful battle fleet the world had ever seen, the fight against the Armada was thought of as the occasion of zits founding. Tactics were said to have been used by the English that did not come into operation until a century or so later. Almost superhuman feats of gunnery and seamanship were ascribed to the English mariners for which there was no documentary evidence.

During the twentieth century, the tale of the Armada campaign underwent a fresh bout of myth making. This time the vast empire of Spain was likened to that of Nazi Germany. Philip's desire to conquer England was compared with Hitler's projected invasion of Britain. The seamen of the English fleet blurred with the gallant fighter pilots of the RAF who faced the Luftwaffe in the summer of 1940.

Nowhere was this version of the Armada campaign epitomised better than in the magnificent 1940 movie *The Sea Hawk* starring Errol Flynn as a Drake-type character and Claude Rains as the silkily menacing Spanish ambassador. In one memorable scene, King Philip II of Spain, played by Montagu Love, is instructing his generals on the conquest of Britain while his shadow moves across a map of the world on the wall behind him to engulf North America. The film is available on DVD and although it contains much that is apocryphal or inaccurate, the battle scenes do capture much of the flavour of the times. I myself was brought up on these various versions of the Armada story, learning about the game of bowls at school and going to Buckland Abbey as a boy to gaze in awe at Drake's Drum.

In recent years it has become possible to get behind the myths and legends to learn rather more about the Armada campaign as it was actually fought. Underwater archaeology has turned up dozens of wrecks. The most spectacular was the *Mary Rose*, a warship that sank some decades before the Armada set sail, but other wrecks have yielded guns, ammunition, coins, jewellery, plates, pots and weapons of all kinds.

Using the information from these artefacts, it is possible to read the contemporary letters, eyewitness statements and other documentation that has survived with a fresh perspective. Opinions and events that were previously baffling make more sense now that we have actual examples of Armada guns to handle. Feats of seamanship that seemed bizarre are perfectly understandable now that we know more about the abilities of sixteenth century ships.

It is time to look again at the campaign of the Spanish Armada and to put it in context.

Cast of Characters

When dealing with a campaign as complex as that of the Spanish Armada it can be easy to lose track of who is who. Some figures enter the story and stay throughout, others appear only once, but most confusing are those who come and go. To help readers sort out who is who, I supply this cast of characters to refer to as the tale unfolds.

Don Francisco de Bobadilla	Spanish soldier and highly experienced commander. During the Armada campaign he served as military adviser to the Duke of Medina Sidonia.
William Borlas	English diplomat. Was acting as liaison officer with the Dutch rebels during 1588.
Lord Burghley, Thomas Cecil	English statesman. Chief Secretary of State from 1558 to 1598. During the Armada campaign he stayed in London attending to paperwork and funds.
Pedro Coco Calderon	Spanish bureaucrat. In 1588 was acting as the chief accountant to the Armada. He later wrote a report on the campaign.
Sir George Carey	English soldier. Commander of the garrison on the Isle of Wight during the Armada campaign.
Captain Francisco Cuellar	Spanish sea captain. During the ill-fated Armada campaign

he commanded the galleon *San Pedro*. He was wrecked on the Irish coast escaped to Scotland and later wrote a detailed account of his adventures.

Sir Edward Denny | English soldier. Commanded the English garrison in Tralee, County Kerry in 1588.

Lady Denny | English gentlewoman. Wife of Sir Edward Denny and acted in his place when he was away from Kerry as the first Spanish ships were wrecked on the Irish coast.

Sir Francis Drake | English sailor born of humble parents in Devon. Through hard work and skill he worked his way up through the ranks of professional seamen and through social ranks ashore to become a knight and the most feared fighting seaman of his age. In 1588 he commanded the English warships based at Plymouth and was appointed deputy to Lord Howard of Effingham for the duration of the Armada campaign.

Elizabeth I, Queen of England | Came to the throne in 1558. She was a Protestant who tried to find a moderate religious policy that would satisfy all but the extremist Protestants and Catholics. She was famously careful with money and understood the financial side of government and international trade better than most rulers of her time. In 1588 she stayed mostly in London, supervising the business of government while her commanders ran the campaign.

Don Diego Enriquez	Spanish soldier who sailed on the *Lavia*. He was known as the 'Hunchback General' due to his bent spine.
Esquival	Spanish sailor, held the rank of ensign in 1588 and commanded a *patache* sent on various missions by the Duke of Medina Sidonia.
Pedro Estrade	Spanish soldier, who in 1588 sailed in the *San Marcos* and later wrote an account of the campaign.
Thomas Fenner	English seaman and follower of Sir Francis Drake, in 1588 he commanded the *Nonpareil*.
Thomas Fleming	English sailor, who in 1588 commanded his own private ship, the *Bark Fleming*.
Sir Martin Frobisher	English seaman and explorer, who had led several voyages to the Arctic in an effort to find a trade route to China. He discovered Frobisher Bay and it is named in his honour. In 1588 he commanded the *Triumph* and led a squadron of the English fleet.
Sir William Fitzwilliam	English soldier, was Lord Deputy of Ireland in 1588. He feared a Spanish invasion and gave orders that all Spaniards who landed in Ireland were to be killed.
Federigo Giambelli	Italian military engineer who gained fame as the inventor of the 'hellburner', a form of floating mine. In 1588 he was working to improve the defences around London and along the Thames Estuary.
Seigneur de Gourdan, Girault de Mauleon	French soldier and bureaucrat, the governor of the city and port of Calais in 1588.

John Hawkins	English sailor, merchant and bureaucrat. Earned a fortune in trade as a young man before entering royal service to improve and maintain the royal navy. In 1588 he commanded the *Victory* and led a squadron in the English fleet.
Lord Howard of Effingham	English diplomat, soldier and seaman, was chosen to command the English fleet during the Armada campaign. He commanded the *Ark Royal* and led a squadron of the fleet as well as maintaining overall command of the entire English Navy.
Thomas Howard	English nobleman and the brother of Lord Howard; in 1588 he commanded the *Golden Lion*.
Earl of Leicester, Robert Dudley	English nobleman, soldier and diplomat, was an old friend and long time supporter of Queen Elizabeth. In 1588 he was in command of the English land forces defending the kingdom, and led the main army that gathered at Tilbury.
Don Alonso de Leyva	Spanish admiral. An experienced and competent commander, who in 1588 commanded the regiment of cavalry from Milan which was being transported in the Armada. He was the most senior army officer in the Armada and had been appointed to take over the Armada if Medina Sidonia died or became otherwise unfit for duty.
Don Alonso de Luzon	Spanish soldier, he commanded one of the Italian infantry regiments embarked in the Armada for service in England.

Don Jorge Manrique — Spanish soldier, who in 1588 was appointed Inspector General of the Armada, bearing overall responsibility for the supply and equipment of the fleet.

Mary, Queen of Scots — was the dethroned monarch of Scotland who was, in Catholic eyes, the legal heir to the throne of England. Her execution in 1587 provoked King Philip of Spain to send the Armada to invade England.

Duke of Medina Sidonia — Spanish soldier, nobleman and diplomat, was appointed to command the Spanish Armada in 1588 despite the fact that he had no experience as a naval commander.

Don Bernadino de Mendoza — Spanish diplomat, in 1588 was the Spanish ambassador in Paris.

Don Hugo de Moncada — Spanish admiral, was in command of the four galleasses during the Armada campaign.

Miguel de Oquendo — Spanish admiral, was commanding the *Santa Ana* and leading the Squadron of Guipuzcoa during the Armada campaign.

Duke of Parma, Alexander Farnese — Spanish-Italian soldier and statesman, and the nephew of King Philip of Spain. In 1588 he was Spanish governor of the Netherlands in the process of fighting a long war against the Dutch Protestant rebels trying to overthrow Spanish rule. He was commander of the Spanish Army intended to invade England in conjunction with the Armada.

Philip II, King of Spain — The richest and most powerful monarch in the world. In 1588 he remained at his palace-headquar-

	ters complex of El Escorial near Madrid.
Don Diego de Pimental	Spanish soldier, commander of a regiment of Spanish infantry embarked on the Armada. He sailed on the *San Mateo*.
Amyas Preston	English bureaucrat, served as secretary to Lord Howard in 1588.
Sir Walter Raleigh	English courtier and soldier, served on land in 1588 organising the supply of the English fleet.
Juan Martinez de Recalde	Spanish admiral, was one of the older and more experienced of the Spanish officers. In 1588 he commanded the *Santa Ana* and led the Squadron of Biscay.
Marquis of Santa Cruz	Spanish admiral, was the original commander of the Armada, but died before the fleet set sail.
Lord Henry Seymour	English admiral, was a well connected nobleman and competent seaman who in 1588 commanded the English squadron patrolling the Straits of Dover and coast of Flanders.
Richard Thomson	English seaman, served in the private warship *Margaret and John* during the Armada campaign and later wrote an account of his experiences.
Don Francisco de Toledo	Spanish soldier, commanded a regiment of Spanish infantry embarked in the Armada. He sailed in the *San Felipe*.
Don Pedro de Valdes	Spanish admiral, was the captain of the *Nuestra Senora del Rosario* and commander of the Squadron of Andalusia.
Diego Flores de Valdes	Spanish admiral, who in 1588 was appointed commander of the Armada of Castile, but before

	the Armada set sail transferred to the fleet flagship to serve as naval adviser to the Duke of Medina Sidonia.
Sir Francis Walsingham	English courtier and bureaucrat, was born of relatively humble parents, but rapidly rose as a government official through talent and hard work. In 1588 he served on the Privy Council, was a trusted adviser to Elizabeth I and ran a highly efficient network of spies spread across Europe.
Sir William Winter	English admiral, came from a distinguished naval family. In 1588 he commanded a squadron under Seymour which patrolled the Flanders coast and escorted English merchant ships to German ports.

I

Seeds of War

With hindsight, war between England and Spain became inevitable at lunchtime on 22 September 1568 when a Spanish nobleman pulled a dagger on an English seaman as the two were sharing a meal of bread and salted fish in the harbour of San Juan de Ullua in the Caribbean. The move was the opening blow in a short but savage fight that had international repercussions and drove the two nations towards war. The dagger strike was itself the culmination of years of distrust, hostility and misunderstandings. Until then, however, the men of both nations had kept their weapons sheathed. It was the spilling of blood on that bright sunny day in 1568 that changed everything.

In some ways the conflict came as something of a surprise. England and Spain had been traditional allies for generations. The hostility that both nations had against France ensured that they had much in common and much to gain from friendship and alliance. Spanish princesses were regular brides for English princes, and as recently as 1554 Queen Mary of England had married a Spanish prince, the future Philip II.

But even as young Philip stepped ashore in England to greet his bride, the problems were starting. Spain, and Philip, were staunch champions of the Catholic faith and of the supremacy of the papacy. Increasing numbers of Mary's English subjects, however, were turning to the new Protestant version of the Christian religion. Unrest broke out against the marriage; in Kent there was even an armed rebellion that was put down with difficulty. Mary was forced to agree to exclude her new husband from all affairs of state and government meetings. When Mary began a bloody persecution of those clergy who refused to submit to papal authority, her foreign husband got some of the blame. Mary died childless in 1558 and the throne passed to her sister Elizabeth.

Philip was by this time King Philip II of Spain. He ruled not only Spain, but also the Netherlands, parts of Italy and the vastly wealthy Spanish territories in the Americas. The political reasons for an alliance with England remained, so he proposed marriage to the newly-crowned Elizabeth. She kept him hanging on for a while without giving a firm answer, but Philip was not one to dally. In 1559 he dropped the idea of an English alliance and instead married Isabella, daughter of King Henri II of France.

The alliance of France with both the Spanish Hapsburgs in the shape of Philip II and the Austrian branch of the Hapsburgs, led by Holy Roman Emperor Ferdinand I, brought years of comparative peace to Europe. The alliance turned its might against the Moslem Ottoman Empire. In 1571 an allied fleet of Mediterranean Christian states crushed the powerful Ottoman fleet at the Battle of Lepanto. Thereafter, Philip's ambitions were for a while played out in the Mediterranean as his fleet came to dominate much of the sea, and his merchants became prosperous on the newly secure trade routes.

Meanwhile, trouble was brewing in northern Europe. Philip had inherited the Netherlands, but apart from spending a few months there in his youth he had had little to do with them. At this time the Low Countries were more industrialised than almost any other part of Europe. The textile industry and its trade routes were making the previously poor agricultural region both wealthy and confident. This made them different from other Hapsburg lands which still gained their wealth from more traditional agricultural sources, or in the case of the Americas from gold and silver mines.

Philip's governor in the Netherlands at this time was his illegitimate sister Margaret, to whom he had given the Duchy of Parma in Italy. She loyally imposed taxes to pay for Philip's wars in the Mediterranean, but did so without any regard for the unique economy of the area. The taxes were deeply unpopular. What made it worse for the Netherlanders was the fact that many of them were taking up the Protestant faith, but Philip insisted that some of their tax money had to go to Rome. In 1566, a deputation of Netherlands noblemen went to see Duchess Margaret with a long list of grievances about taxation and religion. The meeting was tempestuous, and Margaret stormed out. As she did so a courtier asked her: 'What, Madam, you flee from these beggars?' Thereafter the protesters adopted a begging bowl as their symbol.

In 1572 the simmering discontent in the Netherlands broke out into open rebellion. The Beggars, as the rebels were known, seized the city of Brielle as a base and within two years had driven the reach of Philip's government south of the Scheldt. What had begun as a protest movement, had by the mid-1570s become a war for national liberation, fuelled by increasingly bitter religious divisions.

The Dutch rebellion put England's Queen Elizabeth in something of a quandary. She had imposed on her kingdom a religious settlement that placed relatively few duties on her subjects. Only the most extreme Catholics and Protestants were unhappy. By this date, most people in England were moderate Protestants who were only too glad that the increasingly bitter religious wars abroad had passed England by. Sympathy in England was with the Dutch rebels, for both religious and economic reasons. The Dutch rebels were Protestants, and much English wealth was earned exporting wool to the Netherlands.

It was commercial disputes that led to the incident at San Juan de Ullua. Philip had decided that the Spanish territorial possessions in the New World were so important to his government that they should be ruled with a firm hand. This bore down heavily not only with the indigenous population, but also on the Spanish merchants who had settled in the area. They were no longer allowed to trade with English, Scots, French or other foreign merchants. In future all trade was to be conducted with Spanish merchants in Spanish ships operating out of Spanish ports.

Once again, Philip was showing a lack of knowledge of how trade prospered. Not only did the new rules drastically limit the growing prosperity of his lands, but they put an impossible burden on the merchants. There were simply not enough Spanish ships in existence to carry all the trade goods that were available. The situation was made even worse by Philip's occasional commandeering of ships for the use of his government, fleet or army.

In response, the Spanish merchants and settlers in the New World developed an illicit trade carried on through a loophole in Philip's new rules. Trade embargoes of this type were a common tool of diplomacy in the sixteenth century. It was generally understood that individual mariners should not suffer as a result of international disagreements. If a ship were damaged by storm or accident it would be allowed into an embargoed port to undertake repairs, and if the captain did not have enough ready cash on him to pay for those repairs he would be allowed to undertake limited selling of goods to raise just enough money to pay the bills.

The Spanish settlers in the New World and the foreign merchants wishing to trade with them soon learned to exploit this loophole. A foreign captain would put into a Spanish port declaring that it needed to make repairs or buy supplies. As he did not have any cash, he would need to trade and the local Spanish reluctantly agreed out of concern for his plight. Of course, the ruse was undertaken merely so that the goods could be unloaded and traded in the normal way.

One English seafarer who was earning a healthy living out of this sort of subterfuge was John Hawkins. Born in Plymouth in 1532, Hawkins took over his father's merchant business at the age of 23. He made numerous voyages to France, Spain, Portugal and the Canaries before in 1562 he led a fleet of three small merchant ships to trade along the coast of Brazil, then owned by Portugal, and the Spanish colonies in the Caribbean.

On this and a second voyage across the Atlantic in 1565, Hawkins found that the greatest profits were to be made transporting slaves from Africa to the Spanish colonies. At this date there was nothing wrong with trading in slaves. Criminals were often condemned to slavery as a humane alternative to death, and prisoners of war might find themselves similarly enslaved if their own government refused to pay ransom for them. Slaves could be bought almost anywhere, but they were most plentiful and cheapest in western Africa.

On his second voyage, Hawkins had accepted investment from other merchants to boost the number of ships involved, though he maintained command for himself. On the third voyage that left England in October 1567 he did the same. This time one of the investors was Queen Elizabeth herself. She sent two ships, the large Baltic trader *Jesus of Lubeck* of 500 tons and the *Minion* of 300 tons. The small fleet also included three private merchant ships, the *William and John*, the *Swallow* and the *Angel*. Hawkins also took a 50-ton craft named the *Judith*. He gave command of this small ship to a distant cousin who although only 24 years old was showing great promise as a seaman: Francis Drake.

Hawkins' ships were merchant vessels equipped, as was then customary, with a few heavy guns to ward off any passing ship which might attack. The men, of course, were equipped with armour, swords, pistols and other hand guns. The *Jesus of Lubeck* had been converted to a more warlike state some 25 years earlier when she was bought by King Henry VIII, but how much of her weaponry was still aboard in 1567 is unknown. In any case this was a trading expedition, not a military campaign.

Hawkins cruised down to Sierra Leone where he struck a bargain with a local ruler. Hawkins would land men armed with guns to help the chieftain attack a neighbouring tribe. In return Hawkins would get any slaves that were captured. Almost 500 slaves were taken and Hawkins set off to cross the Atlantic. Once in the Caribbean, Hawkins unsurprisingly found that his ships were 'in need of repair'. He called at a number of ports in most of which he was allowed to trade. On 16 September the little fleet was welcomed at San Juan de Ullua.

Unknown to either Hawkins or the Spaniards in San Juan, however, King Philip had decided to crack down on the illicit trading by foreign ships in his colonies. The man he chose for the job was Don Martin Enriquez, who he appointed Viceroy of Mexico. Enriquez was sent off to Mexico aboard a fleet of thirteen warships commanded by Don Francisco de Luxan. It was sheer bad luck that Luxan's fleet reached San Juan de Ullua two days after Hawkins arrived.

Hawkins was understandably nervous when he saw the new arrivals. He sent a messenger out to greet Enriquez and to explain that the English ships were suffering from storm damage, were undertaking repairs and would leave as soon as these were complete. Enriquez hesitated, then agreed. He even gave Hawkins permission to sell a few slaves to pay for the repairs. Next day, de Luxan led his ships into the harbour and demanded that Hawkins vacate the prime berths, which he agreed to do.

Over the next two days Hawkins and his captains made a show of taking down old sails and replacing them with new ones, undertaking assorted carpentry and painting jobs as if repairing damage. The slaves were landed ready for sale, but an auction could not be organised, Enriquez explained, for a couple of days. Spanish gentlemen came over to pay polite visits to the English ships, and the English gentlemen returned the courtesy.

Hawkins, however, was not happy. He knew that he was breaking Spanish law and did not believe that the new Viceroy would let him leave San Juan de Ullua easily. At dawn on 22 September an English sailor reported to Hawkins that during the night he had seen large numbers of men climbing aboard the Spanish ship that lay closest to the *Jesus of Lubeck*. Hawkins eyed the ship warily. There seemed to be nothing unusual about her. A report came in from another English ship making a similar allegation about another Spanish ship.

Hawkins issued orders to be ready for trouble, then sent a Spanish-speaking gentleman off to find Enriquez to ask about the slave sale. The man had instructions to have a good look around on shore for signs of anything untoward. Then a Spanish harbour official arrived with questions for Hawkins and a couple of Spanish gentlemen arrived to pay a visit. Hawkins suggested that they should have lunch. After a final glance around the harbour, Hawkins followed his guests down to the cabin. He beckoned a couple of burly sailors to come down to act as servants at table; it was as well that he did.

Just after noon a trumpet blast sounded harshly from the dockside. That was when one of the Spanish gentlemen pulled out a dagger and lunged at Hawkins. Hawkins punched him aside, and the sailors piled in to overpower the Spaniards. Hawkins ran up on deck as the ominous sound of cannon fire boomed out. Spanish guns from on shore were firing on the *Jesus of Lubeck* while armed men were swarming aboard the *Swallow* and *Angel*. The Spanish warships were now moving out from their moorings and opening fire on the English ships.

Hawkins got his guns into action and had soon inflicted severe damage on de Luxon's flagship. A few minutes later the *Angel* went down and the *Swallow* was captured. The Spanish warships warped round to concentrate their fire on the *Jesus of Lubeck*. A crewman was hurrying around serving beer and handed a cup to Hawkins. Hawkins drank a mouthful, then put the beer mug down on a rail while he bellowed orders. A Spanish cannonball instantly blew rail and cup away, missing Hawkins by inches. Hawkins eyed the smashed rail. 'God who hath preserved me from this shot will also deliver us from these traitors and villains,' he muttered. It was not to be.

The foremast of the *Jesus of Lubeck* came crashing down. Hawkins realised that he could not win. He ordered the *Minion* to come alongside and leapt aboard. The surviving crew of the *Jesus* followed, but then the Spaniards surged on board and the *Minion* captain cast loose. Together with Drake's *Judith* the *Minion* put to sea. The two vessels hurriedly transferred men and supplies so that each had a roughly equal share, then they set sail for Plymouth. Drake arrived first on 20 January, Hawkins five days later. The news of the wholesale bloodshed at San Juan de Ullua spread across England like wildfire.

By chance, four Spanish ships were in Southampton on the day the news arrived from Plymouth. On board the ships was 450,000 gold ducats and 59 chests of silver coin, forming six months of pay for the Spanish troops fighting in the Netherlands. The port governor promptly impounded the lot. Elizabeth approved and confirmed his order. The Spanish ambassador in England, Don Guerau de Spes objected, but was ignored. He then sent a message to the new Spanish governor of the Netherlands, the Duke of Alba, telling him what had happened. Alba arrested every English person he could find and confiscated all their property. Elizabeth retaliated in kind.

Over the months that followed the diplomats slowly worked out a compromise. Alba and Elizabeth released their prisoners and their property. Philip agreed that Enriquez had overstepped the mark by opening fire without warning, and agreed that Elizabeth, Hawkins and their investors were due compensation to be taken from the treasure impounded at Southampton. But the men captured by Enriquez were to stand trial for smuggling. They were all found guilty and imprisoned.

Hawkins was not content and was determined to get his surviving men freed. He let it be known that he wanted to continue trading with the Americas, but this time would do so legally. Spes invited Hawkins to dine. Hawkins let slip that he had quarrelled badly with Elizabeth over the affair and was considering moving abroad if he could find an employer. No need for that, answered the silky Spes who hinted that a generous employer might not be too far off. Spes knew the value of having a senior but disgruntled man as a friend.

In England at this time was an Italian banker named Roberto Ridolfi. Ridolfi specialised in doing business with English Catholics and had become convinced that some of them were deeply unhappy with the Protestant regime of Elizabeth. Handily for Ridolfi there was an alternative to Elizabeth. Mary Queen of Scots had been defeated in a civil war and forced to abdicate her Scottish crown. In 1567 she had escaped imprisonment and fled over the border to England where she hoped that Elizabeth would restore her to her crown. Elizabeth, however, actually favoured the rebel lords who had put Mary's infant son James VI on the throne. Mary found herself in comfortable but nonetheless secure imprisonment in England.

The situation was made more complex by the fact that Mary was a great granddaughter of England's King Henry VII. This made her next in line to the English throne after Elizabeth herself. More importantly, the marriage of Henry VIII to Elizabeth's mother, Anne Boleyn, had never been recognised by the Pope. So far as Catholics were concerned Elizabeth was illegitimate, which made Mary of Scots the true Queen of England. It therefore suited Elizabeth to have Mary under her control. But quite what to do with her was a problem.

There had already been some abortive plots to murder Elizabeth and put Mary on the throne of England by the time Ridolfi arrived on the scene. There had also been more legitimate moves, led by the Duke of Norfolk, to have Mary treated as befitted the heir to the throne.

Ridolfi got in touch with Norfolk and other Catholics as well as with the Bishop of Ross, Scotland's ambassador in England, through whom he made contact with Mary. On a trip to the continent, Ridolfi gained an introduction to Alba. On his return to England the banker held talks with Spes. By this time, the summer of 1570, Ridofli's plot had reached a turning point.

The Duke of Norfolk, an astonishingly rich man, had agreed to fund a rebellion. Other Catholic lords had agreed to join once Norfolk declared himself, and between them estimated that they could raise around 20,000 men. Lord Lumley had agreed to organise the murder of Elizabeth and her leading courtiers. Alba had said that he could spare 8,000 fully trained mercenaries from his campaign in the Netherlands for six months to invade England, but only if King Philip agreed. The Pope had promised to provide funds and to absolve of guilt all involved. The only outstanding problem was how to get Alba's men across the Channel to England. Spes at once thought of the disgruntled Hawkins and all the merchant ships that he had at his command.

Spes was in regular social contact with Hawkins, whose disillusionment with Elizabeth and Protestantism seemed to be getting greater by the day. Without mentioning details, Spes broached the subject to Hawkins. Could Hawkins transport mercenaries from the Netherlands to some undisclosed point? Hawkins readily agreed that his ships were suitable for shipping large number of men and horses, provided that the voyage would not be too long. He said that as well as cash payment he wanted all the men captured at San Juan set free. Over the course of several meetings the details were thrashed out. Hawkins guessed that the movement of men was to invade England; Spes confirmed it. Hawkins agreed to ship the men across the Channel, saying that he could wait for his money, but he needed his men immediately.

Delighted, Spes and Ridolfi worked out the plans in detail, Ridolfi setting off for Madrid to get Philip's backing for the plan. Philip was on the point of agreeing, when a message arrived from Alba. The Duke had been worrying about how he was supposed to get his men over the Channel. When he heard that Hawkins was going to ship them over, he was aghast. He dashed off a letter to King Philip advising him to have nothing to do with the plan: Hawkins could not be trusted.

Philip weighed the evidence and chose to go ahead. Orders were sent to Alba ordering him to muster his troops, verbal messages were carried to Norfolk telling him get ready. Ridolfi was sent back to Italy to get the promised cash from the Pope and the invasion was set for spring 1571. Hawkins was told to get his ships ready and Philip sent orders to release all of Hawkins's men. As soon as the sailors were free they lost no time getting out of Spanish territory by any means possible.

Once the freed seafarers were out of Philip's grasp the trap was sprung. From the very first time he had met Spes, Hawkins had been secretly working for Elizabeth. His playacting at being disgruntled had been a charade designed to flush out any incipient Spanish plot – and it had worked. Elizabeth's chief minister, William Cecil Lord Burleigh, had been infiltrating the conspiracy ever since Hawkins had told him of it. Now he went to Elizabeth who gave orders for the conspirators to be arrested. Spes was expelled from England, as was Ross. Norfolk was put on trial and executed along with a few others. Those on the margins of the plot were fined, imprisoned or watched.

Mary herself denied all knowledge of the plot. The only evidence against her was that she had once met Ridolfi. Elizabeth refused to put Mary on trial on such slender evidence, but did order that the security around the imprisoned queen should be tightened up. Burleigh, however, was convinced of Mary's guilt. He decided that if any future plot were to be revealed he would not move to arrest the conspirators until he had in his hands irrefutable evidence that Mary was plotting to murder Elizabeth.

There was no such doubt as to the involvement of Spain in the plot. Alba, Spes and Philip himself had all been proved to have been active supporters of the move to assassinate Elizabeth and replace her with Mary. Relations between England and Spain predictably hit a new low. Elizabeth was desperate to avoid war. Compared to Spain's vast empire, England was a small nation without much in the way of wealth or manpower to conduct a long war. She decided to endure the plots and insults from Spain.

If Elizabeth was content to endure, Francis Drake was not. He had lost financially at San Juan de Ullua, he had seen friends mown down by Spanish guns and he had drawn the lesson that Spain was his enemy. He had set out to exact revenge. He began in 1570 when he sailed a small ship to cruise the Caribbean, spying out the land and waters. He landed frequently to talk to local tribesmen who were only too happy to tell him all they knew about the Spanish military dispositions.

In 1573 he went back to the Caribbean with two small ships. For months he roamed the area playing havoc with the Spanish. He stopped ships on the high seas, emptied them of their cargoes and anything of value. Some ships he burned, others he kept as prizes. He attacked and looted entire cities. Always, however, Drake was careful to avoid unnecessary bloodshed. The crews of captured ships were always put safely ashore, though in remote places so that it would take them days to walk to the nearest Spanish settlement and raise the alarm. Drake was out to get revenge on the King of Spain, not on his subjects, and wanted to hit Philip where it hurt – in the treasury. He executed this with astonishing thoroughness.

What amazed the Spaniards, and Drake's own men, was his almost uncanny knack for knowing where to go and what to do. It was soon rumoured by the Spanish that he had a magical mirror in his cabin that showed him the location of every Spanish ship at any given moment. Not long after that rumour came a second, that the Devil blew in Drake's sails to give his ships extra speed. By the time Drake left the Caribbean with £40,000 in loot he had acquired a new name. The Spaniards no longer called him Drake but *El Draque* – the Dragon.

Where Drake had led, others followed. Gilbert Horseley of Plymouth took a ship to the Caribbean in 1574 and came back with £2,000 of stolen Spanish treasures. At a time when a skilled workman was lucky to earn £8 a year these were colossal sums of money. By the end of the 1570s there was not a year went by without at least two English ships plundering the Caribbean. Philip was forced to send warships to guard his colonies and trade routes. He protested repeatedly to Elizabeth, but she gave him only fair words in return.

By then Drake had bigger plans. The Caribbean was getting too crowded both with other English raiders and with Spanish defences. Drake decided to go to the Pacific coast of the Americas. The Spanish towns along that coast were quite unprotected, while the shipping was composed almost exclusively of merchant ships with few warships to guard them.

Spanish complacency was due to the fact that only one European expedition had ever sailed from the Atlantic to the Pacific: that of Ferdinand Magellan in 1519. The Magellan Straits were known to be dangerous, treacherous and beset by terrible weather. Magellan had suffered such privations on the trip that the Spanish colonists simply refused to sail ships through the Straits and instead built ships on the Pacific coast of Mexico and South America. At this date it was not known how far south of the Magellan Straits the continent of South America continued, and given the awful weather and dangerous currents nobody was prepared to find out.

Drake believed that he could get through Magellan's Straits and up the west coast of South America without being detected by Spanish ships. He would then have the rich plunder of the Americas at his mercy. But he knew that the expedition was bound to antagonise King Philip almost to the point of war, and so did not dare to sail without the approval of Elizabeth. As a common seaman, however, Drake had no contacts at court, but he did know Hawkins, who by this time was Chief Officer at the Queen's dockyard in Chatham. Hawkins put Drake in touch with a courtier named Sir Christopher Hatton, who agreed to introduce him to the queen. Elizabeth received Drake at court and presented him with a sword telling him 'wear this until we require it of thee'.

Drake was overwhelmed but was not certain if this was an instruction to lay low or permission to embark on his voyage. Hatton put him right, telling Drake that the queen could not officially sanction the voyage for fear of angering Philip, but at the same time was giving unofficial permission so that Drake could injure the Spanish treasury.

In November 1577 Drake set sail with a small fleet of five ships, plus a pinnace – a type of fast, small craft used to carry messages. The journey through the Magellan Straits proved to be more difficult than Drake had envisaged. One ship was wrecked, another had to be abandoned and two more turned for home. Only Drake's ship the *Golden Hind*, a purpose-built warship, got through. Once in the Pacific, Drake went to work in great haste. Coastal merchant ships were snapped up, pillaged and let go, towns captured and held to ransom. Then Drake heard that a large galleon was carrying a vast store of gold and silver from Peru north to Mexico where it was to be moved by mule train to the Atlantic for shipment to Spain.

Drake piled on the canvas and soon after dawn on 1 March he sighted the ship far ahead. Officially named *Nuestra Senora de la Concepcion* the ship was known to the locals as the *Cacafuego*, the 'Shit-fire', as it was the most heavily armed ship in the Pacific. Guns proved to be no defence against surprise. The Spanish captain thought that only Spanish ships were in the Pacific so he allowed Drake to come alongside and was overwhelmed by the rush of Englishmen before he could even draw his sword. The treasure was immense, making every man of Drake's crew rich.

After capturing this great prize, Drake wanted to turn for home. But from the crew of the *Cacafuego* he heard that an English raider named Oxenham had been captured in the Caribbean. Drake sent a messenger to the Spanish viceroy telling him that if Oxenham or his crew were executed he would block the entrance to Lima Harbour with Spanish bodies. It was a bluff, not only was Drake eager to be home but he routinely let his prisoners go free. The threat worked after a fashion, delaying Oxenham's execution for more than a year.

Drake sailed home by way of the East Indies, Indian Ocean and Cape of Good Hope. He came within sight of Cornwall on 25 September 1580. His holds were bursting with looted gold and silver that totalled an astonishing £600,000, but Drake was a worried man. He knew that Philip would be after his head, and feared that if Mary Queen of Scots were now Queen of England the Spanish King would soon get what he wanted. Drake's first act was to hail a passing fishing boat out of Plymouth and ask a simple question: 'Is Elizabeth still Queen of England?' The answer was 'yes'; Drake could go home.

Drake had wisely set aside a proportion of his haul for Elizabeth, and he fully expected to be ordered to make himself scarce for a few months while the diplomatic dust settled. Instead, Drake found himself receiving Elizabeth on the deck of his ship. The Queen knighted Drake for his exploits, a move bound to anger Philip enormously.

The reason for Elizabeth's new willingness to defy Spain openly was that while Drake had been away Philip had been making his hostility to England increasingly obvious. The most blatant action had come in July 1579, while Drake was in the Pacific.

A renegade Irish nobleman named James Fitzmaurice had persuaded the Pope that the Catholics in Ireland were desperate to rise up in rebellion against Elizabeth's overlordship. All they needed, said Fitzmaurice, were weapons. The Pope gave Fitzmaurice enough money to buy weapons, hire mercenaries and pay for transport to Ireland. Fitzmaurice recruited a few mercenaries, but most of his 500 men were fellow Irish exiles or English Catholics who had fled their homeland for their religion.

On 17 July Fitzmaurice and his force landed in Dingle Bay. They built a fort of earthworks at Smerwick as a base and set about making contact with the nearby Irish lords and clans. The reception was not as enthusiastic as Fitzmaurice had hoped, but they received enough support to get through the winter. Next spring, Fitzmaurice sent a message to Spain asking for more arms and reinforcements. Philip was keen to help, but like Elizabeth's endorsement of Drake's voyage, kept it unofficial. He donated 100 cannon, 2,000 muskets and harquebuses plus some 3,000 pikes and swords. Philip asked for 'volunteers' from his army and soon found 800 of them once he made clear their wages would be paid. Finally he contacted one of his admirals, Don Juan Martinez de Recalde and ordered him to take the men and munitions to Smerwick.

When Elizabeth learned of Recalde's mission she sent a squadron of her own warships to intercept. Commanded by William Wynter, the English ships arrived too late to stop the new landing, but found the Spaniards, Irish and English volunteers in low spirits. Fitzmaurice had set off to see an important Irish lord, and being late for the meeting had grabbed a farmer's horse. The Irish farmer did not take kindly to having his horse stolen and a scuffle ensued in which Fitzmaurice was killed.

Winter went straight into action. He bombarded the fort from the sea. A land army then came up under the command of Lord Grey of Wilton, Lord Deputy of Ireland. Grey added his own cannon to the bombardment. After several hours, the defenders asked for surrender terms. Grey was in vengeful mood and said that he would execute any rebel Englishmen or Irishmen in the force, but spare the lives of King Philip's men. The surrender went ahead, and Grey hanged the seventeen renegades out of hand. There then followed a bloody and vicious event.

Grey discovered that the Spanish troops in the makeshift fortress were not there on the orders of King Philip, nor even had his open permission to be there. They had no written warrant or orders from their King that allowed them to be there. Legally, the force was stateless freebooters. Grey ordered them all to be killed. In all, 507 men were butchered before Grey called a halt to the killing. The few miserable survivors were marched off to Dublin to become pawns in the increasingly frenzied diplomatic moves between Elizabeth and Philip.

Drake came home as the repercussions of the Smerwick affair were still being played out. Elizabeth's decision to knight him was an understandable riposte to Philip's support of Fitzmaurice.

By then, however, Philip's attention had moved away from England. In 1580 the King of Portugal died without leaving an obvious heir. Philip was a cousin of the Portuguese Royal Family and had a decent claim to the throne. He recalled Alba from the Netherlands and ordered him to invade Portugal. At the same time Spain's finest admiral, Don Alvaro de Bazan the Marquis the Santa Cruz, was sent with a huge fleet to blockade the Portuguese capital of Lisbon. The two pronged assault worked, the Portuguese caved in and accepted Philip as their monarch, and rival claimants to the throne either submitted or fled.

The acquisition of Portugal was a major triumph for Philip. The Portuguese had the greatest Atlantic fleet of the day, both as regards military warships and merchant craft. They also had an extensive overseas empire and a network of sailing routes and merchant outposts that dominated the spice trade and brought in a fortune. Philip was acquiring his greatest maritime rival and colonial competitor.

The move did not prove to be trouble free. Several Portuguese colonial governors resented being ousted by Philip's replacements, while one rival claimant to the throne enlisted French help and occupied the Azores. Philip sent a fleet led Santa Cruz, supported by a flotilla under Miguel de Oquendo to recapture the islands. It was not until 1583 that Philip was master of Portugal and its empire.

Philip then turned his full attention to the Netherlands. Alexander Farnese, Duke of Parma and son of Duchess Margaret, had been sent to replace Alba and was proving to be highly effective. As a bastard nephew of King Philip he was given considerable freedom of action. Parma himself described his policy as 'carrying a pardon in one hand and a sword in the other'. His combination of ruthless violence against rebels who resisted and generous terms to those who surrendered began to pay dividends. In 1584 William the

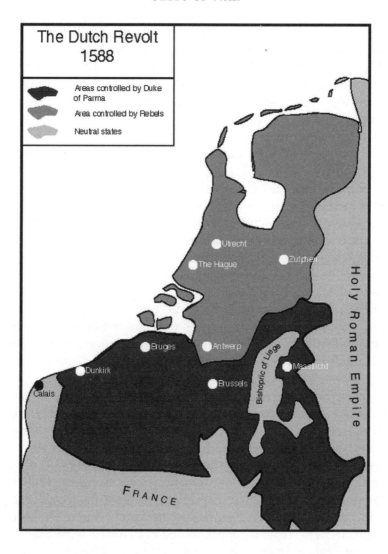

The Dutch Revolt
1588

Areas controlled by Duke of Parma

Area controlled by Rebels

Neutral states

Utrecht

The Hague

Zutphen

Bruges

Antwerp

Dunkirk

Maastricht

Calais

Brussels

Bishopric of Liège

Holy Roman Empire

FRANCE

Silent of Orange was assassinated by a man hired by King Philip. Bereft of their leader, many Dutch rebels capitulated to Parma. Elizabeth began to worry that once Philip had settled affairs in the Netherlands he would turn on England.

The summer of 1585 brought a sudden change. The Iberian Peninsula suffered a dreadful summer that destroyed most of the grain harvest and Spain was threatened with starvation. Philip hurriedly called off his wars and instead concentrated on buying food for his people. He turned even to England, sending emissaries to buy grain and arrange for its transport to Spain. Philip was offering top prices for the grain, and Elizabeth gave permission for the trade to take place. English merchant ships loaded down with grain headed for Spain. When they arrived they were all impounded, their crews thrown into prison and the grain taken without payment.

Elizabeth was furious and took all action she could, short of war. She allowed the Earl of Leicester to recruit volunteers to go to the Netherlands to aid the rebels. The merchants who had lost their ships, cargo and men were given Letters of Marque. These were documents issued by a monarch to subjects allowing them to undertake acts of violence against a foreign state. In times of war the Letters of Marque were unlimited, but in peacetime they had to be strictly controlled. The merchants were given permission to attack any Spanish ship until the loot they had taken equalled the amount of money they had lost.

Sir Francis Drake was also given Letters of Marque that allowed him to recover the value of ships and grain lost by a couple of London merchants, but his secret verbal instructions from Elizabeth went much further. She ordered him to go to the Caribbean and inflict as much damage on Spanish property as he possibly could. Gathering profitable loot was to be a purely secondary considera-tion. Drake did as ordered and spent six months at sea. He came back having made a modest profit and inflicted massive damage.

Not only had Drake burned towns, settlements and ships, but his mere presence had persuaded the Spanish viceroy that it would be too dangerous to send the treasure fleets to Spain. Philip was seriously strapped for cash. He defaulted on loans, could not pay Parma's mercenaries and increased taxation. When Drake came home, Burleigh wrote a report which concluded with the words: 'Truly Sir Francis Drake is a fearful man to the King of Spain'.

Again, the diplomats managed to smooth things over without open war breaking out. Compensation was paid, the Letters of Marque rescinded and things settled down. But as with the furore that followed San Juan de Ullua, the tension had been raised. Most people in Europe were now convinced that a war between England and Spain was inevitable. All that was needed was a spark to start the conflict. That spark was soon to be found in an obscure village in Northamptonshire.

II

The War Begins

An halberdier. The halberd was in origin a Swiss weapon that was adopted and used by most armies across Europe by about 1550. It was a combination pole weapon that was useful for a variety of purposes. The sharp point could be used to thrust at a distance, the broad blade could chop with savage force, while the hook was used to drag men from horses. It was a savage weapon for close quarter fighting that was highly fashionable for half a century or more. This man carries a short sword as a secondary weapon in case the halberd got broken or lost. He wears no armour, though his jacket and hat are both heavily padded as protection against glancing blows from enemy weapons. Halberds remained in favour on ships for some years after they were abandoned by land armies as they were better suited to the confined spaces of a shipboard fight.

After the failure of the Ridolfi Plot that had aimed to put Mary Queen of Scots on the throne of England, Elizabeth had taken steps to prevent any future plot. The first of these was to move Mary to the castle at Fotheringhay in Northamptonshire. Like all castles, Fotheringhay had been built to keep people out, but it was uniquely designed to be effective at keeping people in as well. Elizabeth thought it would make a suitably comfortable prison for Mary.

Elizabeth also promoted the diplomat Sir Francis Walsingham to the Privy Council. Walsingham was given a free hand, and generous funding, to establish a network of spies both abroad and at home. His two main tasks were to discover if and when Spain would declare war and to uncover any plot to kill Elizabeth and place Mary on the throne. He proved to be an inspired choice and quickly built up the most effective espionage network in the world.

In December 1585 Walsingham ordered the arrest of a man named Gilbert Gifford. Gifford had been trained as a Catholic priest, but had publicly renounced the faith and was in outward appearance a loyal subject. Walsingham suspected otherwise and pulled him in for questioning. Gifford professed his loyalty, but admitted that he did socialise with some Catholics whose commitment to Elizabeth was not so firm. Walsingham let Gifford go on condition that he reported back on any suspicious activity that he encountered. The questioning of Gifford seems to have been merely routine and similar to the treatment of hundreds of others but it would prove to yield results that were anything but routine.

In July 1586 Gifford contacted Walsingham to report that he had been asked to carry a letter from a friend of his, Sir Anthony Babington, to a brewer in Northamptonshire. Sensing a link to Mary of Scots, Walsingham asked Gifford for a copy of the letter which turned out to be in code. Meanwhile, Gifford reported that Babington had involved Charles Paget and Thomas Morgan in whatever he was up to. Morgan was a member of the Scottish embassy, another link to Mary.

Walsingham called in his own code experts and asked them to decipher the letter. After several false starts, they realised that only some of the symbols represented letters, while others stood for names, words and even phrases. By comparing how often each symbol occurred they were able to work out which represented very common letters, and which represented rarely used ones. From there they could guess at some words, thus identifying the letters that were harder to pinpoint by the frequency they were used. Context allowed the code breakers to make good guesses at what the symbols for words and phrases meant. They remained utterly baffled as to how to decipher symbols that indicated names.

After much hard work, the code breakers were able to tell Walsingham that Babington's letter was to Mary Queen of Scots. It talked about support for Mary among Catholics in England and France, and described Elizabeth as a usurper. There was certainly enough evidence to have Babington put on trial, but Walsingham and his colleague in government, Burleigh, wanted to entrap as many plotters as they could – and if possible Mary herself.

They alerted Mary's keeper about the messages. It was not long before it was realised that the brewer was placing the letters inside the bungs on beer barrels that he was delivering to Fotheringhay Castle for Mary and her servants.

In the weeks that followed, more letters were sent back and forth. Walsingham learned that Babington was planning to assassinate Elizabeth, Burleigh, Walsingham and a number of leading noblemen. A force of men would simultaneously attack Fotheringhay Castle to release Mary. She would then be escorted to London to assume the reins of power. Babington claimed to have a group of six men who were fully in on the plot, and a large number of others who he was sure would rally to help once the coup was under way. If the English Protestants caused any trouble, Babington said, a Spanish army could be brought in to deal with them.

Walsingham recognised an unlikely scheme when he saw one, but he had to take it seriously. The Babingtons were a wealthy and well connected Derbyshire family. Sir Anthony Babington was a fairly wayward young son who might be expected to dream up some crackpot scheme. Nevertheless the unidentified six gentlemen in the plot might be serious players and in any case, Mary's involvement was worrying. Thus far she had been merely asking Babington for information on the plot and had neither condoned it nor agreed to take part.

Walsingham decided to attempt a ruse. He got Gifford to hand over a letter from Mary to Babington and then got his forgers to add a final sentence in which Mary asked Babington to name his six co-conspirators. Babington did not do so, but the next development was even more serious: Mary wrote to Babington agreeing to the plot. Babington then applied for a passport to travel to Spain claiming business there, but presumably in reality to talk to the Spanish government about the scheme.

Walsingham ordered his arrest along with a number of his friends and relatives. Under torture several of them broke down and confessed all. Walsingham was able to piece together the plot, identify the ringleaders and work out who had known what. Fourteen men were sentenced to death and executed in September.

It was also now very clear that Mary had agreed to a plan to murder Elizabeth and had actively worked to achieve that aim. Walsingham and Burleigh took the evidence to Elizabeth and urged her to have Mary executed. Elizabeth hesitated for two reasons. First she was not certain that she was legally entitled to put a foreign Queen on trial. Second she was worried about the reaction from abroad.

For weeks Elizabeth procrastinated, then in January she agreed that Mary should be put on trial. Mary was found guilty and the court recommended the death penalty. Again Elizabeth refused to take action. Walsingham and Burleigh were convinced that so long as Mary stayed alive there would be plots against Elizabeth and repeatedly urged her to sign the death warrant. Finally, on 1 February 1587 she did so, only to change her mind and demanded that the warrant be torn up. It was too late; Burleigh had already sent it to Fotheringhay Castle and Mary was dead.

There was, for Elizabeth, a sting in the tail. Before she had come under close surveillance, Mary had smuggled out a secret will. She had left her claims to the English throne not to her son, King James VI of Scotland, who was a Protestant, but to a safely Catholic distant cousin: King Philip II of Spain. Even at the time there was a great deal of debate as to how legal Mary's will was. Up to a point the legality of the move was immaterial. It gave Philip a claim to the throne of England. It was now up to him whether he wanted to enforce it in the only way that he could, by war.

The Duke of Parma was in no doubt. He suggested loading an army of 30,000 mercenaries onto Dutch barges, coastal vessels and whatever other craft he could lay his hands on. The army could then be shipped across to England all in one go, to land on Thanet or in the Thames Estuary. London would fall within a week and England would be Philip's. Parma emphasised that speed and surprise were of the essence. If the English knew what was planned they would get their warships into the Channel and sink Parma's barges with ease.

Philip hesitated. He was not a man to be hurried into anything. He particularly did not want to risk Parma's entire army just as it was on the brink of victory in the Netherlands. He sent questions back to Parma asking for more details: facts, figures and demanding to know how Parma planned to undertake the invasion. Inevitably word began to leak out. Pope Sixtus V in Rome heard of the plan and offered to pay a million ducats to Philip on the day that Parma landed in England but by then Parma had gone off the idea. The element of surprise had been lost and he feared what Drake and his Devil-assisted ships would do to barges caught on the open seas of the Channel crossing.

Philip, however, had another plan to invade England sitting on his desk. In 1583 the Marquis de Santa Cruz had come back to Spain from securing Portugal and Portugal's empire for Philip. He had written to Philip advising him that this was the moment to strike at England. With the combined war fleets of Spain and Portugal at his command, Philip heavily outnumbered anything Elizabeth could put to sea. The English navy could be smashed, the sea route to England would be open. An invading army would have little difficulty overrunning a kingdom that had few modern fortresses and no standing army. Philip ordered Santa Cruz to draw up a detailed plan for the campaign – there was little Philip liked better than a detailed plan.

Despite his optimism, Santa Cruz was a realist. He knew that to hold England would be as difficult as taking it. Rebellions and uprisings could be expected to take place for a year or so after the conquest, stopping only once the initial outbreaks had been put down with suitably bloodthirsty thoroughness. He estimated that 64,000 troops would be needed, including cavalry and artillery.

The fleet to carry this huge army would need not only to transport the men and their equipment; it would also have to defeat the English fleet in open battle. The fleet would also be required to secure the supply routes from England to Spain against any attempt at interference by the Dutch or French. He estimated that he would need 150 warships and converted large merchantmen. Then there would be supply ships – Santa Cruz thought that 40 merchantmen would do the job. An assortment of smaller craft and open boats would be needed to carry messages back and forth and to land the troops from the big ships onto the open beaches of southern England; about 300 would be enough. Santa Cruz added that it might be wise to take along some galleys from the Mediterranean. These flimsy craft were not really suited to the Atlantic waters, nor could they out fight English warships, but they could be very useful in calm conditions when the sailing ships of both sides would be useless. Santa Cruz thought 40 galleys would be a good number.

In all Santa Cruz wanted 500 craft operated by 30,000 men as well as the army of 64,000 soldiers. He estimated that the entire two-year campaign would cost some 3.8 million ducats.

Philip replied that he would think about it. The Spanish government did not have 3.8 million ducats, and even if it did Philip would probably think of something more useful to do with them. Although Spain and Portugal between them could probably have mustered such a fleet, it would have meant stripping all other areas of the empire of craft. For the duration of the campaign there would be no ships sailing between Spain and the Americas or carrying spices from the East Indies to Portugal. The economy of the empire would be frozen while ships were engaged against England, Philip's treasury would rapidly empty and Spain would go bankrupt.

Philip never replied definitively to Santa Cruz, but his very silence told the veteran admiral that the plan had not been approved. However, Philip had set his army of bureaucrats to work inspecting the scheme. This had one unintended consequence, the idea of invading England was given a name within the Spanish government. It came to be called 'the Enterprise of England'. Once the plan had a name it was much easier for bureaucrats, admirals and soldiers to talk about it.

Word seeped out that Philip was considering an invasion of England. By 1586 most governments across Europe knew this, and Elizabeth certainly knew it. Money, men and goods were made available to Sir John Hawkins at Chatham for the construction, repair and modification of the Queen's ships.

When news reached Philip that Mary had been executed he went to pray, then began to think. He dusted off the various plans for the Enterprise of England and ordered his officials to look at them again. He wanted a detailed report sent to him by later in March as to what the options there were for the Enterprise of England and would then make a decision. Meanwhile, Philip had already begun diplomatic moves to pave the way for a possible campaign. He wrote to the Marquis de Olivares, his ambassador in Rome, asking him to arrange a secret meeting with Pope Sixtus V. At the meeting Olivares was instructed to

> ...obtain from him a brief declaring that the right to the English crown falls to me. My claim rests upon my descent from the House of Lancaster, and upon the will made by the Queen of Scotland [Mary], of which a copy is enclosed herewith. You will impress upon his Holiness that I cannot undertake a war in England for the purpose merely of placing upon that throne a young heretic like the King of Scotland [James VI] who, indeed, is by his heresy incapacitated to succeed. His Holiness must, however, be assured that I have no intention of adding England to my own dominions, but to settle the crown upon my daughter the Infanta.

In June, Olivares replied that: 'I found his Holiness favourable', but this fell short of the unambiguous approval that Philip had asked for. Philip now changed approach. Instead of asking Sixtus to declare him the rightful King of England, Philip wanted the Pope 'to declare this war a righteous one'. This was rather more vague, but would still secure Philip papal blessing for the campaign. The reason why this was so important was alluded to only indirectly by Philip when he added: 'In the interests of this Enterprise, it is necessary to come to some understanding with certain persons in England.' In other words, Philip was convinced that at least some of the English Catholics would be willing to assist his invasion if it were sanctioned by the Pope.

It was not until 29 July that a firm agreement was made between Philip and Sixtus.

> We will contribute one million gold ducats to wit, 500,000 ducats as soon as the royal fleet shall have touched England and the army has been put on land, and the remaining 500,000 ducats in bi-monthly instalments. That if the kingdoms of England and Scotland are

recovered, as we hope in the Lord they will be, his Catholic Majesty will nominate as king of the said kingdoms someone who will establish and preserve in them the Catholic religion and who will remain grateful to the Apostolic See and accept from it the investiture of the said kingdom.

There are some important points in this agreement, apart from the papal blessing for the campaign and the offer of gold. The first is that the Enterprise was being aimed at not only England, but at Scotland as well. Both kingdoms had Protestant monarchs and were on the same island, but whether tackling both in one campaign was feasible is unlikely.

The second point is that Sixtus was giving Philip the right to nominate the new joint ruler of the two kingdoms. It is not clear if this means that Philip had dropped the idea of putting his daughter on the throne – other evidence seems to indicate that he still aimed to do this. However, it might have meant that he was intending to leave open the question of the girl's husband. Perhaps Philip hoped to marry his daughter to a Catholic English noble – one of those 'certain persons' that he had referred to – who could be expected to be a pliant puppet ruler.

One thing that cannot be deduced from this agreement, but which is now known from internal Vatican documents, is Sixtus's attitude to the Enterprise of England. We now know that Sixtus did not take the idea at all seriously when he signed this agreement. He believed that Philip's bellicose preparations were nothing more than a diplomatic bluff designed to put pressure on Elizabeth. When the Armada actually set sail Sixtus was astonished.

Despite his pledge to put a Catholic on the throne of Scotland, Philip needed to keep the Protestant James VI neutral in any coming war. 'I send to condole the King,' wrote Philip to his ambassador, 'and again offer him my friendship and the goodwill I always bore to his mother.'

France was by this time slipping into a vicious religious civil war. Philip reckoned he could discount French intervention on either side. He did, however, ask his ambassador in Paris, Bernadino de Mendoza, to keep him informed of events, news and gossip.

Mendoza took Philip at his word and over the coming months kept up a constant stream of letters. These contained not just news and views on events in France, but also of what was happening in England. Mendoza did not have a network of spies to rival that of Walsingham, but he had some Frenchmen working for him. These fishermen, merchants and gentlemen were free to go to England and returned with news and gossip. Unfortunately for Philip, Mendoza was in no position to judge what information was true and what was not. All he could do was pass them on.

The Holy Roman Empire, meanwhile, was ruled by Philip's cousin and could be counted upon to be friendly. The attitude of the various Italian states would be crucial and at the very least Philip needed them to remain friendly to Spain. He could not risk moving warships from the Mediterranean to join the Enterprise of England if the moment they were gone the Italians would swoop down to nibble at his dominions. Ideally they should be willing to contribute ships to the campaign. Messages and plenipotentiaries were sent out to gauge the feeling and ask for allies.

While the Spanish diplomatic service was kept busy smoothing the path for the Enterprise, Philip had been studying the report submitted to him on how the conquest of England might actually be achieved. The report reviewed the plans previously put forward by Santa Cruz and Parma. It concluded that Santa Cruz's plan was too expensive to consider. Parma's plan was also ruled out as the barges would be too vulnerable to English warships now that the element of surprise had been lost.

A third option was put forward that was both affordable and practical. The main costs involved in Santa Cruz's plan had been associated with shipping 64,000 men all the way from Spain to England. Without those men to transport, feed and supply, the fleet could be reduced in size drastically. If the only task of the fleet was to defeat the English navy, it could be kept down to manageable proportions. It was estimated that about 50 or 60 warships would be enough to destroy the English warships, even if the freebooters such as Drake actually dared come out to fight. If supply transports, scout ships and messenger craft were included the fleet would need to number about 100 ships.

An army would still be needed to invade and subdue England. That army, it was argued, could be provided by Parma. The bureaucrats writing the report in Spain took Parma at his word that he could find the barges and coastal craft to get his army across to England. They recognised his more recent objections that these small craft would be smashed to matchwood by the English fleet. It was proposed that Parma and his troop-laden barges would not come out until after Santa Cruz's fleet had destroyed or captured the English ships.

At this date, Spanish warships carried large numbers of soldiers who manned the guns, boarded the enemy vessels and generally did the fighting while the sailors managed the ships. Once the English fleet had been dealt with these soldiers could be disembarked from their ships to swell the ranks of Parma's army. Given the intended size of the Spanish fleet, there would be about 10,000 soldiers on board the ships. It was estimated that Parma could spare some 30,000 men from his army in the Netherlands. So long as the troops were not away for more than a year, his remaining forces should be enough to stand on the defensive in the fortresses that they held and so stop the rebels from gaining much ground. The two forces together would total 40,000 men, not much short of the total Santa Cruz had estimated would be needed to conquer and hold England.

There was the possibility that Drake and his comrades would not dare to face the mighty Spanish fleet in a fair fight. After all, the Spanish experience of English freebooters had been that they attacked only when they had a clear advantage. Whenever superior Spanish forces appeared, the English raiders had fled. It was considered that so long as the Spanish fleet was kept in good order the English would not attack. Thus it followed that Parma and his barges could be escorted across from the Netherlands to the Thames estuary by Santa Cruz and his ships even if the English fleet was still intact.

Convoy escort duty is famously difficult to manage and requires a large number of ships if it is to be effective. The planners decided to increase the number of warships in the fleet to take account of this. The increase would in turn require more supply ships and messenger craft. In all the fleet would have to number about 130 vessels.

On 31 March 1587 Philip made up his mind that the new plan could work. With a few amendments Philip approved the scheme and the Enterprise of England was on.

III

Singeing the King's Beard

Musketeer. The musket had become a reliable and useful weapon by the mid-sixteenth century and by 1588 was in common usage. It was lighter than the heavier harquebus, which needed a rest to support the barrel when fired. When first developed the musket was considered inferior as it used a smaller charge of powder and fired a smaller ball than the harquebus, but by the 1580s improved gunpowder made the musket effective at up to 75 yards. Its lightweight and relatively rapid rate of fire, about one shot per minute, made it a handy weapon on shipboard. This man wears armour in the form of an iron helmet, iron breastplate and iron backplate. Such armour was often used in regiments of heavy infantry. He wears a short sword for use at close quarters.

Once he had made the decision to invade England, Philip set his vast bureaucracy to work sorting out the details. Philip had built for himself a vast complex on a hill at the village of Escorial about 30 miles from Madrid. The complex was a combined monastery, fortress, palace and administrative headquarters. It ran to 4,000 rooms, 100 miles of corridors and 86 staircases. At the heart of the complex was a small blue-tiled room in which Philip did his paperwork. A short walk away was the grand church where he could seek spiritual guidance.

On the afternoon of 31 March 1587, messengers began scurrying about the El Escorial carrying instructions, advice and orders. The hundreds of men who toiled away on Philip's military dispositions put aside whatever they had been doing and turned their attentions to the incredibly complex task of getting a huge war fleet ready for sea. Ships had to be gathered together, repaired and equipped; men found, trained and allocated; and supplies gathered, stored and distributed.

Perhaps optimistically, Philip ordered that the great fleet had to be assembled in Lisbon by the end of June, and set sail in July in time to transport Parma and his men to England in August. This would give the Spanish invasion army two months of good weather in which to conquer England, and presumably Scotland, before the northern autumn closed in. The Spanish army could probably campaign into November if needs be, but the autumnal storms would mean that it could not be reliably supplied by sea after early October. Parma would need to have secured at least the main towns with their grain supplies by this time.

One important measure was to keep Elizabeth in the dark for as long as possible. Of course, Philip knew that he could not hope to keep secret the fact that he was preparing a large fleet, but he did his best to conceal its true mission. Almost before the ink was dry on

Philip's orders, the Venetian ambassador, Heironimo Lippomano, was writing back to his government that:

> Every day one hears of fresh preparations for war in various parts of Spain, and especially in Malaga where forty ovens over and above the ordinary are at work continually, preparing biscuits to last a year for a force of 70,000 persons. Frencesco Duartes has been charged with the contract for 30,000 cantaras of cheese, which cost 150,000 crowns and were brought by the twenty Hamburg ships which reached Lisbon a few days ago, but as to the real intentions of his Majesty your Serene Highness will discover them more easily from the enclose report written by the Marquis of Santa Cruz, which I have obtained in great secrecy.

The report which Lippomano was so proud of having obtained had been written to Philip from Santa Cruz a few weeks earlier. It detailed the reports that had come in from the far flung reaches of the Spanish empire concerning the activities of English ships and raiders. It made clear that Santa Cruz wanted to 'attack the English', but whether this meant raiding English ports, invading England or simply seeking the English ships out on the high seas was not specified.

One of Walsingham's agents, a French merchant living in Spain, also picked up the news. He wrote to England:

> There is talk that the King of Spain will make a great army for England of 800 ships, but as yet it seems that there are but small preparations. It seems this is only a Spanish brag and very unlikely in many years for him to provide shipping, mariners and soldiers for such an army – unless the French assist him.

As early as the spring of 1586, Philip had appointed Parma to be his ambassador when conducting talks with the English government. For the most part these talks consisted of detailed and rather tedious discussions about compensation, trade terms and the like. Occasionally, however, Parma's talks did touch on weightier matters. In June 1586 he had broached the subject of the English volunteers serving on the side of the Dutch rebels and asked Elizabeth's ambassador what it would take to persuade her to block any future Englishmen coming to the Netherlands. The ambassadors sent the message back to London, and Elizabeth felt it important enough to write a letter in reply to Parma in her own hand. After the usual pleasantries and formalities, Elizabeth stated:

> You may be persuaded that if any reasonable conditions of peace should be offered to us which tend to the establishing of our safety and the honour and liberty of our neighbours, we shall no less willingly accept them than unwillingly we have been forced to the contrary, seeing that in no way can we do anything more pleasing to God Almighty than by embracing the peace and safety of Christendom of which in these times we who are princes and monarchs have chiefly to think.

In other words, any peace deal had to include the Dutch rebels. Elizabeth suspected that if they were defeated by the Spanish, England would be next. Parma, of course, could not agree to allow the Dutch rebels to form their own state. The talks stalled. Now, however, Parma was ordered to reopen serious, substantive talks with Elizabeth. They were not intended to bring peace, for Philip was intent on war, but Parma was instructed to keep Elizabeth talking and so try to lull her into thinking that the Spanish were not intending an invasion or, if they were, that they were not yet ready to launch it.

In England the news coming in was deemed to be contradictory. Parma's peace talks convinced some that Philip was seeking a compromise and would attack only if Elizabeth remained intransigent. Others thought Philip would attack whatever Elizabeth did. The debates at court swayed to and fro, but there was one need for great urgency: Sir Francis Drake was mustering a force to go to sea. It was essential that two decisions had to be reached quickly. First, was Elizabeth to send any royal ships to sail with Drake? Second, what were Drake's instructions to be?

Drake was now too famous and his proposed fleet too large for him to be allowed to go freebooting on his own initiative. Wherever he went and whatever he did would be interpreted by most foreign observers as an official English action. And if ships of the English fleet went with him it would be obvious that Elizabeth had given him his instructions. Drake himself had no doubts about what his instructions should be. He wrote to Elizabeth's Council of State in late March: 'Give me a fleet and a free hand, and I will smoke the wasps out of their nests. God work to it all in his Glory.'

After much discussion and hesitation, Elizabeth decided to give Drake exactly what he wanted. He was given the vaguest possible instructions as to what he should do, but with the clear aim of doing everything in his power to disrupt the gathering Spanish fleet. The fleet he was to lead was the largest that England had sent to sea since Elizabeth had become queen. There could be no doubting the fact that England and Elizabeth were taking things very seriously.

Drake himself provided four warships of his own. These were small, light and fast with the largest being the *Thomas*, named after his brother, of 200 tons. A group of London merchants paid for seven warships. Although these ships were to sail under Drake's command they had their own commander, Robert Flick, who was responsible to the merchants for the safety of the ships and the costs involved in the voyage. Lord Thomas Howard, Elizabeth's Lord High Admiral, sent one warship. Elizabeth provided two warships, the 600-ton *Elizabeth Bonaventure* and the 500-ton *Golden Lion*. The two royal ships were the largest and most heavily armed in the fleet and Drake took the *Elizabeth Bonaventure* as his flagship. Elizabeth also sent two small pinnaces, and there were another nine small scouting craft provided by private men.

Elizabeth also sent William Borough. Borough had orders to be responsible for the welfare and costs of the Queen's ships. He was also appointed to be the vice admiral of the expedition. Borough was aged 51 at this date and had spent almost his entire adult life in the navy and was respected both by Elizabeth and by his men. It was, however, some years since he had been at sea. In recent years he had been in charge of dockyard works, making sure that ships were repaired on time and on budget and ensuring that the docks had all the men and materials that they needed. He had done a good job and had worked hard and nobody doubted his diligence or his loyalty. His abilities as a fighting commander were, however, untested.

Drake and Borough got off to a bad start during a stormy meeting on 11 April. Drake had been desperate to get to sea for weeks and he believed that the best chance the English had of defeating a Spanish fleet was before it had even set sail. Drake had been agitating for permission to attack since the autumn of 1586, months before Philip had even decided to invade England. Now that he had the crucial written permission he wanted to get on with the job before the less warlike noblemen in London persuaded Elizabeth to change her mind. Borough, however, believed that the fleet should not sail until everything was ready, all the stores were on board and a plan had been agreed. Drake overruled Borough and the fleet set sail from Plymouth on 12 April.

It was as well that it did so. On the very day that Drake and Borough had been arguing, Elizabeth had held a meeting of her Council to listen to the latest proposals from Parma. These seemed promising, and Elizabeth decided that she did not want Drake to spoil any chance that there might be of a negotiated peace. She sent a message to Plymouth changing Drake's orders significantly. Instead of having a free hand he was ordered to restrict his actions to capturing Spanish ships on the high seas and then bringing them and their crews back to England to act as hostages.

The messenger carrying the orders arrived in Plymouth two days after Drake had set sail. He quickly boarded a royal pinnace and set off in pursuit but the vessel had the most dreadful mishaps. First it ran into contrary winds, then some rigging frayed and broke and then supplies ran low. The commander had no choice, he said, but to return to Plymouth at once. The commander was a cousin of Sir John Hawkins, which might have had something to do with the run of bad luck.

On 26 April Drake was off Lisbon, though out of sight of land. He captured a small fishing smack and questioned the crew, who were clearly terrified to be in the presence of the infamous *El Draque*. They told Drake that Santa Cruz was in Lisbon with a sizeable fleet of warships. A second fleet, they said, was gathered at Cadiz.

Drake called a council of war on board the *Elizabeth Bonaventure*. At this date it was usual for the commander of any sizeable military expedition to call a council of war to discuss any changes of plan or unexpected news. In a fleet made up of ships drawn from a number of sources, as Drake's was, it was essential. The usual arrangement was for the commander to outline the issues to be discussed and the information that was to hand. The most junior officer would speak next, giving his opinion. The next most junior would speak second and so on until the deputy commander had his say. The commander would then round up the discussion, summarise the points raised and then give his view of what should be done and how it should be achieved. If nobody objected, the commander would then issue his detailed orders. If the task was particularly complex, the orders might take the form of written instructions to each captain prepared by the commander's secretary and delivered by pinnace an hour or so later.

It was this sort of a council of war that Borough came on board the *Elizabeth Bonaventure* expecting to take part in. Those captains who had sailed with Drake before knew better. As soon as the captains were gathered in his cabin, Drake spread a chart of Cadiz harbour on the table. He pointed out the shoals, where the shore batteries were located and where he expected the Spanish ships to be anchored or berthed. He then said that he would lead the attack in the *Elizabeth Bonaventure,* ordered the other captains to follow him as fast as they could and advised them to watch his flagship for signals. He rolled up the map and everyone started to leave.

Borough realised that the meeting was over and objected. Nobody had been given the chance to have their say other than Drake. There was no proper plan, he protested, and no scouting had been done to find out where the Spanish ships really were, how many there were nor how strong they were. Drake and the others were astonished, they believed they would charge into Cadiz, take the Spaniards by surprise and work things out as they went along. Drake glanced around at the others to make sure he had their support then told Borough: 'We shall not stay at all.' Drake was already piling on the canvas before Borough got back to his ship.

In Cadiz all was bustle and excitement. The orders to get a vast fleet ready for June had prompted every shipyard worker into action, and labourers had been hired in from the surrounding countryside to help out. Soldiers had marched into town and armourers were at work making and repairing weapons and armour of every kind. When a straggling line of ships came into sight over the north-western horizon an hour or so after noon, nobody paid them much attention: no doubt it was more warships coming to join the gathering fleet.

The port governor was slightly concerned that he could see no flags on the approaching ships, so he sent out six galleys to investigate. The galleys reached the ships when they were about two miles from the harbour entrance. There was a sudden boom of cannon fire. The lead ship had run up an English flag and fired a broadside at the nearest galley. The Spanish vessel lurched drunkenly as it went out of control. Another broadside smashed into a second galley, which began to settle in the water. Both limped towards the shore, where they ran aground and were abandoned. The four remaining galleys turned about and fled back toward Cadiz harbour.

The harbour was crammed with 60 ships, most of them in the deeper outer harbour and around 20 in the shallower inner harbour.

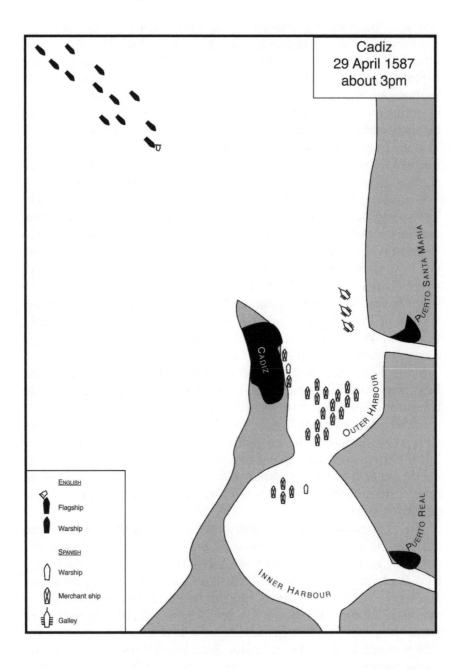

Cadiz
29 April 1587
about 3pm

PUERTO SANTA MARIA

CADIZ

OUTER HARBOUR

PUERTO REAL

INNER HARBOUR

ENGLISH

Flagship

Warship

SPANISH

Warship

Merchant ship

Galley

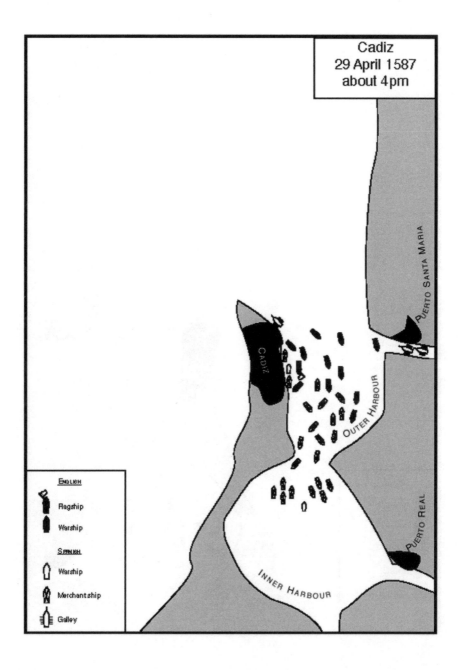

Cadiz
29 April 1587
about 4 pm

PUERTO SANTA MARIA

CADIZ

OUTER HARBOUR

PUERTO REAL

INNER HARBOUR

English
Flagship
Warship

Spanish
Warship
Merchant ship
Galley

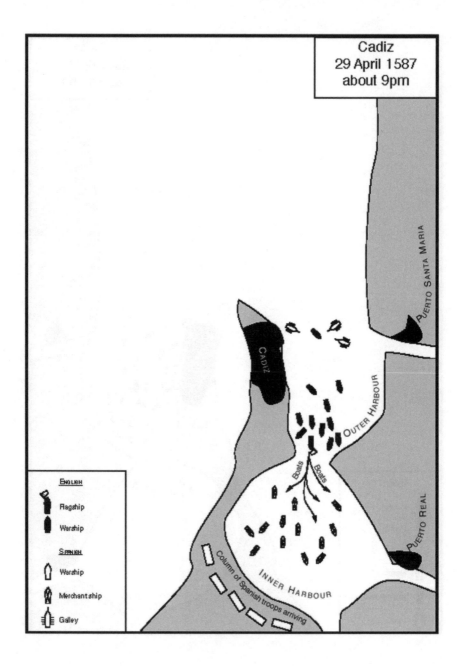

Cadiz
29 April 1587
about 9pm

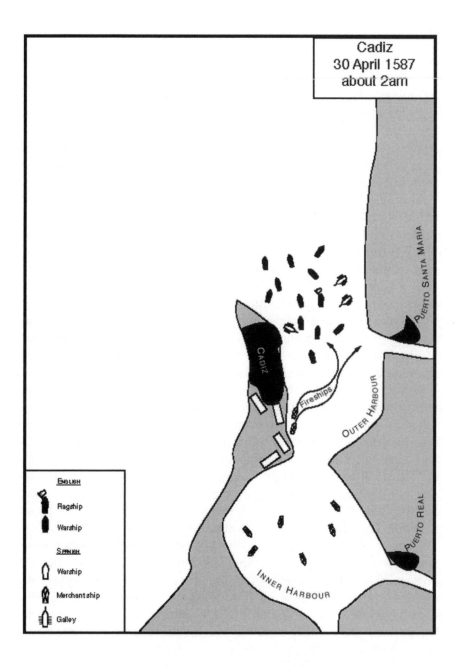

Few of the ships were ready for sea as most of them were either under repair, being converted for war use or had their crews on leave while they were supplied with provisions. Only two ships of any size were ready for war: a 1,000 ton armed merchant man and a 700-ton trader converted for war by having extra guns fitted.

As the English ships came into the harbour, the smaller ships that had crews on board fled to the inner harbour. The two larger vessels began firing their guns, but most ships simply bobbed at anchor. On shore the population of Cadiz panicked: the city gates were slammed shut, but hundreds were outside the city. They rushed to the gates, pounding and shouting to be let in. More than two dozen were killed in the stampede, but the governor refused to open the gates.

Meanwhile, Drake had led the assault on the Spanish ships. The 700-ton ship was surrounded by four English warships and sent to the bottom. The larger vessel was abandoned by its crew after a short battle. Drake then began the methodical business of destruction. Each Spanish ship was boarded in turn. If it was fit for sea, Drake put a small crew on board and gave them orders to head for England. If a ship was not in a condition to sail, it was stripped of anything useful then set on fire. By midnight the harbour was illuminated by blazing ships.

Ashore the Spaniards had now reopened the city gates and were manhandling a large cannon from the citadel's sea-facing defences down to the quayside from where it could reach the anchored English ships. A column of hundreds of veteran soldiers had arrived under the command of the local nobleman, the Duke of Medina Sidonia. Borough thought it was time to leave but Drake was not content. He fired a gun to attract attention, then launched his ship's boats loaded down with men and headed for the inner harbour. The other captains followed suit, even Borough.

Once in the inner harbour, the armed men began scrambling aboard the smaller Spanish ships. The crews were overcome one by one and the craft set alight. Then the great cannon on the quayside opened fire. Its first shot hit Borough's *Golden Lion*, bringing him racing back to order it out of the harbour. He only blundered into the path of the waiting galleys, which pounced on the lone ship. Drake had to come back to rescue his second in command.

Then a flat calm fell and the English ships were immobilised. For some hours they could be moved only by being towed by their boats. They were forced to spin back and forth, always trying to present their deadly broadsides to the more nimble galleys. Then the wind got up and Drake led his force back out to sea. He claimed to have sunk or captured 37 craft whereas the Spanish admitted to a loss of 24 ships. The discrepancy may be due to Drake counting smaller craft, which the Spanish ignored, and it may be that some craft that Drake had thought thoroughly aflame had been rescued and repaired.

Either way, Drake had only just begun. He headed south toward the Straits of Gibraltar and called a council of war to explain his plans. He intended to find a secure anchorage, landing a force to watch for any advancing Spanish troops, and then sally out to attack the coastal craft bringing supplies from Philip's Mediterranean territories to the gathering fleet. Borough objected that the orders from Elizabeth did not give Drake permission to land troops and invade Spain. Drake countered that his orders did not forbid him from doing this but Borough refused to condone the plan. Drake told him to put his objections in writing and the gathered captains waited while Borough angrily scribbled out his objections. Drake took the note, folded it up and put it in his pocket. He then ordered the arrest of Borough for insubordination and ordered for him to be locked in his cabin on board the *Golden Lion*.

The fleet moved off to capture the small harbour of Sagres. From there Drake spread out to capture or destroy as many coastal craft as he could. Over the next 20 days he captured 100 craft, some of them one-man fishing smacks. The biggest haul was a small flotilla of traders carrying 1,700 tons of wooden barrel staves. It would prove to be a crucial haul. By the twentieth day the number of victims was declining as word got around that *El Draque* was on the scene. Drake upped anchor and set sail for the Azores.

Suddenly the *Golden Lion* bore off to the north leaving behind a rowing boat which hurriedly splashed over to Drake's ship. In the boat was the captain of the *Golden Lion*. He reported that there had been a mutiny stirred up by the imprisoned Borough. The crew had decided to go home, but the captain had preferred to stay with Drake rather than with his ship. Drake was furious. He convened a hurried court martial and had Borough convicted of mutiny and condemned to death. By the time he got to England Drake's anger had subsided and he agreed to drop proceedings. He did not, however, forgive Borough and the incident rankled with both men.

When Drake reached the Azores he ran into the main treasure fleet of the year heading to Spain from the East Indies. After some hard fighting, the English captured the great merchant ship the

San Felipe. The ship and her cargo were worth £114,000 making it the greatest single prize of Drake's career. In all, the voyage had captured over £140,000 worth of plunder. Elizabeth took £40,000, the merchants who had provided ships another £40,000 and Drake pocketed £17,000. The rest was divided up amongst the crews.

Drake gleefully reported that he had 'singed the beard of the King of Spain'. The damage he had inflicted had two immediate consequences. First, the date of the Enterprise of England had to be deferred from 1587 to 1588. Second, Philip's credit rating among the bankers of Europe was badly damaged. He now had to pay extra interest on any loans that he raised.

The delay in the sailing of the Armada and Drake's exploits along the coast of Spain had more long term effects. For the first time the Spaniards had seen the English fighting against even odds, and despite assurances that the English had no stomach for a fight they had done well. Confident talk that the English freebooters would run from a fair fight died. The idea that the great Spanish fleet had only to sail up the Channel to secure victory was abandoned. Those involved now expected that hard fighting would be required.

Of much greater importance was the fact that on 9 February 1588 the 62-year-old Marquis of Santa Cruz died of a sudden fever. His death was a serious blow to Philip. Santa Cruz was not only the finest and most experienced admiral in Philip's service, but he was the only seaman on the Spanish side whose reputation was unsullied by defeat or shipwreck. Philip had plenty of other able and experienced admirals, but none of them had the prestige and authority to be the obvious choice to command the campaign. Philip knew that if he appointed any one of his admirals to the prestigious command, the others would be bound to resent being passed over. They might refuse to serve in the campaign in a secondary role or, even worse, might agree and then do only a half-hearted job.

Philip wracked his brains for a suitable commander and found his answer, strangely enough, in Drake's raid on Cadiz. The cost of the raid to Philip's treasury had been in the region of 160,000 ducats. It would have been many times worse if Drake had landed his men and managed to capture the city. The bulging warehouses of Cadiz had been filled with vast quantities of weapons, ammunition, sails, ropes, spars, food, pitch and a host of other commodities needed by a warfleet at sea.

Drake had had no intention of landing and getting drawn into a land battle for which he was not equipped, but the Spaniards did not know this. They gave the credit for stopping Drake from landing to the local nobleman who, entirely on his own initiative, had led a column of 3,000 men at breakneck speed down to Cadiz – marching to the sound of guns. That man was Alonzo Perez de Gusman el Bueno, 7th Duke of Medina Sidonia.

Aged 38, Medina Sidonia belonged to one of the oldest, noblest and richest families in Spain. He had behind him a solid record of taking on tasks for King Philip and was a soldier of distinction and an administrator of genius. Sidonia had played a leading role in Alba's invasion of Portugal in 1580 and had done much to win over Portuguese opinion by his efficient and effective handling of government finances in the years that followed. When he led his men to the relief of Cadiz he was serving as Captain General of Andalusia, only one rank below the King in the government hierarchy of Spain.

Philip decided that he had found his man. Brave, resourceful and talented, and above all the man who had bested the dreaded *El Draque*: Medina Sidonia was a perfect choice thought Philip. In both military and social senses he outranked every fighting admiral in Spain. None of them could possibly feel passed over if Medina Sidonia was given command. Even before Santa Cruz had died of his fever, Philip wrote to Medina Sidonia ordering him to go to Lisbon to take over when the old admiral died.

When he received the letter informing him of the honour being bestowed to him, Medina Sidonia was appalled; he was a soldier, not an admiral. He had never commanded a ship, let alone a fleet. And on the few occasions when he had gone to sea he had been violently seasick. On 16 February he sat down and wrote a thoughtful and lengthy letter to Philip explaining why his appointment to command the great Enterprise of England was a terrible mistake.

I first humbly thank his Majesty for having thought of me for so great a task, and I wish I possessed the talents and strength necessary for it. But, sir, I have not health for the sea. Besides this, your worship knows, as I have often told you verbally and in writing, that I am in great need, so much so that when I have had to go to Madrid I have been obliged to borrow money for the journey. My house owes 900,000 ducats, and I am therefore quite unable to accept the command. I have not a single real I can spend on the expedition.

Apart from this, neither my conscience nor my duty will allow me to take this service upon me. The force is so great and the undertaking so important that it would not be right for a person like myself, possessing no experience of seafaring, to take charge of it. I possess neither aptitude, ability, health, nor fortune for the expedition. But, besides all this, for me to take charge of the Armada afresh without the slightest knowledge of it, of the persons who are taking part in it, of the objects in view, of the intelligence from England, without any acquaintance with the ports there, or of the arrangements which the Marquis [of Santa Cruz] has been making for years past, would be simply groping in the dark, even if I had experience, seeing that I should have suddenly and without preparation to enter a new career.

I conclude that in view of the representations I make to you here, his Majesty will permit me not to undertake the voyage. I am incapable of doing so for the various reasons I have stated. I therefore do not reply to your question about the defence of this coast during my absence as I shall remain here to attend to it myself and serve his Majesty here as I have always done.

I send this reply with all speed after commending the matter very earnestly to God.

King Philip was having none of it. His response began:

The undertaking being so important in the service of our Lord which has moved me to collect these forces, and my own affairs depending so greatly upon its success, I have not wished to place so weighty a business in any other hands than yours. Such is my confidence in you personally, and in your experience and desire to serve me, that, with God's help, I look for the success we aim at.

And so the Duke of Medina Sidonia set off for Lisbon with a heavy heart. He was to find that he was to command not just a routine naval taskforce but the most powerful war fleet the world had ever seen.

IV

The Spanish Armada

Pikeman. This heavily armoured individual wears a helmet with breastplate, backplate and thigh guards. His main weapon is a pike about seventeen feet long and he carries a short sword as a side arm. Men equipped like this were not usually carried on board ships as the weapon was too long and unwieldy to be much use in fighting. However, the Armada did have several regiments of land infantry that were intended to be used once the invasion of England took place. We do not know if any of them fought on board using their land gear, but it seems unlikely. This figure is included by way of comparison. Certainly such men would have been included in Parma's army.

When the Duke of Medina Sidonia arrived in Lisbon to take command of the great Armada, he found himself faced by various problems. Some were practical, others financial and not a few involved the personal relationships between his officers. But by far the most esoteric was a prophecy.

For half a century, people across Europe had been looking forward to 'the Year of the Eights' – 1588 – with some trepidation. In the 1520s a German scholar named Philip Melancthon had announced that from a study of the Bible, historical chronicles and other sources that the history of the world was divided into cycles of 80 years. These, he reckoned, had been getting progressively worse. The cycle that ended in 1518 had culminated in Martin Luther's defiance of the papacy and the birth of the Protestant faith. The cycle ending in 1588 would, he confidently predicted, be even worse: 'If this year, total catastrophe does not befall, if land and sea do not collapse in total ruin, yet will the whole world suffer upheavals, empires will dwindle from everywhere will be great lamentation,' he wrote in one of his more cheerful passages.

Other scholars had since got to work on Melancthon's figures. They had studied the relevant passages of the Book of Revelations, the Book of Daniel and the Book of Isaiah and come up with predictions even more dire. God's vengeance was at hand. They could not agree, however, on exactly what would happen. A French scholar speculated that the target of God's vengeance would be 'Jezebel' – who he identified as Queen Elizabeth of England. A Spanish fortune teller risked a nasty death by announcing that it would be Spain that would fall – she was lucky to get away with a lengthy prison sentence. Numerous other rumours flew about, but all agreed that the 'Year of the Eights' was going to be terrible. The rumours were sweeping through the sailors and soldiers gathered for the Armada like wildfire. Medina Sidonia ordered sermons to be preached, fortune tellers to be arrested and every officer to speak out confidently that the Armada was 'lucky'. By April it seemed that the rumours were under control.

That left the vast mass of organisational work that needed to be done. In his letters and files, Medina Sidonia made frequent complaints about the terrible mess that he had found on arrival. He may have exaggerated, but there can be no doubt that the great fleet was far from being ready to sail. The Duke set his considerable administrative talents to work and slowly he began to bring order out of chaos. Perhaps Media Sidonia's greatest contribution to the campaign was getting the Armada ready to sail at all.

The Duke's job cannot have been made easier by the constant stream of advice and instructions arriving from the bureaucrats at Philip's monastic-palace-fortress of El Escorial. Philip knew very well that Medina Sidonia was no admiral and had no experience of war at sea. He sought to make up for this deficiency by drawing up a detailed plan and giving the hapless commander the most precise instructions as to what he should do in different eventualities.

All of Philip's orders and Medina Sidonia's preparations were built on long years of Spanish naval supremacy, itself built on generations of experience of fighting at sea. Ever since history had been written down there had been two basic methods of winning a battle at sea. The first was by ramming, the second was by boarding. In ancient times ramming had dominated, though by the sixteenth century it was boarding that was becoming more usual.

For ramming to be effective, the attacking ship needed to have both great manoeuvrability and a ram capable of penetrating the hull of an enemy vessel. This meant that the ship needed to be powered by oars so that it was independent of the wind. The rigs of ships at this period meant that they could not sail particularly close to the wind. If a ramming ship relied on sails, it would not be able to manoeuvre during a battle with the agility needed to be effective. By the sixteenth century it was usual for galleys to have one or at most two banks of oars, each oar being pulled by more than one man.

Most navies with galleys used slaves to man the oars. The condemnation of English mariners to the galleys was a particular grievance of Elizabeth that she raised several times with Philip. Drake made a point of releasing galley slaves whenever he could. On one occasion he even set free 100 Turks and arranged for their transport back to Constantinople.

Because ramming ships were oar-powered, they had to be built as lightly as possible. Oars could convert muscle power into motion very effectively, but only if the craft to be moved was neither heavy nor had a hull cluttered with seaweed, shellfish and other fouling. The hulls were therefore constructed of thin planking and light frames. They were also generally narrow, being up to five or six times as long as they were broad. The ships were hauled up out of the water when not in use, allowing the hulls to dry out and so kill off any weeds or shellfish that had accumulated.

The ram was fitted to the front of the ship, being an extension of the keel. It was usually positioned on the waterline and was sheathed in bronze to increase its ability to smash through the timbers of an enemy ship. In battles between galleys, the key to success was the ability to move faster and turn more quickly than the enemy. In that way it would be possible to get on to the flank of an enemy galley, then ram it to inflict a hole so large that the enemy ship would soon sink.

The light construction, elongated shape and low freeboard that were necessary to make a galley an effective fighting ship meant that they were highly vulnerable to storms and bad weather. They were used most often in the Mediterranean where huge waves were less common, even in stormy weather, and where a sheltered port of anchorage was rarely far away. When they did venture into the Atlantic, galleys were utilised almost exclusively as patrol craft to guard the entrances to harbours.

It was in this role as harbour guards that galleys had encountered Drake at Cadiz. The freedom of galleys to move against the wind made them highly effective at approaching, halting and questioning merchant ships heading for port. Drake had cruelly exposed their vulnerability to cannon fire. The lightweight construction of a galley meant that any well aimed shot would cause serious damage, while at the same time making it impossible for the galley to mount heavy cannon. By the 1580s most galleys had a large platform built just behind the bow on which three or four cannon could be mounted, facing forwards over the ram. This gave them some firepower, but it remained significantly inferior to that of sail-powered ships.

The second method of fighting at sea was to board the enemy's ship, defeating the crew in hand to hand combat as on land. This technique called for men trained and equipped as soldiers to be ready to do the boarding, once the sailors had manoeuvred the ship into an advantageous position. Ideally, overwhelming force should be brought into play. This usually meant either having a ship that carried more men than the enemy's or bringing more of your ships into the fray than your opponent. Surrounding and isolating an enemy ship with several of your own was the usual tactic.

To make the attack more effective, it had become usual to equip some of the soldiers with bows, crossbows or the more up to date firearms such as muskets and harquebus. While the ships were manoeuvring, these men would shoot at the enemy in the hope of inflicting casualties. Once ships came alongside, the men armed with missile weapons would shoot furiously onto the enemy's decks to kill or wound as many of the opposing crew as possible. Those soldiers armed with hand weapons, such as pikes or swords would then swarm on to the enemy ship to kill the crew and take possession of their ship. It was usual for the assaulting crew to attach their ship to the victim vessel with grappling irons and ropes. They could be thrown by hand, but there was also a variety of contraptions designed to be dropped from yardarms or shot from crossbows that aimed to fix the two vessels firmly together.

Height is a great advantage when fighting hand to hand or with bows and crossbows. For this reason, from about 1250 onwards ships were fitted with what were known as sterncastles and forecastles. At first these were temporary structures placed on merchant ships when they were needed for war. By about 1380, however, they had become permanent wooden structures on both warships and merchant ships, there being relatively little difference between the two.

By the mid-sixteenth century the castles could be twice as tall as the hull of the ship but they were usually flimsily built. Their purpose was to give the soldiers in them greater height from which to fight, and so long as their timber sides could stop an arrow that was considered good enough. In any case these towering structures would have made the ship dangerously top heavy if they had been built of more substantial timbers. They were sometimes constructed not of solid wood, but of mere framework on which was perched a wooden fighting platform surrounded by canvas sheeting. This arrangement went by the name of 'cagework'.

The large castles had an unavoidable effect on the sailing qualities of the ships that carried them. The tall wooden panels acted rather like permanent sails, but sails that gave considerably more sideways motion than did the actual sails that were rigged to drive the ship forwards. The most problematic structure was the forecastle. When a ship sought to steer into the wind, the forecastle would inevitably catch the wind and tend to slew the bows back downwind. A ship with a large forecastle was unable to sail as close to the wind as one without.

It was partly for this reason that forecastles tended to be smaller than sterncastles. The large number of big merchant ships that were routinely converted to war use had a forecastle that was composed of a permanent lower section and a temporary upper section. When in use as trading vessels, the upper sections were removed. When chartered for war work, the ship would have it upper cagework installed, a process that took several days. One of the tasks that Medina Sidonia had his carpenters undertake was the installation of these upper forecastles.

The rather unwieldy nature of sailing ships with high castles was not too much of a problem given the boarding battle tactics used by navies. A commander would naturally seek to engage an enemy force less powerful than his own or to flee from one that was stronger. Flight was not always possible, at which point battle would be joined.

It was generally the case that safety lay in keeping a fleet of ships in tight formation so that all the ships were within bowshot of each other and therefore in a position to help each other. It was not unknown for ships to go into action lashed together, though this practice had fallen out of favour after about 1450. Efforts were often made to disrupt an enemy's formation by feints, moves to attack a flank and similar ruses. The objective was to isolate one or more ships so that they could be surrounded and overwhelmed by superior numbers of boarders surging forward from several different ships. This was not always possible, so actions between larger fleets often climaxed with large numbers of ships lashed together into a vast floating battlefield with soldiers fighting a mass of battles and actions. Ultimate victory went to the side that could gain an advantage in hand to hand fighting across the battlefield cluttered by masts, bulwarks and capstans and interspersed with castles and fighting platforms. In such battles casualties among fighting men were usually high. A defeated fleet might find that the men on ships that could not escape were annihilated. Ships tended to be captured, not sunk, as the weapons used were designed to kill humans not to inflict structural damage on the ships themselves.

When guns were invented they were fitted into the existing tactics and practise of naval warfare. Galleys had a few guns mounted so that they fired forward over the ram, considerably increasing the impact of the weapon. On ships with high castles that used boarding tactics, guns were essentially used to increase the killing power of the arrow and crossbow bolt fusillade that preceded the boarding. Men armed with muskets or the harquebus had replaced archers and crossbowmen by the 1580s. They crowded onto the castles and fighting platforms, pouring bullets on to the enemy decks as the ships closed.

Most ships' castles also had rather heavier guns with a bore of an inch or more. These were designed to shoot bullets over a greater distance than handheld muskets and would then be reloaded with a handful of pellets or even broken pieces of scrap iron. As the ships were lashed together these guns were fired again, their load spraying out in a horrific fan similar to that of a gigantic sawn off shotgun. The aim was to clear the enemy decks of men able to fight so that the boarders armed with swords and pikes could get across and secure a section of the enemy deck before the opposing soldiers could respond.

As larger cannon became available they tended to be used in a not dissimilar way. At first a ship could carry only one or two of these weapons and they had to be mounted on the top deck so that they could fire over the ship's bulwarks. But their enormous weight would make the ship top heavy if too many were used. Having one each side in the waist of the ship was not an unusual arrangement.

In about 1510 a French shipwright invented the gunport. This was a small, watertight door set into the side of the ship. It was kept shut most of the time, but could be opened during battle to allow the barrel of a cannon to be pushed out and fired. The gunport allowed the big, heavy guns to be mounted on the lower decks, which meant that each ship could carry more of them.

By the 1550s, most larger warships had eight or ten large cannon mounted on a lower deck and firing through gunports. These guns did not much alter the tactics of sea fighting. Their range might have been up to a mile, but fired from the heaving deck of a ship by a gun captain peering through a gunport they were accurate at only a fraction of that range. They were used to augment the missile weapons deployed as ships closed prior to boarding. A cannon might be fired two or three times before the ships locked together. Thereafter, the decisive fighting would take place on the upper decks, which the lower heavy guns could not reach. The gunners would abandon their weapons and dash up on deck to join the real fighting. Typically a warship went to sea with about 15 rounds for each heavy cannon and 25 for the lighter weapons mounted in the castles.

When fighting in fleets, ships were expected to carry out only a limited number of manoeuvres before they closed for boarding. Battle plans were usually worked out in advance at councils of war. The fleet commander would instruct his captains of signals that would convey specific orders to put the battle plan into action. A red flag on the foremast would mean one thing, a blue flag on the mainmast something else. Usually one of the heavy cannon would be fired as a signal was made to call every captain's attention to it.

Because the masses of canvas and billowing smoke tended to obscure vision in a sea fight, it was usual for larger fleets to be divided up into squadrons of no more than 20 ships. Each squadron had its own commander and signalling system. The squadron commanders being responsible for passing on orders from the fleet commander, but also having some freedom of decision making to ensure the best use of battle conditions in their immediate areas, of which the fleet commander was not aware.

As the Duke of Medina Sidonia marshalled his fleet for war, he followed this traditional pattern. It had developed slowly over the previous 200 years, since guns had first appeared on ships, and had proved to be highly effective. It had the further advantage that all the admirals and most of the captains in the Armada knew and understood this method of fighting.

In the Spanish Armada as it was being formed in Lisbon there were a number of different types of vessel. Many of the varieties were designations that meant more to the men of the time than they to us today. The principal fighting ships were termed 'galleons'. These were purpose-built warships, nearly all of them owned by King Philip himself, though a few were contributed by allies or rulers hoping to curry favour. The Duke of Florence, for instance, sent one of the largest galleons in the Armada. It was called *Florencia* in Spanish accounts. This was not the vessel's name but merely meant 'from Florence'.

The galleons had some distinctive features in addition to their high castles and fighting platforms. The tall superstructures were heavy and might have made a ship prone to rolling over. To remedy this, the galleons were built wide at the waterline, but narrow on the upper decks. This pronounced inward sloping of a ship's sides was known as the tumblehome or housing-in. The majority of wooden sailing ships had this feature, but it was most pronounced in the galleons.

Necessary as the tumblehome was to the stability of the ship, it did mean that the topmost decks of the castles were too far from their counterparts on an enemy ship for a man carrying weapons to stand any chance of jumping from one to the other. Boarding an opposing ship therefore involved swarming over the sides of the section of deck between the two castles. Only there was the gap between two ships lashed together narrow enough for a soldier in armour to leap across. This section was also the most vulnerable to gunfire as it was overlooked by the castles. A principle aim of the gunners in the castles was to kill or disable their counterparts in the opposing ship so that they would not be able to inflict massive casualties on the boarders as they formed up in the waist to attack.

Vessels designated simply 'ships' were large merchant vessels that had been converted to war work. Chartering ships to a ruler during a war could be a profitable business, so most of the larger merchant ships were designed with an eye to such conversion. Their castles could be as tall and imposing as those of galleons, they could carry as many men and they could mount just as many guns.

The main differences were to be found in the internal construction of the vessels. Galleons were purpose built to carry large numbers of men for long voyages, ships were not. Conditions on a converted merchant ship tended to be considerably more cramped and uncomfortable. This should not have made much difference to the fighting abilities of the ships concerned, but on a long campaign like the intended invasion of England could lead to lower morale, outbreaks of disease and other problems.

At this date most craft called 'ships' were those that were later termed 'carracks', though technically this term more properly refers to a type of rig. Carracks were generally about 2.5 times as long as they were wide and had a pronounced tub-like shape with rounded bows and stern. The distinguishing features of the carrack were the masts and rigging. It had three or four vertical masts, the front most of which was raked forward slightly. At the bow was an additional mast that struck out forwards at a steep angle, the bowsprit as it was later to be generally known. The first two masts, the foremast and mainmast, carried two large square-rigged sails each. The hindmost mast, or masts, were termed the mizzens. They carried triangular lateen sails.

This arrangement proved to be very efficient, so much so that it later came to dominate ship design and is often termed simply 'ship-rigged'. The square sails on the foremast and mainmast provided the main motive power for the ship, especially when running downwind. The Spanish cut their sails so that they were very full, billowing out as they caught the wind to provide the maximum possible speed. The lateen sails at the rear were most useful when the ship was beating up into the wind. They were highly efficient at pushing the bows into the wind and so keeping the ship on the correct heading, close to the wind.

The 'hulk', called the *urca* in Spanish, was a type of merchant ship that came from the Baltic. The differences between a ship, or carrack, and a hulk are not now known for certain as no detailed drawings of a hulk have survived. So far as can be deduced the differences were related to the fact that hulks tended to carry cargoes of timber in the form of planks and poles, while ships tended to carry more general cargoes packed into barrels or sacks. Presumably the interior layout was very different, but the exterior of the ships does not seem to have differed obviously.

Hulks were notoriously poor sailors, though well able to withstand storms and bad weather. The hulk seems to have lacked the full carrack rig at this date, though it would adopt it within a few decades. The foremast and mainmast of a hulk usually carried only one sail each. This sail was very large and square rigged. It was controlled by a mass of stays, reefs and other ropes so that it was almost as flexible as the carrack's two sail arrangement, but called for much more in the way of seamanship and delicate fiddling to work.

It was probably this rig that made it difficult to handle with any precision. When in use as a merchant ship this was not much of a problem, but when used in a military situation when keeping station with other ships was of importance, the hulk proved to be less than satisfactory. Hulks were not, therefore, converted into warships as often as carracks or ships. In the Armada they seem to have been used almost exclusively as store transport ships, though they had a few light guns added to them for the campaign.

Similarly the differences between the two types of small craft that sailed with the Armada are not now clear. The patches and zabras were both used much as the English used pinnaces.

They were small vessels that seem to have carried only about a dozen men each. They were used to scout ahead of the fleet, carry messages between ships, land to collect water and provisions and a host of other duties. They were not, as a rule, used in battle though there are a few instances on record of these small craft taking part in raids.

The Armada also took with it two types of oared warship. There were four galleys equipped with rams and a few heavy cannon pointing forward. They were included because the Marquis of Santa Cruz had read an account of a French raid on Portsmouth that had taken place in 1545. A sudden calm had settled down during the fighting, rendering the sailing ships on both sides helpless. A couple of French galleys had rowed out to bombard the English warships, inflicting much damage. It was considered that galleys would be of use only in calms and were not intended to play a significant role in a battle fought under any other conditions.

Rather different were the four galleasses that had been contributed by Naples. These awesome ships were a hybrid between the oared galley and fully rigged ship. Each one was about 150 feet long and was shaped very much like a galley. It had a ram at the bow and was powered by oars. The construction of the hull was much more solid and heavier than a conventional galley. The ship carried three masts, rigged in a similar fashion to the conventional galleon and there were no castles. The main armament, in addition to the ram, were a number of heavy cannon mounted along the sides of the ship under the oars. A number of lighter cannon were mounted on a fighting platform built over the bows, with a smaller number of similar guns at the stern.

The basic idea of the galleass was that it would combine the sailing qualities and gunfire hitting power of a galleon with the agility and manoeuvrability of a galley. The type had performed well in the Mediterranean where it was highly respected as a fighting vessel. Medina Sidonia and his admirals had great hopes for the galleasses. They mounted heavy guns and could move more nimbly than any ship other than the galleys.

The English had had galleasses in their fleet during the 1540s although these craft had been smaller and lighter than the Mediterranean galleasses. The oars were located under the gundeck which meant that the guns could fire at any time without risk of shooting off the oars, but had the drawback of allowing only

Galleass. The galleass was a hybrid warship which first appeared in the 1520s and remained in use until the early seventeenth century. Essentially it was an oared galley fitted with an extra deck on which cannon were mounted. It was an attempt to produce a ship able to move in dead calms, or to move directly upwind, which had the firepower of a galleon. It was first produced in the Mediterranean, where it remained most popular, but within a decade or two was being used in Atlantic waters. Outside of the Mediterranean the main use of this type of ship was as a harbour guard. The oars enabled her to work in or out of a port regardless of the wind direction or state of the tides, while her guns made her able to halt any ship that was attempting to evade customs or seeking to leave without paying harbour dues. The English used them at major ports as early as 1535 and in 1588 London was guarded by two of these ships. The galleasses used in northern waters tended to be quite small and restricted to inshore work. The oarsmen were free men, hired at a rate of pay similar to that of an unskilled farm labourer. Galleasses from Italy and Spain – including those sailing with the Armada – were substantially larger warships that were expected to take their place in large scale sea battles. The oars on these ships were manned by slaves or convicts. There were two main varieties of galleass, those with the guns below the oars and those with the guns above the oars. Having the guns located lower down made for a more stable craft and enabled larger guns to be carried, but meant that the oars had to be lifted in unison out of the water every time the guns were fired. It is thought, but by no means certain, that all the Armada galleasses had large guns fitted below the oars.

lighter guns to be fitted. They fell out of use in the 1560s and the design was abandoned. One reason that they were abandoned was that the English did not use galley slaves, and recruiting sailors to pull oars was difficult to say the least.

The size of all these ships was conventionally given in tons or tonnage. Confusingly this had nothing to do with the actual weight of the ship. It was instead a measure used by port authorities to decide how much quayside to allot to a ship, and consequently how much to charge the ship for putting into harbour. The measurement had originated in northern Europe in the twelfth century when it had equated simply to how many barrels of a standard size – the tun – the ship could carry. By the 1450s this system had changed in English ports due to continual disputes between harbour masters and ship's captains over how many barrels a ship could hold and therefore what harbour dues it should pay. The new English system allowed for a quick and easy computation of a ship's tonnage by the harbour master that could not be gainsaid by the captain. The tonnage was calculated by measuring the length of the ship in feet, multiplying that by the maximum width, or bream, and then multiplying that by the depth of the hold beneath the main deck. The resulting figure was divided by 100.

This system had the advantage of not only being quick and easy, but that it could also be used to measure the tonnage of warships. These warships did not actually carry any tuns, or standard barrels, but they had a length, width and height that could be used to calculate harbour fees. The system was refined from time to time, but was to remain in place until 1890.

By about 1500 all nations had adopted a similar method of calculating a ship's tonnage for the purposes of harbour fees, rental payments and the like. The Spanish system was rather more complicated than the English system, taking into account the height of the ship out of the water as well as the depth of its hold. The Spanish system resulted in a similar result for merchant ships as the English, but tended to produce a higher figure for warships. Thus a warship that in the English reckoning would have been 500 tons would by Spanish calculations come out at about 650 tons. It is worth bearing this fact in mind when comparing the sizes of opposing warships during the Armada campaign. As a rule of thumb, the figures given for Spanish galleons is something of an overestimate compared to English warships.

Having got all his ships together, Medina Sidonia adopted the customary practice of dividing his Armada into a number of squadrons – confusingly also called 'armadas' in Spanish documents. The ships of each of these squadrons were expected to sail and fight together, allowing Medina Sidonia a degree of flexibility in his battle and sailing arrangements.

Medina Sidonia put himself in command of the Squadron of Portugal, the most powerful fighting force in the Armada. It was composed of ten large, powerful galleons. Nine of them were from Portugal: *San Martin, San Juan, San Marcos, San Felipe, San Luis, San Mateo, Santiago, San Cristobal, San Bernardo*, while the tenth, *Florencia*, was from Florence. At 1,000 tons, the *San Martin* was the largest and most powerful of these galleons. It was also Medina Sidonia's flagship. The squadron included two zabras.

The Squadron of Biscay was commanded by Admiral Juan Martinez de Recalde, who had transported the troops to their ill fated campaign in Ireland that ended at Smerwick. He had ten large ships: *Santa Ana, Gran Grin, Santiago, La Concepcion de Zubelzu, La Concepcion de Juanes de Cano, Magdalena, San Juan, Maria Juan* and the *Santa Maria de Montemayor*. Recalde also had four pataches. The *Santa Ana* was chosen as the flagship of the squadron, but at the last minute Recalde was to move to the *San Juan*, apparently as it was the largest vessel in the squadron.

The Squadron of Castile was led by Admiral Diego Flores de Valdes. He had ten galleons, though these were rather smaller than those in the Squadron of Portugal. They were the *San Cristobel, San Juan Bautista, San Pedro, San Juan, Santiago el Mayor, San Felipe y Santiago, Ascencion, Nuestra Senora del Barrio, San Medel y Celedon* and *Santa Ana*. The squadron also had four ships: *Nuestra Senora de Begona, Trinidad, Santa Catalina* and *San Juan Bautista*. Diego Flores also had two pataches.

The Squadron of Andalusia was commanded by Don Pedro de Valdes. He had one galleon, the *San Juan*, and a hulk which contrary to custom had been converted to be a warship: the *Dequesa Santa Ana*. Don Pedro also commanded eight large ships: *Nuestra Senora del Rosario* (the flagship), *San Francisco, San Juan de Gargarin, La Concepcion, Santa Catalina, La Trinidad, Santa Mara del Juncal* and *San Bartolome*. He had only one patache.

The Squadron of Guipuzcoa was led by Migeul de Oquendo. This consisted of nine ships: *Santa Ana* (the flagship), *Santa Maria de la Rosa, San Salvador, San Esteban, Santa Marta, Santa Barbara, San*

Buenaventura, La Maria San Juan and *Santa Cruz*. There was also a large hulk the *Doncella*, though to what extent this had been converted to war use is not clear. Oquendo had two pataches.

Martin de Bertondona commanded the Squadron of the Levant, which consisted of ten ships. Bertondona's flagship, *La Reganzona*, was the largest ship in the entire Armada at 1,249 tons. The other vessels in the squadron were *La Lavia, La Rata Encoronda, San Juan de Sicilia, La Trinidad Valencera, La Anunciada, San Nicholas Prodaneli, La Juliana, Santa Maria de Vision* and *La Trinidad de Scala*. Most of these ships were Italian, as the names such as 'de Sicilia' or 'de Scala' would suggest.

The Storeship Squadron was led by Juan Gomez de Demida who had his flag in the *Gran Grifon*. His command also included *San Salvador, Perro Mariono, Falcon Blanco Mayor, Castillo Negro, Barca de Hamburg, Casa de Paz Grande, San Pedro Mayor, El Sanson, San Pedro Menor, Barca de Danzique, Falcon Blanco Mediano, San Andres, Casa de Paz Chica, Ciervo Volante, Paloma Blanca, La Ventura, Santa Barbara, Santiago, David, El Gato, Essayas* and *San Gabriel*.

There were a further 23 small vessels, assorted zabras and pataches, held under the command of Don Antonio Hurtado de Mendoza. These craft were to be loaned out by Don Antonio to whichever squadron commander needed them at various times, though Medina Sidonia had first call on the fastest and best.

Don Diego de Medrano commanded the four galleys: *Capitana, Princessa, Diana* and *Bazana*. The four Galleasses of Naples – *San Lorenzo, Zuniga, Girona* and *Napolitana* – were commanded by Don Hugo de Moncada.

In all there were 130 ships carrying 29,453 men, of whom 19,000 were soldiers. There were also 180 monks, five physicians, five surgeons, four priests and 71 hospital staff. All admirals and commanders had a personal staff of treasurers, officials and servants. The staff of Medina Sidonia himself totalled 50, the others had less than half that each.

The fleet flagship also housed 22 gentlemen, and most of the other flagships had their own gentlemen. These young men were almost exclusively the sons of noblemen and *hidalgos* who were sailing with the Armada to gain military experience and useful contacts. This was quite usual at the time in all military commands of all nations. The gentlemen had no set duties, but were expected to obey any commands given to them and to play a full role in any fighting that took place. They, or their families, were usually expected to pay their own way. Securing a position as a gentleman on the flagship was a highly rated honour, and much sought after. Before he sailed Medina Sidonia would have been pestered by letters and personal visits from many noblemen seeking a place for their son.

As he was preparing for sea, Medina Sidonia made a few changes in the command structure of the Armada. Santa Cruz had been an experienced sailor and admiral, but Medina Sidonia was neither and felt that he was going to need some help. He appointed two men to come on board the *San Martin* to advise him on day to day matters. For naval affairs he chose Don Diego Flores de Valdes, appointing Gregorio de las Alas to command the Squadron of Castile in his place.

The choice of Diego Flores proved to be a mistake. Of all the squadron admirals he was the least experienced and most junior in terms of previous commands. On both counts the most senior man in the Armada was Recalde, and he resented being passed over for the honour of advising the fleet commander on the decks of the flagship. To try to smooth his feelings, Medina Sidonia made Recalde the Vice Admiral of the Armada, but the move failed to mollify the veteran sea dog. Even worse, Diego Flores was on famously bad terms with his cousin, Don Pedro de Valdes. Although the origins of the feud are unknown, it is clear that Don Pedro regarded Diego Flores as an incompetent upstart who owed his position to flattery of his seniors rather than to any actual talent. Don Pedro never missed an opportunity to pour scorn on Diego Flores's advice nor to question orders from the decks of the San Martin.

The choice of a military adviser proved to be no less fraught. Medina Sidonia chose well when he appointed the highly respected veteran soldier the Marquis de Penafiel, but Penafiel flatly refused to move to the flagship. He had taken great care in the choice of the crew of his ship, the *San Marcos*, and said that he much preferred to go to war with men he knew and trusted. Medina Sidonia then turned to Don Francisco de Bobadilla, who agreed to serve. Bobadilla was a very experienced soldier, but most of his experience had been on land. He was not accustomed to boarding enemy ships or in the sailing tactics that made such boarding possible. At least nobody had a grudge against him.

On 11 May Medina Sidonia wrote to King Philip announcing that at long last everything was ready. The ships began to move down the Tagus River from Lisbon to the sea. The river was narrow just below Lisbon Harbour, which made it easy to defend but meant that the Armada had to move off a few ships at a time. As they arrived in the mouth of the Tagus the ships anchored to await the others. It took two weeks to complete the move.

At dawn on 29 May a bugle call sounded out from the decks of the flagship *San Martin*. It was picked up and repeated from ship to ship. The anchors were lifted and the sails set. The Armada was on its way to England.

V

The Voyage to England

As the Spanish Armada steered north from the River Tagus, the Duke of Medina Sidonia must have pondered over his orders. These came direct from King Philip in El Escorial and were a curious mixture of pedantic precision and vagueness. As events were to prove, they were self-contradictory and would cause Medina Sidonia a good deal of trouble, though this was not clear on 29 April as the great fleet spread its sails.

The orders from King Philip came in a number of different documents, of which the two most important had been written on 1 April. The first might be termed the General Instructions as it covered a wide range of matters. The second could be considered the Secret Instructions since they were for the eyes of Medina Sidonia only – an almost exact copy was sent by fast courier to the Duke of Parma in the Netherlands.

The General Instructions opened in conventional fashion, then addressed what Philip considered to be the most important point:

> In the first place, as all victories are the gifts of God Almighty, and the cause we champion is so exclusively His, we may fairly look for His aid and favour, unless by our sins we render ourselves unworthy thereof. You will therefore have to exercise special care that such cause of offence shall be avoided on the Armada, and especially that there shall be no sort of blasphemy. This must be severely enforced, with heavy penalties, in order that the punishment for toleration of such sin may not fall upon all of us. You are going to fight for the cause of our Lord, and for the glory of His Name, and consequently He must be worshiped by all, so that His favour may be deserved. This favour is being so fervently besought in all parts that you may go full of encouragement that, by the mercy of God, His forces will be added to your own.

The King then moved on to give instructions regarding the campaign ahead.

> You will sail with the whole of the Armada, and go straight to the English Channel, which you will ascend as far as Cape Margate, where you will join hands with the Duke of Parma, my nephew, and hold the passage for his crossing in accordance with the plan which has already been communicated to both of you.
>
> It is important that you and the Duke should be mutually informed of each other's movements and it will therefore be advisable that before you arrive thither you should continue to communicate with him as best you can, either by secretly landing a trustworthy person at night on the coast of Normandy or Bolougne, or else by sending intelligence by sea to Gravelines, Dunkirk or Nieuport. You must take care that any messengers you may send by land shall be persons whom you can thoroughly trust so that verbal messages may be given to them. Letters to the Duke may be sent in the enclosed cipher.
>
> Although it may be hoped that God will send fair weather for your voyage, it will be well, when you sail, to appoint a rendezvous for the whole fleet in case a storm may scatter it.

Philip's letter goes on to give advice about fighting battles at sea, warnings against pursuing booty rather than victory and the wisdom of giving written orders to any officers sent on a mission that would take them out of sight of the flagship. There is also a strongly worded paragraph about the need to act in conjunction with the Duke of Parma and a warning of the disasters that occur when senior commanders fall out. Philip continues:

> It must be understood that the above instructions about fighting only hold good in case the passage to England of my nephew the Duke of Parma cannot otherwise be assured. If this can be done without fighting either by diverting the enemy or otherwise, it will be best to carry it out in this way and keep your forces intact.
>
> In the event of the Duke establishing himself on shore you may station the Armada at the mouth of the Thames and support him, a portion of your ships being told off to hold the passage of reinforcement etc from Flanders, thus strengthening us on both sides. If circumstances at the time should, in the opinion of the Duke and yourself, render another course desirable you may act in accordance with your joint opinion; but on your own discretion alone you will

not land or undertake anything on shore. This you will do only with the concurrence of the Duke, your sole function on your own account being – what indeed is the principal one – to fight at sea.

You will have to stay there until the undertaking be successfully concluded, with God's help, and you may then return, calling in and settling the affairs in Ireland on the way if the Duke approves of your doing so, the matter being left to your joint discretion.

There are several important points within the General Instructions. The first is that the Medina Sidonia is instructed to head for 'Cape Margate' and wait there while the Duke of Parma's army is ferried across the England. This headland is better known as the North Foreland and the anchorage off it as The Downs, and is not a sheltered harbour, but an open area of sea. It is protected from the west by Kent and from the east by the sandbanks of The Goodwin Sands. To the south, the distant coast of France offers some protection, but it is open and unprotected to the north. It was a tolerable anchorage for a large fleet, such as the Armada, for most of the time, but if a strong north wind blew it was unusable. Relying on it to remain safe for the Armada for the several days that would be needed for Parma to move his army was taking something of a risk.

Secondly, no mention is made of a point on which Parma had been most insistent. That is that the Armada had to guard his barges and small craft while they crossed the sea from the Netherlands to a landing point in the Thames Estuary. And it was not only the English that he was worried about, the Dutch Sea Beggars were also a potent threat. The seaborne arm of the Dutch rebel movement had by this date established a firm grip over the coastal waters off the Netherlands.

Those coastal waters, as Parma knew but Philip does not anywhere acknowledge, were unique. They were fringed by vast shoals and shifting sandbanks that ensured that the entrances to harbours were complicated, while the coastal waters were always changing and usually treacherous. In the twentieth century heavy dredging has changed the coastal aspect and made ports such as Rotterdam easy of access for even the biggest ships, it was not so in 1588. The big warships of the time were unable to navigate the Dutch coasts in safety.

The Sea Beggars used local craft called 'flyboats'. These were wide, flat-bottomed craft with a shallow prow and deep stern and were powered by a spritsail rig – akin to that of a modern racing yacht. A spritsail allowed a small craft to sail nimbly into the wind, and to change direction with agility – just what was needed for negotiating shifting sandbanks. Armed with cannon, the flyboats would have been able to race in to smash the fragile barges of the Duke of Parma and drown his men with ease.

Parma had a few flyboats of his own, but nowhere near enough to protect his barges, still less to defeat the Sea Beggars. He had warned repeatedly that the Armada would need to help him against the enemy flyboats. Nowhere in any orders or instructions sent to Medina Sidonia is this problem mentioned. It is true that the Armada had a squadron of 22 armed pataches and zabras. These may have been intended to defeat the flyboats, but if so this is not specified.

It is also noticeable that Medina Sidonia is told to sail straight to Cape Margate and is banned from landing in or raiding England unless Parma agrees. This would seem to rule out one of the options that had been discussed in the previous months and which Santa Cruz had seemed to favour: the capture of the Isle of Wight.

In 1545 a French raiding fleet had landed soldiers on the island, securing most of it while the ships anchored in the stretch of sheltered water between the island and the mainland. The experiences of the French force had been studied by Santa Cruz. Having sacked the island, the French had been confronted by England's main war fleet and had withdrawn to France.

For the Spanish Armada it could be different. The Isle of Wight could be a vital staging post. A key problem with transporting Parma's army was the need to guard a huge number of flimsy, flat-bottomed barges all at the same time across a wide stretch of the North Sea. These problems could be erased by the capture of the Isle of Wight. With the island secured, the Armada could send off a number of large warships that could collect Parma's soldiers in batches, bringing each contingent back to Wight before returning for the next. The process would take several days, but would be less dependent on good weather than for the Armada to anchor in the Downs while Parma shipped his men to the Thames Estuary. Once Parma's army was assembled on the Isle of Wight it could be transported quickly and easily to the adjacent English coast. Certainly there were difficulties, not least getting the men ashore on to a defended coast, but the main maritime problems would be solved by the capture of the Isle.

Now Philip was ruling out the idea. We do not know why he did so, as no explanation is given in the documents that have survived, or even if Medina Sidonia had been informed of the earlier plan, still less the reasons why it was being abandoned. Subsequent events would seem to indicate that he had not.

Some historians have sought to make much of Philip's injunction that Medina Sidonia was to avoid fighting the English fleet if he possibly could. It has been theorised that Philip was worried that the English might win any such battle. However, the context makes it clear that this is not what was concerning Philip. He remained confident that his Armada could deal with the English freebooters and Elizabeth's weak navy and was more concerned with the need for Medina Sidonia to keep his force intact.

After all, Philip had other uses for his armada. He specifies one: 'settling affairs in Ireland' but the needs of his far flung overseas empire would demand many warships. The affairs in Ireland that needed settling were, as in England, mostly religious. The majority of the native Irish were Catholics, but the ruling English were Protestant. In fact the situation in Ireland was nowhere near as straightforward as Philip imagined.

Elizabeth's role as 'Queen of Ireland' was very different from that of monarchs in other nations. The monarch in Ireland had only limited powers and did not rule in the sense that Elizabeth ruled in England or Philip ruled in Spain. Instead power mostly rested with local noblemen, who were often clan chiefs as much as noblemen in the conventional sense of the word. The Irish fought private wars with each other, made treaties as they wished and lived by their own laws.

Various English monarchs had sought to entrench their rule over Ireland by sending over English soldiers, but none had been particularly successful. By Elizabeth's time her direct rule expanded over an area around Dublin, known as the Pale. Beyond the Pale, she had to work through the local chiefs and nobles. There were garrisons of English troops scattered across Ireland to keep an eye open for any serious trouble and to try to stop disputes between Irish lords turning to violence, but they were few and far between. In 1588 there were about 8,000 English troops in Ireland, mostly in or near Dublin. There were some 4,000 Irish that Elizabeth might have been able to rely on, but for the most part the armed men of Ireland followed the orders of their lords and clan chiefs, not Elizabeth.

It had long been a policy of England's enemies to foster rebellion and discontent in Ireland. War between the Irish lords, or even better between a lord and the King, would drain men and resources out of England. Philip himself had been happy to conduct this sort of action but he now envisaged the Armada doing something quite different.

Once England was subdued, the Kingship of Ireland would pass to Philip's daughter and to whoever Philip chose as her husband. This was why Philip ordered Medina Sidonia to 'settle' Irish affairs rather than foment rebellion. If the King of Ireland was a Catholic, thought Philip, the indigenous Irish would have neither need nor desire to continue to fight against the monarch. He must have fondly believed that Ireland would fall into his lap like a ripe plum once England was disposed of.

In fact, the main issue between the native Irish and their Queen Elizabeth was not so much religion as power. It was the efforts of the kings to convert the loose, informal overlordship of the King of Ireland into a centralised, effective monarchy like that of England that had first sparked the trouble. The earls and lords of Ireland deeply resented being told what to do and fought against attempts to do so. The struggle had been going on for generations, starting long before there were any religious differences between the two nations. It was likely that the Irish chieftains would fight against efforts by Philip's puppet ruler every bit as violently as they did against Elizabeth.

The Secret Instructions were much shorter than the General Instructions, and there were good reasons for Philip's strict order that neither Medina Sidonia nor Parma should reveal them to anyone. They were concerned with how Medina Sidonia and Parma should behave if it proved impossible for Parma's army to be transported over the North Sea to England. In such circumstances Philip instructed Parma and Medina Sidonia to bully Elizabeth into signing a peace treaty. The military might of the army and the naval might of the Armada were to be used to inflict damage on England and the English until Elizabeth agreed.

Philip's demands for a treaty were very clearly spelled out:

The first is that in England the free use and exercise of our holy Catholic faith shall be permitted to all Catholics, native and foreign, and that those who are in exile shall be permitted to return.

The second is that all the places in my Netherlands which the English hold shall be restored to me.

The third is that the English shall recompense me for the injury they have done to me, my dominions and my subjects – which will amount to an exceedingly great sum. This third point may be dropped. You are to use it as a lever to obtain the other two.

With regard to the free exercise of Catholicism, you may point out to them that since freedom of worship is allowed to the Protestants in France, there will be no sacrifice of dignity in allowing the same privilege to Catholics in England. If they retort that I do not allow the same toleration in Flanders as exists in France, you may tell them that their country is in a different position, and point out to them how conducive to their tranquillity it would be to satisfy the Catholics in this way, and how largely it would increase the trade of England and their profits since, as soon as toleration was brought about, people from all Christendom would flock thither in the assurance of safety.

Philip must have known that these conditions would have been unacceptable to Elizabeth. Even if she were minded to permit Catholics to practise their faith openly in England, she could not be expected to allow the return of the exiles. Many of them had, after all, sworn to murder her. Nor was Philip willing to give anything in return, except to allow Drake and the other freebooters to keep what they had already got. He did not offer to recognise Elizabeth as legitimate ruler of England, nor to make any concessions in the Netherlands. Still, he probably thought that it was worth trying.

In the event it was none of these orders and injunctions that would prove to be of the most immediate use to Medina Sidonia. It was the advice about agreeing a rendezvous point that would be used first.

Within two days of leaving the Tagus, the Armada was buffeted by strong headwinds. As he had predicted, Medina Sidonia was desperately seasick, but at least steady progress was being made. On 10 June he sent a patache north to report to the Duke of Parma that the Armada was on its way. That same day, one of the hulks, *David Chico*, lost a mast and had to go back to Galicia for repairs. Medina Sidonia told the captain to follow him north to England as soon as he could.

On 18 June a great storm blew down from the north and scattered the Armada. On 20 June Medina Sidonia and most of the ships put into Corunna, but 34 craft were missing. Much to his embarrassment, Medina Sidonia had not set Corunna as the rendezvous, but the Isles of Scilly and he had been unable to get there. Even worse,

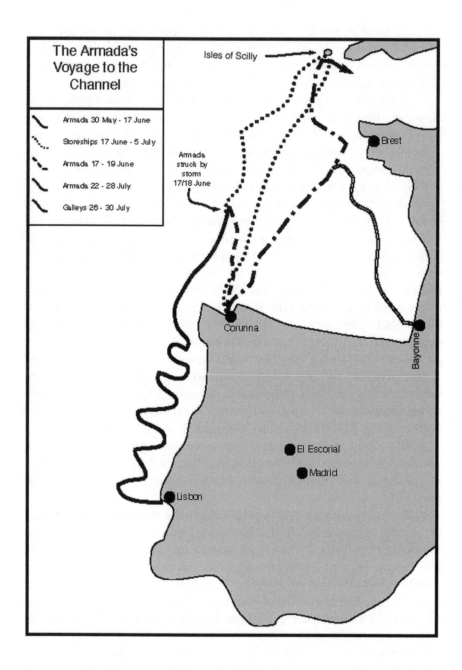

The Armada's
Voyage to the
Channel

Armada 30 May - 17 June

Storeships 17 June - 5 July

Armada 17 - 19 June

Armada 22 - 28 July

Galleys 26 - 30 July

Isles of Scilly

Brest

Armada
struck by
storm
17/18 June

Corunna

Bayonne

El Escorial

Madrid

Lisbon

he had added an extra sentence to his orders that read: 'should any ships be separated from the Armada, they are not to return to Spain on any account. The punishment for disobedience being death with disgrace.'

As soon as the wind moderated, Medina Sidonia sent a patache racing north to the Scillies to round up any ships that had gone to the rendezvous point. About 30 ships had got to the Scillies, some individually, others in groups, and they now turned back south to rejoin the Armada.

The ships, mostly store ships, had not been wasting their time. On 1 July one group of nine Spanish ships had encountered two small ships coming south from Ireland. The Spanish hurried to attack, using their favoured boarding tactics but things did not go quite according to plan. The *El Gato* rammed the first of the new arrivals so hard that she was knocked over on to her beam ends and began to sink.

The hapless crew scrambled on to the Spanish ship, but two had been killed in the collision. They turned out to be Irishmen heading for Spain with a cargo of wheat who were most indignant at the way they had been treated. They told the Spanish a tale of English barbarity in Ireland, laying emphasis on how badly Catholics were treated. No doubt they hoped this would ensure they were well treated, and it did.

Meanwhile, the *Paloma Blanca* was closing with the second ship. She was successfully boarded and the four men found on board taken back to the Spanish ship for questioning. They were Scots carrying coal to Brittany and knew very little about events in England or the movements of the English warships. A strong wind then got up and the Spanish cast the Scottish ship adrift, keeping the hapless Scots on board to be carried back to Spain.

Paloma Blanca later ran into a patrolling English warship. The Spanish captain ordered all the soldiers on board to hide out of sight in cabins, then pretended to be an unarmed and poorly manned merchant ship. As he had hoped the English ship closed to investigate, the soldiers then rushed out to pour a devastating volley into the English vessel. This was the moment for boarders to surge forward, but much to the Spaniards' disgust the English ship bore away, circled the Spanish ship and then headed off back toward England.

The captain of the *Paloma Blanca* was jubilant, and when he heard of the incident so was Medina Sidonia. The English warship had behaved just as the Spanish had been hoping that the English would. Just like the freebooters, they had closed quickly enough on an apparently helpless merchant ship, but had fled as soon as real fighting was called for. Their morale soared.

The patache sent to round up the ships off the Scillies was commanded by an enterprising young man named Ensign Esquival. He decided to push on and scout out the English coast, a decision fraught with danger. Esquival was sailing into enemy waters in a tiny vessel. There would be plenty of English ships about, including warships on patrol. But there would also be fishing boats, French coastal traders, German merchant ships and a host of others. Esquival could not be certain of the identity of any ship until he got close, and by then it might have been too late to get away.

Nevertheless, Esquival pushed on. He sighted Cornwall and at dusk on 1 July pushed into Mount Bay. He was within two miles of land. 'A sail passed to leeward at two leagues distance,' Esquival later reported. 'I wanted to chase her, but the pilot opposed it as we were uncertain of catching her and it was late.' A strong north wind then got up and blew the patache out to sea. 'At four o'clock a wave passed clean over us, and nearly swamped the craft. We were flush with the water and almost lost, but by great effort of all hands the water was baled out.'

Soon after dawn on 3 July, Esquival tried to get back to the English coast, but found his path blocked by six warships strung out across the open sea. Clearly these were English ships on patrol looking for the Armada. He turned about and fled south without being seen. When he got back he found that the entire Armada was once again together.

While Esquival was off the coast of England, Medina Sidonia had been holding a council of war. Unlike Drake, Medina Sidonia conducted his meetings according to convention. The question he posed was whether the Armada should put to sea with the ships that were ready, or wait for the storm-damaged ships to be repaired. All the officers present agreed that it would be best to wait. All except Don Pedro de Valdes who could not resist having a go at his hated cousin Diego Flores. Don Pedro spoke up for setting sail at once, then added that the storm damage would not be great because 'the storm that overtook them was not very violent, unless for reasons of their own any of the vessels wished to make bad weather of it.' It had been Diego Flores who had advised Medina Sidonia to put into port and everyone knew it.

As things turned out, there was a far more pressing reason for the Armada to stay in port. Large quantities of the stores taken on board at Lisbon and Cadiz had gone rotten and were quite inedible. The reason was quickly found: the barrels in which the salt cod, bacon, cheese and other foods had been sealed had warped, allowing air to get in and spoil the food. The use of unseasoned barrel staves was the problem, and that had been made necessary by the destruction of so many seasoned staves by Drake the previous year.

It was probably in Corunna that the men of the Armada heard a relatively unimportant piece of news that was later to have a profound impact on the campaign. An Italian military engineer by the name of Fedrigo Giambelli had left the employment of the Dutch rebels and had been hired by Queen Elizabeth. Giambelli was an acknowledged genius. He was at his best building defensive works, and had come to be greatly feared by Parma. Giambelli's real talent was with gunpowder, his explosive devices and booby traps were bloodily effective.

It took several weeks to restock the ships with food and drink and to repair the storm damage that had been sustained. The Armada was ready to sail on 20 July and Medina Sidonia held another council of war. It was decided to leave as soon as a southerly wind came up. The wind blew on 22 July and the Armada sailed.

On 26 July the fleet was becalmed in deep fog in the Bay of Biscay. That evening a wind got up which by nightfall had become a squally storm lashing the Armada with rain. The great Atlantic rollers did not cause problems to most of the ships, but the Mediterranean galleys were soon wallowing in the waves. They sent a message to Medina Sidonia, then fled for the shelter of French ports. Two of the galleys ran aground and were wrecked. The galley slaves broke free and ran ashore, fleeing their Spanish masters. One of the slaves was a Welshman named Gwynn. Penniless and destitute, he made contact with English merchants in France and headed for home.

During the night another ship went missing. This was the mighty 768-ton *Santa Ana* of the Squadron of Biscay. She never rejoined the Armada, but her captain Juan Perez de Mucio, had not given up. After putting into a Breton port for quick repairs, he entered the English Channel alone seeking news of the Armada. He would eventually get to Le Havre only to learn that the Armada was far to the east and that the English fleet blocked his path. He was to stay where he was awaiting orders that never came.

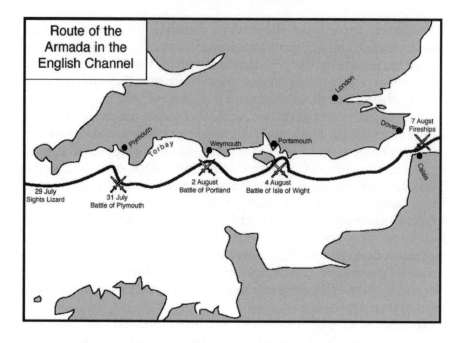

Route of the Armada in the English Channel

Meanwhile, the Armada had paused at the Scillies to reform then pushed on into the English Channel. At 4pm on 29 July the coast of England was sighted. Medina Sidonia ordered a three gun salute to be fired. Almost at once a lookout spotted a column of smoke rising from the land, then another further away. The Spanish took these to be a signal that they had been sighted.

Fast pataches went out and captured two fishing boats, the crews of which were interrogated. Both reported that the main English fleet was at Plymouth under the command of Lord Howard and Drake. Medina Sidonia called another council of war where it was decided to head for Plymouth. If it proved possible to attack the English fleet with a prospect of success this would be attempted, if not the Armada would push on towards Cape Margate.

By the evening of 30 July the Armada was approaching Plymouth. They saw a great gaggle of vessels strung out across the sea to the east, and counted 76 ships – something of an overestimate. Medina Sidonia consulted Diego Flores and Bobadilla. The two men agreed and were confident the English fleet was disorganised after getting out of Plymouth in a hurry. More importantly they were downwind of the Armada. This gave the Spaniards the advantage of what was termed the weather gauge. In the days of sail, being upwind of the enemy meant that you could decide when and where to attack, while he could only react to your movements. In the context of Spanish boarding tactics, this would allow the Armada warships to manoeuvre so as to isolate some portion of the English fleet and overwhelm it before the rest could come to its rescue.

Medina Sidonia was jubilant. The English were at his mercy but it was getting dark, so he decided to start the battle at sunrise next day. The night proved to be cloudy and blustery. At about 2am a break in the clouds allowed the moon to shine for a few minutes. Five English ships were spotted between the Armada and the shore. Then the clouds closed over again and darkness returned.

At dawn, just after 5am, the Spaniards prepared for action. Medina Sidonia, Diego Flores, Bobadilla and the rest peered eastward through the gloom toward the last sighted position of the English fleet. As the light improved they spotted first the six ships close to the shore, one of which was huge, but to the east there was nothing but empty sea.

Then a cry of alarm came from the lookout, who was pointing west. There on the horizon, upwind of the Armada was the English war fleet. Somehow they had sailed right around the Armada in the night to gain the weather gauge. The Devil must have blow in *El Draque's* sails once again. Even as the baffled Spaniards gazed at the English ships they saw flags break out and sails unfurled. The English were piling on the canvas and coming down to attack.

The battle was about to begin.

VI

The English Fleet

Race built galleon. This ship is based upon the ship *Revenge*, commanded by Sir
Francis Drake in the Armada campaign. Other English ships built specifically
for war under the guidance of John Hawkins would have been similar. The rig is
similar to that used by the Spanish galleon. A key difference was that the square
rigged sails on the foremast and mainmast were designed to be much flatter so
that they did not belly out when filled by the wind. This made it easier to work
the ship to windward, but did require more careful handling, especially in rough
weather. The main differences between this and the traditional galleon are to be
found in the hull. The stern castle has been greatly reduced in size and height,
while the forecastle is now little more than a level of planking over the heads
of the gunners on which the sailors could stand to work the sails. This sleeker
profile was matched by having a substantially thinner cross section, not obvious
on this side view. The two features combined to make this type of ship much
more nimble to sail, quicker to change course, faster in all strengths of wind
and, perhaps most important, able to sail closer to the wind. The armament is
of the long-barrelled, long-range culverin type of cannon. The heavier guns are
located on the lower deck, the lighter weapons on the upper deck. The decks are
open all along their length to enable the gunners to coordinate their firing. The
crew sleep alongside the guns, except for the officers who have cabins at the rear
of the ship.

When Drake returned from his expedition to Spain, few people could have been left in any doubt that Philip was mustering a huge war fleet, nor that England was the intended target. How he intended to use it and what England should do by way of response were questions that were nowhere near as easy to answer as to pose.

Queen Elizabeth herself was certain that it would be best to avoid war if at all possible. Wars were expensive affairs and Elizabeth was always acutely aware of the need to retain the support of her people, so she abhorred heavy taxation and sought to avoid the expenditure that made it necessary. Ideally she wanted peace to replace the tense stand-off with Spain that had prevailed for some years.

In 1587, the fighting in the Netherlands had made trading up the Rhine possible only intermittently. Merchants had tried bypassing the Netherlands by using Hamburg, but the move had been only partially successful. The wool trade that accounted for some 80 per cent of England's overseas trade had been severely reduced. Elizabeth needed peace, so in the late summer of 1587 she sent ambassadors and negotiators to the Netherlands to hold talks with the Duke of Parma.

Parma had previously proved himself to be open to sensible arrangements when he had been approached and had agreed to local truces and prisoner exchanges. Now Philip had given Parma the power to negotiate a peace in the Netherlands. Elizabeth hoped that she could extricate England from the Dutch revolt, bring peace to the region and so allow trade to flow unhindered.

Elizabeth gave her instructions to Dr Rogers, an experienced diplomat, and his team which included Sr James Croft, Dr Dale and, when important issues needed dealing with, the Earl of Derby. The peace deal that Elizabeth favoured was effectively a return to the status quo before the outbreak of the Dutch revolt. She

The great seal of Elizabeth. This follows the formal design established more than 450 years earlier by the Norman monarchs of England. On one side she is shown holding the royal regalia, on the other she is shown on horseback.

A half crown issued by Elizabeth. One of her most long lasting reforms was to establish a coinage which contained set and consistent weights of precious metals. Her predecessors had at times reduced the silver content and so caused inflation.

A farthing issued toward the end of Elizabeth's reign. At this time all smaller coins were minted in sterling silver, so the farthing was a very small coin indeed. It did not prove popular and was soon discontinued.

A half sovereign issued by Queen Elizabeth. Gold coinage was relatively new to England at this time and the coins were issued only in small numbers.

A halfpenny of Queen Elizabeth. Unlike the farthing, the halfpenny proved to be a success and continued to be minted after Elizabeth's death.

A silver penny of Queen Elizabeth. The penny had been the basic unit of English money since about AD 750 and would continue, with minor variations, until the decimalisation of the currency in the 1970s.

A twopence coin of Queen Elizabeth. This innovation in coinage did not prove popular as people preferred the penny or groat, worth four pennies, when conducting trade.

Drake's coat of arms emblazoned on the stern of the replica *Golden Hind* in Brixham, Devon. Drake adopted the arms after being knighted by Queen Elizabeth I in 1580 after his return from his voyage around the world.

Errol Flynn stars in the Hollywood movie *The Sea Hawk* in which he played a character based on that of Sir Francis Drake.

A first day cover of British stamps issued in 1988 to celebrate the 400th anniversary of the Armada campaign.

A Victorian engraving of Sir Francis Drake. Drake was the most famous seaman of his age. He gained command of his first merchant craft, a small coastal trader working the English Channel at the age of only thirteen.

Mary Queen of Scots from a portrait of her during her time as monarch of Scotland. Her reign proved to be disastrous for Scotland as she favoured first one faction then another without apparent reason.

A shilling minted during the reign of Queen Mary I of England. She insisted on giving her husband, Philip of Spain, equal prominence on her coinage and to listening to his advice, much against the wishes of her nobles and Parliament.

King Philip II of Spain as a young man. His first marriage to Mary of Portugal brought him into Portuguese affairs and he was to seize the throne after his son by Mary, Don Carlos, died without children.

Queen Elizabeth enters
London in 1558 just
a few days after she
became Queen. Elizabeth
had always been popular
with the lower orders of
society and her accession
was widely celebrated.

Queen Elizabeth as a
young queen. Elizabeth
moved quickly to
stifle the religious
disputes that were
tearing Europe apart by
imposing a compromise
religious policy that
satisfied all but the most
extreme supporters of
the various sects.

The bluff bows of the *Golden Hind* replica in Brixham, Devon, were typical of ocean-going ships in the sixteenth century and were designed to combine strength with stability, especially in heavy seas. The sail layout of the *Golden Hind* replica in Brixham, Devon, with two square rigged sails on the foremast and mainmast and a lateen rig on the mizzen was the usual form of layout in the later sixteenth century for most ships. It combined flexibility with ruggedness, though it was not as effective in lighter winds as were later forms of rigging.

Opposite above: Mary signs the document of abdication of Queen of Scotland in favour of her son, King James VI. By 1567 Mary had managed to alienate most nobles and found it impossible to recruit a reliable army. She was imprisoned in the castle of Lochleven by the Earl of Murray and others.

Mary Queen of Scots shown on her voyage back to Scotland from France after the death of her first husband, King Francis II of France. She was to find that her northern kingdom was a turbulent place wracked by religious divisions and murderous disputes between the nobles.

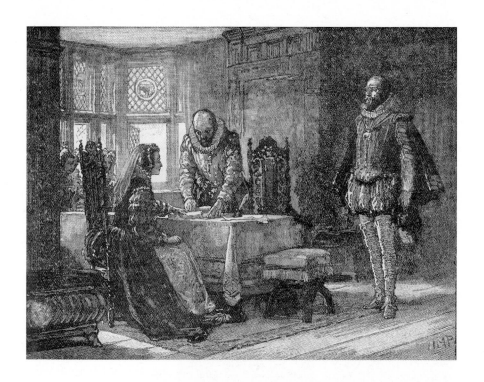

William Cecil, Lord Burghley, was a junior bureaucrat under Henry VIII and Edward VI who advised Elizabeth during the reign of Queen Mary and, after Elizabeth came to the throne, rose to the very highest positions in government.
In 1588 he was Lord High Treasurer with overall responsibility for royal expenditure.

The Ship Inn in Exeter is a rare survivor in that city from the sixteenth century. It was in this inn that merchants would hold meetings with sea captains to discuss business. The inn has not changed much over the years, though now it is more popular with the city's students than with sailors. Sir Francis Drake was often in Exeter when ashore, and local tradition has it that his favourite hostelry was the Ship Inn, which still stands just off the city's high street and is close to the great cathedral.

Opposite above: The trial of Mary Queen of Scots in Fotheringay Castle, Northamptonshire. The trial began on September 1586. The crux of the issue was whether or not Mary knew that Anthony Babington, whose plotting she had encouraged, was planning to murder Queen Elizabeth.

Drake is knighted by Queen Elizabeth on the deck of his ship the *Golden Hind*. The act of knighting the privateer showed beyond doubt that Elizabeth approved of his methods of conducting undeclared war against Spain.

The scene on 8 February 1587 as Mary Queen of Scots is informed that
Queen Elizabeth has signed her death warrant. She was executed a
few hours later. The death of Mary was the event that caused Philip of
Spain to order the Armada campaign to take place.

Opposite above: The Spanish Inquisition was run by a small group of monks and clerics dedicated to rooting out heresy. The ruthless methods used by the Spanish Inquisition were to become notorious, while its execution and imprisonment of English travellers was a frequent cause of friction between England and Spain.

King Philip II of Spain in a formal portrait painted about 1560. By this date Philip was already the champion of religious orthodoxy and supporter of the papacy against Protestantism, a stance that would lead him into war with England.

King Philip II of Spain receives a foreign ambassador in his private chambers at his palace-office-monastery complex of El Escorial. Once he had taken up residence at El Escorial, Philip rarely left, running his vast empire on the basis of written reports that he received here.

A replica carvel built in the early twentieth century for use in a film.
The simple rig and tall sides of this ship were typical of Spanish vessels in the
mid-sixteenth century.

El Escorial, King Philip's main residence outside of Madrid was an austere and chilly palace dominated by bureaucrats and officials. The large church was included so that Philip could seek divine guidance and support in his task of running the Spanish Empire.

St Michael's Mount off the south Cornish coast is a familiar landmark. In 1588 the first craft of the Spanish Armada, a patache commanded by Ensign Esquival came here and escaped from an English patrol only with difficulty.

Dover Castle was fully manned in 1588 and served as headquarters for the Kent militia on the south coast. Seymour and his squadron operated out of Dover harbour as they patrolled the Straits throughout the spring and early summer.

Sir Walter Raleigh was a leading courtier and seaman during the reign of Queen Elizabeth. In 1588 he had charge of the supply system keeping the English fleet ready for action.

Identified as the 'Earle of Nottingham', just one of his many titles, this portrait of Lord Charles Howard of Effingham shows the English commander about 20 years after the Armada battles.

The *Triumph* as she was originally built. This was the largest and one of the oldest ships in the English fleet in 1588. By that time the towering sterncastle and forecastle had been cut down to make her more weatherly, but she was still the biggest and most imposing ship in the fleet.

The entrance to the Chatham Dockyards, Kent. It was in these dockyards that Hawkins worked tirelessly for more than a decade to perfect the design of the race built galleon and to have the royal fleet converted to the new style of ships.

The sign for the Ship Inn at Exeter displays a spirited painting of an Elizabethan war galleon in heavy seas. The painting is modelled on the *Revenge*, Drake's command during the Armada campaign.

The harbour at Mousehole on the south coast of Cornwall. It was a small trading vessel from Mousehole on a voyage to Brittany that was the first English vessel to sight the ships of the Armada in the mouth of the Channel.

Sir Francis Walsingham was an English diplomat who in 1588 was running the English spy system for Queen Elizabeth.

A Victorian view of the famous game of bowls played on Plymouth Hoe by Drake, Howard, Hawkins and others as the Spanish Armada came into sight. Drake's determination to continue with the game has become legend.

Sir Francis Drake in an engraving based upon a contemporary portrait. Drake won great riches through his personal war against King Philip of Spain that began when Drake's ship was attacked without warning by the Spanish in 1568.

The Downs anchorage lay to the south of what the Spaniards called 'Cape Margate'. According to King Philip's instructions the Armada was to anchor here to rendezvous with the army of the Duke of Parma. Here the southern end of the refuge is seen from Deal beach.

Opposite above: A small craft heads out to sea past the old Kingswear Castle at the mouth of the River Dart in southern Devon. The small fort was built during the reign of King Henry VIII to guard the entrance to the harbour at Dartmouth.

The Armada as it appeared off Plymouth. The crescent shape of its tight formation can be clearly seen, as can the looser fleet of the English to the left.

The castle at Dartmouth was built in 1488 as the very first fortification designed in England to mount cannon. In 1588 the guns were manned by the Devon militia but saw no part in the fighting. The main bastion of Dartmouth Castle faces down the Dart toward the open sea. In 1588 the long range culverins mounted here would have been able to pound any ships coming up the river long before they could retaliate.

Drake accepts the surrender of Don Pedro de Valdes. The capture of this important Spanish nobleman and admiral was a coup for Drake which made for a good start to the campaign for the English.

The Spanish Barn in Torquay. The prisoners brought ashore from the captured Spanish ships the *Nuestra Senora del Rosario* and *San Salvador* were brought here to be kept safe under lock and key until their ransom was arranged some months later by the Duke of Parma.

An engraving of Sir Martin Frobisher based on a contemporary portrait. The yorkshireman was a highly respected seaman and navigator who undertook several voyages of exploration to the Arctic as well as trading voyages to Africa.

Lewes Castle in Sussex. Although by 1588 such medieval fortifications were obsolete, the castle acted as a centre for the local militia and a storehouse for military supplies. Gunpowder from here was sent to the English fleet as it fought up the Channel.

The small port at Rye had been given upgraded and modernised defences by 1588. The harbour was overlooked by modern cannon mounted on this gun platform built around the older citadel of Ypres Tower, now a museum.

The Armada off Calais.

Opposite below left: Queen Elizabeth in an engraving taken from a formal portrait. She came to the throne only after her brother Edward and elder sister Mary had died childless. In the early years of her reign she received many foreign suitors, including Philip of Spain, but rejected them all.

Opposite below right: John Hawkins was the architect of the English fleet that faced the Spanish Armada. He had spent years perfecting new ways of building ships so that they could use long-range guns as their main weapons in battle.

The great Naval Monument in the city of Oporto. The men who have served in Portugal's navy are commemorated here. The premier fighting ships of the Armada were drawn from Portugal and several had Oporto as their home port.

The replica *Golden Hind* in Brixham, Devon, is open to the public and offers a good view of what life was like aboard these sixteenth century sailing ships. The *Golden Hind* was a converted merchant ship adapted to carry heavy guns and a fighting crew. Although Drake remodelled her according to his new ideas on naval warfare, she was still very different from the race built galleons that were beginning to be produced at this time.

Opposite below: Deal Castle was designed to withstand the heaviest of artillery in the sixteenth century. The low profile of the walls made them difficult to hit, while their great thickness and rounded shape enabled them to withstand such shot as did hit home.

Sir Francis Drake in middle age. By the time of the Armada campaign, Drake was the most respected sailor in England and had a proven talent for warfare.

Elizabeth walks on Richmond Green, Surrey, with a group of courtiers. Elizabeth travelled much around her kingdom in order to meet and cultivate the support of the lesser gentry and merchants.

Deal Castle, a powerful fortress built by King Henry VIII in the 1530s and brought up to date for the campaign of 1588. The castle was manned by a company of Royal gunners to man the big cannon, plus a company of the local militia who provided infantry support in the case of a siege.

The main dry moat at Deal Castle was designed to frustrate attempts to capture the fortress by attacking infantry. The gunports in the lower walls to shoot at any enemy troops who got into the moat.

The town gate to the port of Rye on the Sussex coast. These defences were unable to withstand a determined siege by a modern army in 1588, but could have held off raiders and were part of the national defence strategy.

Lulworth Cove on the Dorset coast. In 1588 this small anchorage was considered to be a possible landing place for Spanish raiding parties and so was guarded by a detachment of the local militia. History repeated itself in 1940 when worries about a German raid led to a squad of the Home Guard being posted here. On neither occasion did a landing actually take place.

The town of Rye in Sussex was in 1588 surrounded by medieval stone walls, hastily improved by the addition of a few earthworks. The town's main contribution to the war effort, however, was to pay money to equip a merchant ship for war service and send her fully manned to Plymouth.

Opposite below: The main gun platform at Dartmouth Castle. The weapon visible here is a nineteenth century cannon, but it occupies the same position as the culverins that were the main armament of the coastal defences in 1588.

118. Robert Dudley, Earl of Leicester, was a talented courtier and a favourite friend of Queen Elizabeth. In 1588 he had command of England's land defences and commanded the army that gathered at Tilbury to resist a Spanish landing.

Death of Sir Philip Sidney at the Battle of Zutphen.

The death of Sir Philip Sidney at the Battle of Zutphen was one of the most famous incidents in the English campaign in the Netherlands, conducted to support the Protestant rebels against rule from Spain.

London in Elizabethan times. The houses and shops on London Bridge can be clearly seen in the foreground. During the Armada campaign, Elizabeth spent most of her time in London from where she could keep an eye on events, and where she could be protected.

The camp at Tilbury was well organised by the Earl of Leicester who ensured that the army had plenty to eat and drink, and that sanitary arrangements were impeccable.

Queen Elizabeth rides through the camp at Tilbury to be cheered by her soldiers. The visit did not take place until after the Armada had already been defeated, though nobody on land was aware of the fact.

Below: A ship of the Spanish Armada is wrecked on the coast of Ireland, as imagined by a Victorian artist. There were few survivors of such wrecks, and those that did get ashore were often killed by the locals for plunder or hanged by English troops fearful of Spanish invasion.

Irish warriors as depicted by a Tudor artist. The Irish were only loosely controlled by the English at this date. Rebellions, private wars and feuds were common.

The wreck of the galleass Girona within sight of Dunluce Castle was a tragedy that cost the lives of over 1,200 men.

suggested that the rebels should return to their allegiance to their hereditary lord, Philip of Spain, and that in return Philip would confirm the hereditary rights of the seventeen Dutch provinces.

It had been an attempt to impose new taxes on the Dutch that had sparked the trouble, though the underlying discontent had been caused by Philip's attempts to impose direct royal rule and so circumvent the traditional rights and powers of the local councils and nobles. Elizabeth was hoping that the huge cost of the Dutch war would tempt Philip to abandon his policy of direct rule in return for peace.

The return of the traditional powers of the provinces would also, Elizabeth believed, solve the religious difficulties. Philip wanted Catholicism to be the only religion in his realms, but the Dutch rebels wanted to be free to practise Protestantism. Under the traditional arrangements, it was up to the provincial governments how to impose laws and what punishments to inflict on those who broke them. If Philip wanted to make Protestantism illegal he could do so, but those provinces where Protestants were strong could opt to impose only token punishments. It seemed a sensible compromise to Elizabeth, but then she was neither an ardent Protestant like the rebels nor a strict Catholic like Philip.

There were other matters that would need to be sorted out – not least the fact that Elizabeth had refused to recognise Philip as the legitimate King of Portugal – but Elizabeth viewed these more as bargaining points than substantive issues. She was confident that some sort of deal could be reached. What she did not realise at first was that Philip had ordered Parma to conduct the negotiations with the sole aim of fooling the English into thinking that a peace treaty could be agreed. He was to spin out the talks as long as he could, raise fresh difficulties and find new issues to discuss for as long as he could.

Parma acted exactly as instructed. He managed to spend more than two months discussing where the talks should take place, and only then moved on to the more tricky issues of what should be discussed and how the negotiations would be conducted. Croft, Dale and Rogers were frustrated and confused by the seemingly interminable talks about talks. Derby, on the other hand, began to suspect the truth. He told Elizabeth that he suspected they were being tricked and predicted that Philip would attack England as soon as he felt able to do so.

Back in England others had already come to the same conclusion. Drake had been saying so for years, and as the autumn of 1587 brought an end to the campaigning season he urged Elizabeth to let him prepare a fresh expedition in the spring to repeat the success of his attack on Cadiz. Sir John Hawkins supported Drake, and Sir Walter Raleigh also spoke out. Others were not so sure, fearing either that the Armada might slip past the English ships or that Drake's expedition might be struck by a storm and scattered. In the end it was Elizabeth who put a stop to the clamour for an attack on Spain. She was still hoping for peace and preferred to wait until the spring.

Meanwhile, she knew that preparations for war had to be made. The most pressing problem was who was to command the English fleet, and how should it be deployed. The second question would very much be a decision for whoever was the answer to the first.

On 21 December Elizabeth announced that the supreme commander of English ships for the coming year would be Lord Charles Howard of Effingham. It proved to be a good choice, though not everyone thought so at the time. There were plenty of men more experienced at sea fighting than Howard – such as Drake, Hawkins, Frobisher and Winter – but Howard was no landlubber. His father had been Lord High Admiral during the 1550s, and young Charles had spent much of his teenage years at sea or around the docks. During the early years of Elizabeth's reign, Howard had held a few short naval commands and had commanded land forces, but had spent most of his time as a courtier and diplomat. He had acquired a reputation for administrative skill and for preferring a cautious policy over a bold one.

Howard's first acts were to confirm two appointments that had already been made. Sir Francis Drake was to remain in Plymouth to command the ships there and Sir William Winter was to command the ships operating out of London. Winter's task was an arduous one: he was to keep constant patrols cruising off the Dutch coast to keep watch for any sign that the Duke of Parma was putting to sea. If the Spanish barges did come out, Winter was to intercept and destroy them.

Howard was to appoint other commanders as the weeks passed. Lord Henry Seymour was given a flotilla to patrol the Straits of Dover and Sir Walter Raleigh was sent to Devon to organise the shore-side of things, gathering supplies and ensuring the ports gave priority to the warships when it came to repairs and stores.

Sir Martin Frobisher was given command of a squadron composed of the older ships in the fleet, including the *Triumph* which he took for his flagship. At this date Frobisher was best known as a merchant-adventurer. He had led three expeditions to the Arctic in search of both a route to China and minerals worth mining. He found neither, but did at least show that they were not there. He had undertaken one plundering voyage to the Caribbean and so had some experience of fighting the Spanish. His seamanship was beyond doubt, and his administrative skills were formidable, on the other hand Frobisher had a reputation for being touchy and quarrelsome and neither Winter nor Drake would have anything to do with him.

Sir John Hawkins was given command of the royal ship *Victory* and with it a group of the newest and most modern ships in Elizabeth's navy. Hawkins began by issuing standing orders that were remarkable for their brevity and common sense. He told his men to 'Serve God daily, love one another, preserve your victuals, beware of fire and keep good company'.

The choice of Hawkins to command the newest warships was understandable as nobody had been more responsible for their creation than he had himself. On his return from the disastrous voyage that ended in the bloodshed of San Juan de Ullua, Hawkins had married the daughter of Benjamin Gonson, Treasurer of the Navy. His father-in-law got him a job, hoping to use Hawkins's experience of long sea voyages and combat. In the event, Hawkins quickly came to dominate the Navy Board, the panel of noblemen appointed to oversee the navy. In 1577 he succeeded Gonson as Treasurer and thereafter was free to implement his ideas, constrained only by the amount of money Elizabeth gave to the Board.

Hawkins' ideas were revolutionary, but not unique, and he was supported by Drake, Winter, Frobisher and others. This group was highly controversial in its claim that the way everybody else conduced war at sea was wrong. Moreover, they wanted Elizabeth to place faith in them and trust them to protect England at sea. It was an astonishing demand, and Elizabeth was taking a huge risk in backing Hawkins.

The key to the ideas of Hawkins and his supporters was that the gun was by the later sixteenth century the most important weapon at sea. They dismissed the ram as useless and the tactics of boarding as clumsy and wasteful of human life. So far as Hawkins was concerned, it was the gun that would win battles and believed that ships should be designed to carry guns and tactics formulated to use the guns most effectively. The guns that Hawkins wanted to use were the new-style guns that were generally termed 'culverins'.

The older types of guns were, he thought, ineffective and should be discarded. Cannons and port pieces were despised by Hawkins, although when he entered naval administration these were by far the most common guns on English ships.

Cannons were made of iron to a design called the bobbin-barrel. Iron foundries at this date were able to produce plenty of cast iron, but this was brittle and would shatter to fragments if used in a gun barrel. Wrought iron combined strength and resilience, but could be made only in relatively small pieces. A cannon barrel was therefore built up of several sections of wrought iron, each one forming a tube about twelve inches in length and ending in a lip. The tubes were placed end to end and sealed with molten lead.

Inevitably the tubes did not fit exactly, so it was usual to use a cannonball that was slightly smaller than the supposed bore of the gun, resulting in inefficient firing. Gasses escaped around the sides of the cannonball, reducing the speed of the ball and hence both its range and hitting power. The fact that the cannon ball could shake slightly as it ran up the barrel also made these weapons inaccurate at anything much over 200 yards, less when fired from the moving deck of a ship. As the gun was used, the lead solders would crack and so allow gases to leak out, further reducing the gun's effectiveness.

These guns were breech loaded. The rearmost section of the barrel was removable and was sealed at one end to form a chamber. Into this chamber was rammed the gunpowder and wadding. The ball was then placed in the barrel just in front of the breech. The breech tube was then put in place, secured with a wooden wedge and the gun was ready to be fired. Lifting the breech in and out was a three-man job due to its weight. Usually two or three spare breeches were kept near the gun so that they could be loaded ready for use. After a gun was fired, the used breech had to be lifted out, washed out with water to remove any burning fragments of powder and then dried before it could be reloaded. It was a slow and cumbersome procedure.

In general, cannons were wide barrelled so that they fired a very heavy ball. These weapons could inflict massive damage, but as they were so slow to reload they tended to be used only once or twice before the boarding began.

When Hawkins started service there were six types of cannon used by the navy. The canon royal had a diameter of 8.5 inches, fired a ball weighing 66lb and used 27lb of gunpowder each time it was fired. The canon itself was slightly smaller having a diameter of 8 inches, a shot weighing 60lb and used 27lb of gunpowder.

The canon serpentine, bastard canon, demi cannon and cannon petro were progressively smaller. The cannon petro had a diameter of 6 inches, fired a ball of only 14lb and needed 14lb of gunpowder. This family of guns were to remain the standard heavy guns of most navies for many years, and dominated the firepower of the Armada.

Hawkins, however, favoured the very different culverin style of gun. These guns were made from bronze and were cast all in one piece. They took the form of a long, hollow tube which was closed at one end. The fact that they were made in one piece meant that they did not have the weaknesses of the iron chambered guns. The bore was smoother, allowing for a ball of tighter fit to be used, and the barrel did not leak at the joins. This made it possible to use a greater charge of powder which would fire a ball further, more accurately and with greater hitting power.

The guns were muzzle-loaded. Before it was fired, the gun was loaded with powder from a measuring scoop, topped by cloth wadding to hold it in place. A ball and further wadding was then rammed down on top of the powder and pushed firmly into place with a ramrod. After firing, a wet sponge mounted on a long pole was used to wash out the barrel to remove burning embers before the next load of powder was pushed in. The process of loading and firing was quicker than in the older cannon.

Like cannon, culverins were produced in a range of sizes. The culverin itself had a diameter of 5.5 inches and fired a 17lb shot using 10lb of powder. The range of guns decreased through the basilisk, the demi culverin, the bastard culverin, the sacre and the minion to the falcon which had a diameter of 2.5 inches, fired a 2.5 lb shot using 2.5lb of powder.

The advantages of the culverin were increased by new techniques of gunpowder manufacture that were also being introduced at this time. The basic components of gunpowder are carbon, a nitrate and sulphur. Given the technology of the time, carbon meant charcoal and nitrate was saltpetre. The actual combination of charcoal varied depending on which type of wood was used to make it and the techniques used during manufacture. Saltpetre was produced by allowing great piles of excrement and urine to decompose inside wooden barns, the saltpetre being deposited on the walls and beams as the mass rotted down. Again, the composition of the resulting chemical varied greatly depending on the techniques used.

At first, gunpowder had been produced by grinding the three constituents down into a fine powder and then mixing them together.

This had the disadvantage that the three different powders tended to separate out as a barrel was moved about, so that they needed remixing before use. Around 1450 a process known as corning was developed. This involved stirring water into the powder immediately after it was first mixed to produce a paste which was formed into small granules about the size of a grain of corn – hence the name. When they dried out the corns remained stable, allowing the gunpowder to be used without remixing.

Gunpowder manufacturers soon realised that corning stabilised the mixture so that each corn had the precise proportion of ingredients as had the whole batch. They gradually learned that by combining different types of basic ingredients in different proportions they could produce different types of gunpowder. Gunpowder that exploded very quickly was good for demolition and explosions, guns required a slower burning powder that would smoothly accelerate the ball up the barrel.

By about 1550 the combination of improved gun and gunpowder manufacturing had produced an awesome new weapon in the culverin. However, the new guns and the new powder were both significantly more expensive than the older forms. Because sea captains used boarding tactics in which the guns were fired once or twice as the ships closed, the greater range and accuracy of the culverin were of little practical use. Unsurprisingly most ships carried a mix of guns, with cannons in the majority.

Hawkins suggested the entirely novel idea that sea battles should be fought with guns alone, that there should be neither boarding nor ramming. In a battle fought along Hawkins's lines the opposing ships would stay at a distance from each other and bombard each other with gunfire until one sank or surrendered.

To fight this type of battle effectively, a captain would need not only good guns but also a ship designed to use them. Hawkins, Drake and others identified the key features of such a ship to be the ability to carry a large number of heavy culverins and the ability to sail nimbly and with agility so as to outmanoeuvre the opposing ship. The most obvious way to increase the number of guns on a ship was to increase its length. The heavy culverins were already conventionally mounted on the lower deck where they would not make the ship top heavy, and were fired through gunports. Making the ship longer allowed more guns to be placed side by side on the lower deck. After some experimentation it was found that the best arrangement was to have two gundecks running the length of the ship. Culverins or basilisks were put on the lower deck and demi culverins or bastard culverins on the upper deck.

Because boarding was no longer to be used, there was no need for the towering castles. The forecastle was cut away completely to be replaced by a simple deck over the heads of the guncrews on the forward part of the ship. The sterncastle was likewise discarded, but no so completely as the forecastle. The rear third of the ship was decked over. The rear sixth of the ship had a second higher deck, the poop, raised about four feet above the deck below. It was here that the captain stood to direct the ship. The added height gave him a clear view of what was going on throughout the ship and allowed his shouts and trumpet calls to be heard by the crew.

The removal of the castles greatly improved the sailing abilities of the ship. In particular the lack of a forecastle allowed the ship to keep its head into the wind more consistently and so sail much more closely to the wind. Hawkins went further. He discarded the great billowing sails that bellied out to catch us much wind as possible. Instead he insisted on tighter, thinner sails that remained taut and so allowed the captain to position them much more precisely. Again the result was to allow the ship to sail closer to the wind.

The abandonment of boarding meant that the ships no longer needed to carry any soldiers. Without the need to provide cabins for officers, sleeping space for troops and storage for food and weapons, the ships could be made smaller and slimmer while still carrying the same number of guns together with the ammunition and stores for a lengthy voyage. The resulting warship was called a 'galleon' by Hawkins and others as it was a ship specifically built for war, but it was a very different type of ship from the Spanish galleon. It was recognised, however, that these ships were something new and they came to be termed 'race-built' galleons.

So radical was the new design, that the shipwrights asked to build the ships had trouble understanding what was required of them. Hawkins therefore came up with another entirely novel and unheard of idea: He drew pictures of what he wanted the finished ship to look like. Up to this date nobody had ever drawn up plans for a ship before. Each vessel was built by eye according to a preconceived idea in the head of the master shipwright. The customer would explain what sort of craft he wanted and how big it was to be, after which the shipwright got on with the job. But Hawkins wanted very specific features in his new ships, and only detailed drawings could adequately explain what he intended.

It took some years for the different aspects of this new style to be perfected. The first ship to be built entirely to the new style was probably the *Revenge*, launched at Deptford in 1577. She was rated at 441 tons and carried 34 heavy culverins on two decks. Of these two pointed forward as bowchasers and two backward as sternchasers. The remaining 30 guns were arranged with 16 on the lower and 14 on the upper decks. During the Armada campaign the *Revenge* would serve as Drake's flagship.

The new ships were not only purpose built for war, but could not be used for anything else due to the restricted space below decks that could be converted for the carriage of goods. Similarly for merchant ships to be converted to the new style was not straight-forward. While a race-built galleon might be five times as long as it was broad, merchant ships had a ratio of about three to one.

English merchant ships were converted to war for the Armada campaign and they served successfully. The conversion was achieved not by adding castles, as did the Spanish, but by cutting gunports in the lower hull and mounting culverins to fire through them. The resulting vessels packed as much firepower as the race-built galleons, but were rather less agile. They remained, however, significantly better sailors than their Spanish opponents.

The tactics for the use of these new style weapons were slowly developed. The first written evidence for what was to become the standard English use of these ships comes from the attack by Winter on the Spanish forces in the fort at Smerwick, Ireland, in 1580. He had used his ships in turn to bombard the fort. Each ship went through the same manoeuvres. It first sailed toward the fort and fired its bowchasers as it came within range. The ship then turned to one side to fire all the guns of the side facing the fort. It then turned about to fire the guns along its other side before turning away and firing the sternchasers as it made off. The next ship then came in to repeat the procedure while the guns on the first ship were reloaded.

When an English ship met an enemy on the high seas, Hawkins envisaged that the English captain would use his ship's superior handling characteristics to stay out of cannon range while firing his culverins at the enemy – a distance of perhaps 700 yards. The gunfire was intended to inflict casualties and damage the enemy ship to such an extent that she would surrender or sink. Later wooden fighting ships would have massively thickened sides to withstand incoming cannonballs, but at this date even purpose built warships had comparatively thin sides that could be penetrated by gunfire.

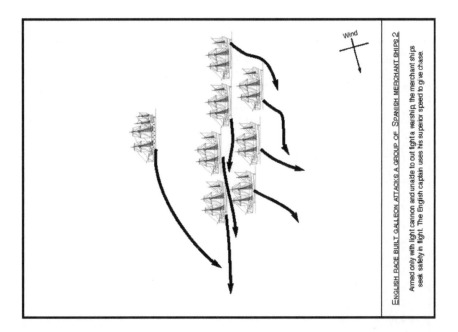

ENGLISH RACE BUILT GALLEON ATTACKS A GROUP OF SPANISH MERCHANT SHIPS 2

Armed only with light cannon and unable to out fight a warship, the merchant ships seek safety in flight. The English captain uses his superior speed to give chase.

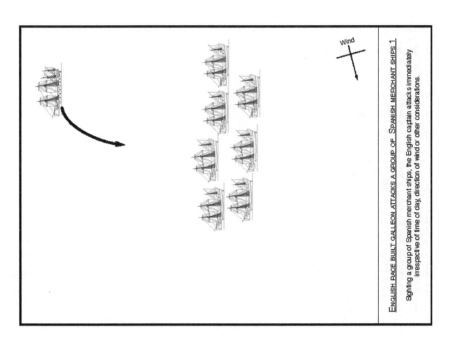

ENGLISH RACE BUILT GALLEON ATTACKS A GROUP OF SPANISH MERCHANT SHIPS 1

Sighting a group of Spanish merchant ships, the English captain attacks immediately irrespective of time of day, direction of wind or other considerations.

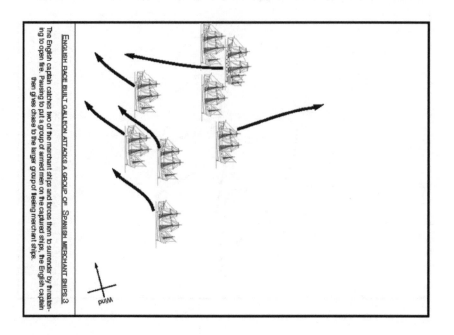

English race built galleon attacks a group of Spanish merchant ships 3

The English captain catches two of the merchant ships and forces them to surrender by threatening to open fire. Pausing to put a group of armed men on the captured ships, the English captain then gives chase to the larger group of fleeing merchant ships.

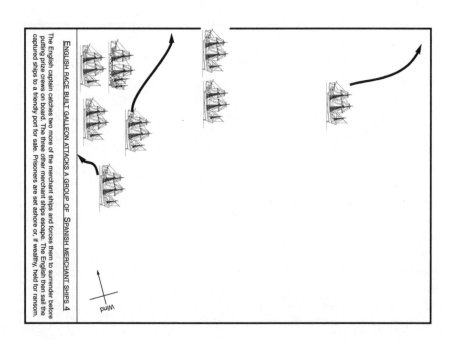

English race built galleon attacks a group of Spanish merchant ships 4

The English captain catches two more of the merchant ships and forces them to surrender before putting prize crews on board. The three other merchant ships escape. The English then sail the captured ships to a friendly port for sale. Prisoners are set ashore or, if wealthy, held for ransom.

In the event, captains were to find that the vagaries of gunfire accuracy at sea meant that they needed to get closer than Hawkins had envisaged. To be reasonably certain of a culverin shot hitting a target the size of a ship, it needed to be fired from about 300 yards. This was well within cannon range, but these guns were even less accurate so the perils of return fire were not too serious. To inflict serious damage the shot needed to be fired from even closer.

When an action was to be fought between groups of ships, the English preferred to adapt Winter's tactics as used at Smerwick. The English ships would attack one after the other, swooping in at high speed to fire a broadside, turn about to fire again and sail off out of range to reload. The ships did not form anything as formal as a single line ahead, but instead each captain chose his own route in and out again. The commander of the group of ships would show the way, and the others would reform on his ship after the assault. The commander would then decide if a second attack was needed, and if so how and where it should be delivered. If possible, the English sought to isolate one or more enemy ships from the general formation. Those ships would then be targeted and surrounded so that they could be subdued by gunfire.

Unlike the Spanish, the English had no experience of fighting in large fleets. None of the English commanders had handled fleets of more than a couple of dozen ships in action. Facing up to the 130 ships of the Armada was going to be a novel and disconcerting experience for them.

As the spring of 1588 brought good sailing weather to the seas off England, the debate about how best to defeat the threat of the Armada erupted afresh. Drake wanted to take his Plymouth fleet down to the coast of Spain and harry the enemy. At this date, Drake had at Plymouth eight of the new race-built galleons belonging to the queen and about 40 private ships of various sorts. The details of his plan are given only vaguely in his written report, probably because he had not worked it out himself. He was not one for preconceived plans but for boldly taking advantage of circumstances. He probably intended to go to Spain to destroy and capture whatever he could while avoiding open battle.

Elizabeth refused Drake's suggestion, even when Hawkins supported him. The two then turned to Howard and explained their idea to him. At first Howard preferred to stay in home waters, but eventually he was won over and wrote to Elizabeth suggesting that Drake should be allowed to go. Elizabeth's reply surprised

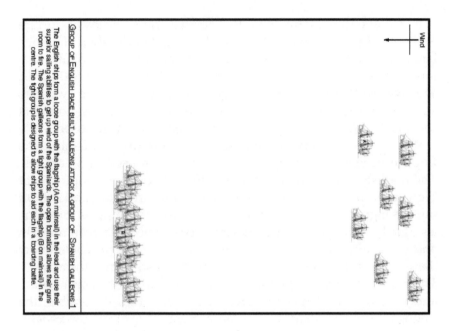

GROUP OF ENGLISH RACE BUILT GALLEONS ATTACK A GROUP OF SPANISH GALLEONS 1

The English ships form a loose group with the flagship (A on mainsail) in the lead and use their superior sailing abilities to get up wind of the Spaniards. The open formation allows their guns room to fire. The Spanish galleons form a tight group with the flagship (B on mainsail) in the centre. The tight group is designed to allow ships to aid each in a boarding battle.

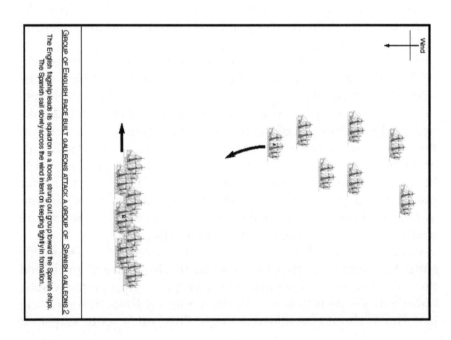

GROUP OF ENGLISH RACE BUILT GALLEONS ATTACK A GROUP OF SPANISH GALLEONS 2

The English flagship leads its squadron in a loose, strung out group toward the Spanish ships. The Spanish sail slowly across the wind intent on keeping tightly in formation.

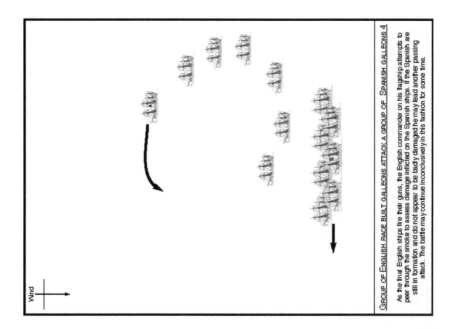

GROUP OF ENGLISH RACE BUILT GALLEONS ATTACK A GROUP OF SPANISH GALLEONS 4

As the final English ships fire their guns, the English commander on his flagship attempts to peer through the smoke to assess damage inflicted on the Spanish ships. If the Spanish are still in formation and do not appear to be badly damaged he may lead another passing attack. The battle may continue inconclusively in this fashion for some time.

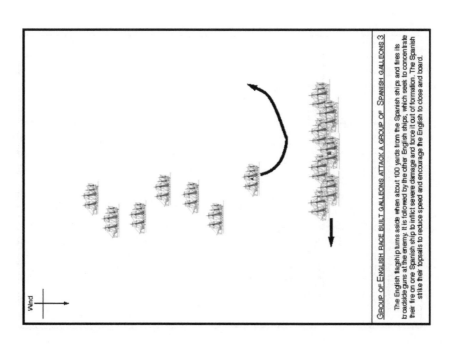

GROUP OF ENGLISH RACE BUILT GALLEONS ATTACK A GROUP OF SPANISH GALLEONS 3

The English flagship turns aside when about 100 yards from the Spanish ships and fires its broadside guns at the enemy. It is followed by the other English ships, which seek to concentrate their fire on one Spanish ship to inflict severe damage and force it out of formation. The Spanish strike their topsails to reduce speed and encourage the English to close and board.

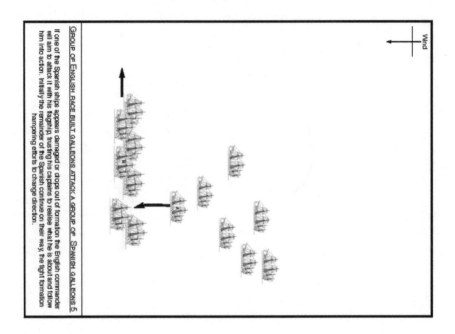

GROUP OF ENGLISH RACE BUILT GALLEONS ATTACK A GROUP OF SPANISH GALLEONS 5

If one of the Spanish ships appears damaged or drops out of formation the English commander will aim to attack it with his flagship, trusting his captains to realise what he is about and follow him into action. Initially the remainder of the Spanish continue on their way, the tight formation hampering efforts to change direction.

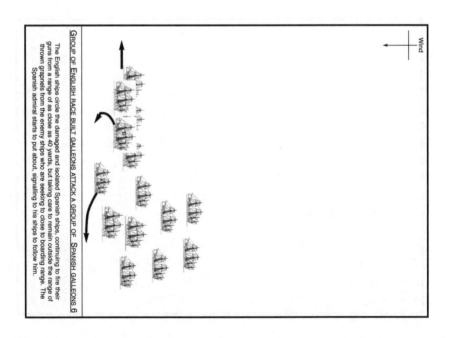

GROUP OF ENGLISH RACE BUILT GALLEONS ATTACK A GROUP OF SPANISH GALLEONS 6

The English ships circle the damaged and isolated Spanish ships, continuing to fire their guns from a range of as close as 40 yards, but taking care to remain outside the range of thrown grapnels from the enemy ships who are seeking to close to boarding range. The Spanish admiral starts to put about, signalling to his ships to follow him.

them all. She now ordered Howard himself to go and to take with him the entire English fleet, except for Seymour's Dover patrol and Winter's North Sea fleet.

Accordingly, Howard left London along with Frobisher, Hawkins and all their ships. He arrived in Plymouth on 2 June. Ever tactful, Howard knew that his arrival could not fail to annoy Drake who was thus losing his independence of command. Howard therefore promoted Drake to be second in command of the entire English navy for the forthcoming campaign and gave him a specially embroidered flag to fly from his foremast.

Word then came from London ordering that they should not set out. The negotiations with Parma were looking promising and Elizabeth did not want to provoke war. Drake fumed, believing that war was inevitable. Unknown to anyone in England the Armada had left Lisbon nine days earlier.

On 29 June a small trading bark left Mousehole in Cornwall heading for France, where it was to pick up a cargo of salt and return. The craft was entering French waters when it encountered a patrolling French warship. The French craft altered course and came within hailing distance of the Cornish vessel. 'As you love your life,' bellowed the French captain, 'do not go on. The Spanish fleet is up the coast.' He waved his arm to the west, then passed on.

The Cornish master held a hurried discussion with his men. They decided that the salt should be abandoned. Instead they would sail directly west to try to find the Spanish ships. In an unarmed bark this was bravery indeed, but every Englishman knew that what their fleet needed most was definite news of the Armada. Three hours later the Cornishmen saw masts and sails coming up over the horizon. They kept steadily on, veering off to make sure they stayed up wind of the ships. As the range narrowed, it was obvious that somebody on the ships had spotted the small bark. Three of the ships turned to intercept him. The Cornish captain decided it was time to go. He had counted nine ships, the largest of about 800 tons and the smallest around 200 tons. He noticed that each of them had a red cross painted on its foresail.

When he got back to Mousehole, the Cornish captain wrote out a quick report and rode with it to the home of Sir Francis Godolphin, who sent a rider to take it to Plymouth. It was the first firm news of the Armada, but not the last. Before nightfall two other craft had come in with sightings of Spanish ships. There were fifteen south of the Scillies and six north of the islands.

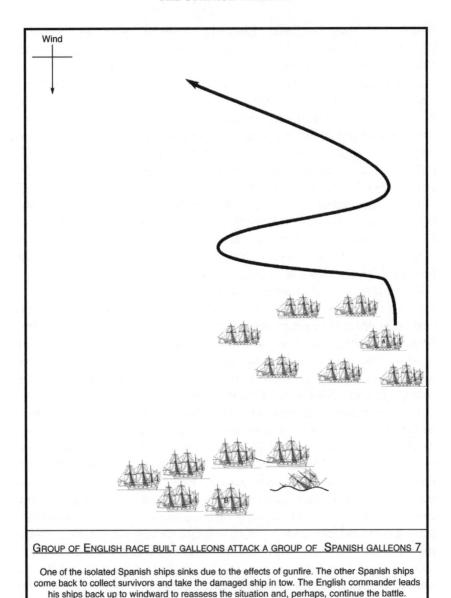

Wind

GROUP OF ENGLISH RACE BUILT GALLEONS ATTACK A GROUP OF SPANISH GALLEONS 7

One of the isolated Spanish ships sinks due to the effects of gunfire. The other Spanish ships come back to collect survivors and take the damaged ship in tow. The English commander leads his ships back up to windward to reassess the situation and, perhaps, continue the battle.

Howard at once put to sea. He led most of the English ships toward the Scillies, while Drake led a smaller force toward Brittany. By the time they got to their stations there were no Spanish ships to be seen. The vessels had been the storeships rounded by Esquival in his patache and they had by this date

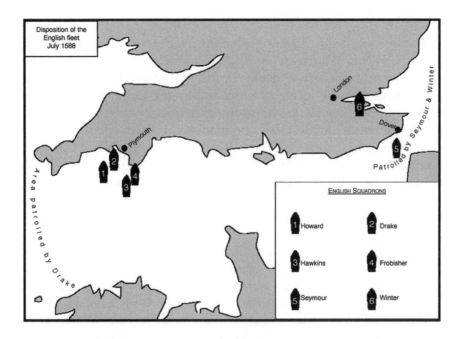

Disposition of the
English fleet
July 1588

ENGLISH SQUADRONS

1 Howard   2 Drake

3 Hawkins   4 Frobisher

5 Seymour   6 Winter

turned south to rejoin the Armada at Corunna. Drake did, however, pick up the Scottish merchant ship that had been captured by the *Paloma Blanca*. The Spaniards thought that they had moved the entire crew to their own ship for questioning, and had later cast it adrift when they thought it was sinking. Yet here it was with three men and the cabin boy left aboard limping on for France. The Scots told all they knew, then passed on. Drake now knew that the mystery ships had been storeships scattered by a storm, not the great Armada itself.

Meanwhile, one of Howard's scout ships ran into what it took to be an unarmed Spanish merchant ship. The English craft closed intending to overawe the enemy with a show of gunfire, only to receive a mass of musketry in response and a salvo of cannon fire. The scout hauled off, having orders to report back with sightings not to get involved in battle. Thus English orders to avoid a fight were mistaken by the Spanish as fear of open battle. Natural enough in the circumstances, but a mistake that would later lead the Spanish into trouble.

Howard and Drake raced back to Plymouth. Wherever the Armada was, it had been dispersed by a storm and possibly damaged. Now was the time to strike. They hurriedly took on fresh

stores, then put to sea. They did not get far before the wind swung
around to the south. The English ships might have been relatively
good at sailing into the wind, but they still needed to tack labori-
ously to and from across the Bay of Biscay. In the end Howard gave
up, not having enough food on board to get all the way to Spain
against the winds. He led his ships back into Plymouth on 22 July.
It was the same day that the Armada left Corunna.

Waiting for Howard in Plymouth was a letter from Lord Burleigh
complaining that the bill for fresh food and wages had not been
filled in correctly. Howard was in no mood to be refused what he
needed for the campaign. He sent the bill back again, with a cover-
ing note that by the standards of the time was blistering:

> I have caused Sir Francis Drake and Mr Hawkyns [sic] to consider of
> your charges, for that our company grow into great need and many
> occasions in such an army doth breed sundry great and extraordi-
> nary charges. I have sent herein enclosed an estimate thereof, pray-
> ing your Lordship that there may be some care had that we may be
> furnished with money – without which we are not able to continue
> our forces together.

When he got this letter, Burleigh complained to Walsingham about
Howard, but was told bluntly that his job was to make sure the fleet
had what it needed to fight at sea.

Unlike the heavily bureaucratic Spanish government systems,
those of England were traditionally informal and personal. The monarch would appoint a man to do a job, give him the money and leave
him to get on with it. As a result historians do not have the same level
of documentation about the English fleet in 1588 as they do about the
Spanish Armada. We do not know the names of all the ships, only
what they consumed in terms of wages and supplies and who had to
be paid. The records do, however, give the overall figures.

The Royal Navy consisted of 34 vessels ready for sea – though
one of these was a galley which patrolled the entrance to London
and never left the Thames. Of the rest, thirteen were large galleons
of over 500 tons, eight were of between 200 and 400 tons while
another twelve were classed as small being under 200 tons. Most of
these craft were in Plymouth, though Winter had some.

Drake had command of 34 converted merchant ships of up to
400 tons. Another eighteen converted ships were under Howard's
command. Also based at Plymouth were fifteen merchant ships

which had not been converted. These were tasked with keeping the warships and converted merchantmen supplied. Another 20 ships were under Howard's command but do not seem to have been based at any port in particular. There were 23 ships provided by private individuals and merchants. These craft could in theory go wherever their owners liked, but in practice they attached themselves to Drake's command and followed his lead.

Lord Seymour led his Dover Patrol from the decks of the *Rainbow*, one of the newest of the race-built galleons. She was rated at 500 tons and carried a useful armament of six culverins, twelve demi-culverins, seven sakers and one minion. He also had with him the other new race-built galleon, the *Vanguard*. This ship was also of 500 tons, but she carried four culverins, fourteen demi-culverins, eleven sakers and two minions. In addition to these ships Seymour also had three older royal ships which had undergone conversion to make them more like race-built galleons. Finally, he had 23 converted merchant ships, the largest of which was only 160 tons.

In all the English had 197 ships compared to the 130 in the Armada. Most of them were much smaller than their opponents. Moreover the English were equipped for the new style of gun fighting and nobody knew if Hawkins's master plan would lead to success or defeat. Nor were all the ships available for battle. There were only 54 ships in Plymouth with Howard and Drake. The rest were with Winter or Seymour or were escorting English merchant ships to Hamburg or Antwerp. It would take time to get all the English ships together. But time had just run out.

On 29 July, Thomas Fleming came racing into Plymouth on board of his scout ship. He had been on patrol off the Isles of Scilly when he sighted a vast fleet coming from the south-west. He had waited just long enough to make sure it was the Armada, then he had turned about and raced for Plymouth. What happened next has passed into legend.

When Fleming jumped ashore he asked for Howard, and was told that while the ships were being reprovisioned the admiral was up on Plymouth Hoe. Fleming ran up the hill to find Howard, Drake, Frobisher, Hawkins and a group of ship's captains chatting and playing bowls. Hurrying up to Howard and the senior officers, Fleming blurted out his news. The Great Armada had come at last. Howard at once began gabbling at his officers. Stores had to be loaded more quickly, gunpowder supplies had to be confirmed, ships had to get to sea, men had to be recalled from shore leave. The messengers and captains began milling about in confusion. Nobody seemed to know who was where or exactly what needed doing.

'Gentlemen,' Drake's voice cut through the hubbub. The seamen fell silent and turned toward Drake who calmly proceeded to bowl his ball across the green. Having taken his turn, Drake smiled and continued. 'Gentlemen. There is time enough to finish our game and beat the Spaniards too.'

What Drake had remembered, but the others had not, was that the tide was against them. Plymouth has many advantages as a naval base, but with a south-westerly wind blowing – which it was – the only way to get out was to ride the outgoing tide. At that moment the tide was coming in. The English fleet could not get out for some hours to come, and there was no need to panic. Drake was right.

When the tide did turn the English ships began working their way out to sea. The modern warships went first, followed by the converted merchantmen attached to Drake's command. By the later afternoon of 30 July, as the Armada came into view, most of the fleet was out of Plymouth Sound and was gathering between the mainland and the Eddystone rocks, which is where the Spanish saw them. Only Frobisher and the older ships were still in the Sound. They would get out during the evening.

Exactly how the English managed to get up wind of the Armada that night is unknown. None of the English seaman involved wrote about it in their accounts. Only Howard mentioned the incident, stating: 'We did what we could to work for the wind.' It is unlikely that the abilities of the English ships to sail into the wind was enough. More likely is the idea that the English rode the tide.

The tides in the seas off Plymouth would have been known to Drake and all the West Country captains, perhaps half the total in the English fleet at this point in the campaign. In places the tide can run at seven knots, while being almost still elsewhere. If the English got into a strong current heading west it would have carried them right around the southern flank of the Armada and put them upwind and south-west of the Armada by dawn. However, they managed it; the English had got the weather gauge by dawn. The fighting could begin.

But the English had one problem, and it was a serious one. They did not know what Medina Sidonia intended to do, nor did they really know how they were going to stop him doing it.

VII

The Battle off Plymouth

Ever since he had arrived in Plymouth, Howard had been debating with his senior officers how best to tackle the Spanish Armada. There was general agreement that they would need to fight with their guns, as Hawkins had long advocated. Beyond that there had been much to discuss. The main problem was that nobody in England knew what Medina Sidonia intended to do.

As the English saw things, there were three basic options open to the Armada, though each had a number of possible variants. First, the Armada could land an invasion force itself, probably somewhere along the south coast of England. Second, the Armada might head for the Netherlands to pick up Parma's army and transport that to England. Finally, it could land troops to seize a port, then bring Parma's army over and land it through that port.

There had been other possibilities raised over the winter of 1587–88 – that the Armada might land an army in Ireland, Scotland, or France – but these had been generally discounted by the spring of 1588. One possibility that remained a concern longer than most was that the Armada would put into a French port. To do so without taking losses, would require the consent of the King of France. It was not until late June that Walsingham received assurances from the King of France that he would remain neutral in the coming struggle and would not permit the Armada to use French ports.

In formulating his battle plans, Howard needed to bear in mind that his paramount mission was to stop a sizeable Spanish army landing on English soil. The occasional raiding party might be tolerated, but no more. It followed that Howard needed to stop two things from happening. He had to block any move by a sizeable number of Armada ships to get into any English port or safe anchorage and he also needed to stop the Armada making contact with Parma and his army.

If Howard were to stop the Armada, or a large part of it, landing on the south coast he had to decide which were the most likely places where Medina Sidonia would try to do this. In May he had received a message from the Privy Council, a committee of senior noblemen and ministers that was chaired by the Queen or, if she were not present, by Walsingham. The message identified the Isle of Wight as the most likely landing place:

Three things he [Medina Sidonia] will principally respect:
First, where he may find least resistance and most quiet landing.
Secondly, where he may have best harbour for his galleys, and speediest supplies out of Spain France and Flanders.
Thirdly, where he may most offend the realm [England] by incursions, and force her Majesty by keeping many garrisons to stand upon a defensive war.
There is no doubt to be made, but landing in the Wight – which with an army of 8,000 men, divided into four parts, he may easily do, the force of the Island being unable to resist them with that force – in very short time they may so fortify themselves and possess those parts and places that lie convenient for passing over our supplies are by nature more than three parts fortified, that he may keep in safe harbour his galleys to make daily invasions into the firm lands, where they shall perceive the standing of the wind will impeach her Majesty's ships to come to their rescue. So that all the castles and sea towns of Hampshire, Sussex and Dorsetshire will be subject to be burnt, unless her Majesty will keep garrisons in those places, the number and charge whereof will be no less exceeding than how long they shall be forced to continue uncertain.

That this idea was not very far off the mark is shown by a late addition that King Philip added to the Secret Instructions that he gave to Medina Sidonia and to Parma. After outlining the basis of a peace deal with England, Philip added that Elizabeth could best be brought to reason if some aggressive raids were carried out against England. He gave details of only one such projected assault:

It would be very influential in bringing them to these or the best conditions possible, if the Armada were to take possession of the Isle of Wight. If this be once captured, it would be held, and would afford a shelter for the Armada, whilst the possession of it would enable us to hold our own against the enemy. In case of failure of the principal design [ferrying Parma's army to the Thames Estuary] and if nothing else can be done, you may jointly discuss and decide with regard to this.

If the Isle of Wight was the obvious choice for kings, noblemen and bureaucrats in London and Madrid, things did not seem so obvious to Howard, Drake, Hawkins and Frobisher. They had no real idea how many soldiers were on board the Armada and if the Spanish fleet was bringing with it enough men to mount an invasion, they would not need the Isle of Wight to use as a base. Instead, they could either seize a port, or simply land the soldiers onto some sheltered beach. In the Netherlands, the Spaniards had perfected the art of living off the land, stripping hostile areas of food and provisions as they passed. Any such port or landing ground would need to have an anchorage big enough to hold the entire Armada for the few days needed.

The south coast of England had several such places. Plymouth Sound was the first area to offer a large, secure anchorage and a port. Torbay did not boast a port, but did have wide sandy beaches on which troops and supplies could be landed, plus a large and sheltered bay in which the Armada could drop anchor. Weymouth, like Plymouth, had a large anchorage and a port and as already mentioned there was the Isle of Wight. Beyond that the coastline had neither port nor anchorage large enough to hold the Armada until the Downs roadstead, called Cape Margate by the Spaniards.

If Howard was to stop Medina Sidonia from landing he had either to defeat the Armada in open battle or get the two fleets into such a position that a landing would be impossible. Quite clearly, Howard had decided not to bring the Armada to a battle of annihilation. If this had been his object he would have remained downwind of the Armada, blocking the access to the Channel so that the Spaniards would need to fight a major battle to get past him. By manoeuvring upwind, Howard had allowed the Spanish Armada free access to the Channel. He must have had another plan.

None of the English accounts of the campaign spell out what this plan was, but it can be deduced from what happened over the following days. At each battle, the English ships followed a set pattern of action. They sought to push the Spanish ships past the possible landing place, blocking their access and crowd the Armada together, disrupting its formation to make any organised landing impossible.

If this plan worked, the Armada would be shepherded all the way up the Channel to the coast of the Netherlands. That would leave the Spaniards with only one option, to ferry Parma and his men over the North Sea. This was, as we now know, the Spanish plan all along. To disrupt this projected invasion, Howard needed either to stop the barges carrying Parma's men from coming out or to separate them from the warships of the Armada. As things stood, Seymour and Winter were blocking the barges in port by the simple expedient of cruising up and down off the coast to show that English warships were in the area.

This did not go down very well with the Dutch admiral, Lord Justin of Nassau. He had a formidable fleet of coastal flyboats that were, like the English, armed with long barrelled guns of the culverin family. He was desperate for Parma to leave the Netherlands and try to invade England. The Dutch rebels were being pushed remorselessly back by Parma on land. If the veteran Spanish troops with their experienced Italian and German mercenaries could be caught at sea in unarmed barges it would be another matter entirely. Justin was confident that he could massacre the lot.

Justin's plan was to keep a few craft coasting along the shoreline between Dunkirk and Sluys, the two main ports in Parma's hands. These would be disguised as fishing smacks and coastal traders. As soon as the crews spotted Parma's barges getting to sea they would race east to Justin's home port of Flushing where the main Dutch flyboat fleet was kept. Justin estimated that he could get his gunboats among the Spanish barges before they had got out of the maze of sandbanks and shoals to a place where Spanish warships could protect them.

More than once the Dutch tried to persuade the English to withdraw Seymour and Winter, but without success. The negotiations between Parma and Elizabeth's ambassadors were dragging on. Parma had refused to include the Dutch ambassadors in the talks, and their only input was by way of Elizabeth's representatives. The Dutch were understandably worried that Elizabeth might agree a separate peace with Parma, while Elizabeth was concerned that Justin's apparent commitment to a naval battle that would save England might not be as firm as it appeared.

Winter for one was desperate to be away from his tedious patrolling. He wrote to Walsingham begging him to persuade the Dutch to take over from him along the coasts of the Netherlands.

Sir, I suppose that if the countries of Holland and Zealand did arm forth but only the shipping which the Lord Admiral [Justin] at his departing delivered unto our admiral in writing that they would send from those parts to join with us here, and that was 36 sail of ships of war, and that it were known to the Prince [Parma] those did nothing but remain in readiness to go to the seas for the impeaching of his fleet whensoever they did come forth, I should live until I were young again or the Prince would venture to set his ships forth.

We do not know what Howard's plan was for defeating the projected invasion by the combined forces of Parma and Medina Sidonia actually was. We know, of course, what he eventually did, but not if this was what he had in mind at sea off Plymouth at dawn on 31 July. What we do know is that he was astonished by what the Armada did that morning.

English mariners were accustomed to sailing in small, loosely organised squadrons. They had little experience of sailing in large fleets, and none of adopting any sort of formation at sea. In English fleets, each captain chose how best to follow the flagship of his admiral. As a result, English fleets generally adopted a triangular sort of a formation when travelling, with the flagship at the front and the other ships straggling roughly behind. When action beckoned, the ships adopted a longer, thinner formation so that the ships could adopt the new tactics of gun fighting, but it was still left to the individual captains where they should put their ships to best advantage.

The Spanish, and more particularly the Portuguese, had a very different tradition. Their fleets were precisely ordered and formed according to a prearranged plan agreed in advance by the fleet commander in a council of war with his captains. The captains were highly adept at keeping tight formation in all but the roughest seas. Even the clumsiest sailing ship was expected to hold its station in a formation. The commander would choose a formation that would allow the poor sailors to maintain position, even if this was at the expense of the better sailors. Keeping precise formation was considered more important than allowing freedom of action to captains of the better ships.

The fighting formation of the Armada had been agreed weeks earlier. As the English warships bore down, Medina Sidonia had a gun fired from his flagship the *San Martin*. It was the signal for the

Armada to adopt formation. What had until then been a gaggle of ships without any apparent formation slowly shook itself out as the ships slipped into position. The English were astonished to see the fleet adopt a tightly knit shape akin to that of a crescent moon, with the trailing tips of the crescent pointed backward toward the English fleet, the blunt nose of the crescent pointed east along the Channel.

Leading the Armada at the very peak of the curve was Medina Sidonia in the *San Martin*. Immediately behind him came Don Hugo de Moncada with his four powerful galleasses. To Moncada's starboard was the Squadron of Portugal, to his port was the Squadron of Castille. Medina Sidonia maintained control of the Portugal Squadron, while the Squadron of Castile was now under Gregorio de las Alas. Thus the three most powerful fighting squadrons of the Armada were clustered in the centre and front.

Tucked in behind the leading three squadrons were the store-ships, transports and the like – 23 ships commanded by Juan Gomez de Medina. To Medina's starboard was the Squadron of Guipuzcoa, ten fighting ships under Miguel de Oquendo. To Oquendo's starboard and slightly behind him was the Squadron of the Levant composed of another ten fighting ships commanded by Martin de Bertondona. Together Oquendo and Bertondona made up the right wing of the crescent.

On the opposite flank, to Medina's port, was the Squadron of Andalusia. These ten warships were commanded by Don Pedro de Valdes. To his port and slightly behind him was the Squadron of Biscay under the veteran Juan Martinez de Recalde.

The warships seem to have adopted the standard battle formation of the Spanish Navy. This was for the ships to be drawn up in two lines abreast, one behind the other, a formation designed for a battle of boarding tactics. The front line would crash into the enemy fleet to get the battle underway, grappling the opposing ships and seeking to overwhelm isolated ships. The second line would then crowd in where the admiral felt that they would do most good. Unlike the English, the Spanish did not intend to fire off many broadsides of guns, so a line ahead formation was deemed unnecessary. The mass of attack was best delivered by a large number of ships striking the enemy fleet at all at once, which meant a line abreast.

The position of the pataches and zabras commanded by Don Antonio de Mendoza in this formation is not clear. These small craft were not expected to play an active part in any fighting, nor did they do so. As a result none of the commanders bothered to specify where they were positioned. It would make sense for them to be somewhere near the middle of the crescent where they would be sheltered from English attacks. Since their central purpose was to carry messages or go out scouting on the orders of Medina Sidonia it would also make sense if they were close to his flagship. Perhaps they were located in front of the storeships of Medina and between the squadrons of Portugal and Castile.

It was customary for an army (and in Spain a fleet as well), to be divided into three. The Vanguard went first and was traditionally composed of a small fighting force surrounded by a cloud of scouts and messengers. Behind that came the Centre which had the bulk of the most effective ships. Behind that came the supply ships. Bringing up the rear was a third fighting force, about the same size as the Vanguard, termed the Rearguard.

The division into three 'battles' was based on the formation adopted by an army marching along a road. For a fleet at sea this internal division made less sense, but was adopted by most navies as it allowed for a degree of flexibility in battle, while fitting in neatly with the bureaucratic demands of the home government when it came to paying wages, sending supplies and such like.

For the Armada, the Vanguard was composed of the Levant and Guipuzcoa squadrons and command was given to Don Alonso de Leyva. De Leyva was not an admiral, nor even a seaman. He was a land general who commanded the cavalry embarked on board the Armada. Officially he was the second in command of the expedition, though in practice his role was to control any landings that took place and to cooperate with Parma. De Leyva sailed on the *Rata Encoronada* in the Levant Squadron. This was a large ship at 820 tons that housed not only de Leyva but also his staff officers, secretaries and servants.

The Rearguard of the Armada was composed of the Biscay and Andalusia squadrons and came under the command of Recalde. The Centre was composed of the galleasses plus the squadrons of Castile and Portugal, all commanded by Medina Sidonia.

Medina Sidonia had chosen to adopt this formation because of his main aim in the campaign was to get the Armada safely up the Channel. He had expected the English fleet to seek to bar his entry into the Channel, to be in front of the Armada. That was why the prime fighting ships were at the front of the crescent formation. He hoped to bear down on the English fleet, striking an opening and decisive blow with his most powerful forces.

However, Medina Sidonia was well aware of the English preference for gun fighting from a distance. He expected them to spend some time swooping about seeking to harass the Armada by dashing up to the flanks, firing a broadside and then bearing off. To counter this the Vanguard and Rearguard were positioned on the flanks of the storeships, thus protecting the relatively undefended merchantmen from English guns, while at the same time positioning Spanish ships with guns on the flanks where they could shoot back.

The backward sweeping tips of the crescent were a trap. Any English ships which sought to attack the vulnerable storeships in their unprotected rear would soon find themselves in trouble. The tips of the crescent would steer inward to surround the English ships and bring them to a boarding battle.

There is no doubt at all that the Spaniards still expected and hoped for the campaign to come to a climax in a battle based on boarding tactics. They knew all about the English preference for gunfire and manoeuvre, some of them had even experienced it. However, they believed that such tactics could not win a pitched battle. If the English sought to stop the invasion, they would need to destroy the Armada. And that, the Spanish firmly believed, could be achieved only by getting to close quarters and boarding. The English believed otherwise and were now going to put their ideas to the test.

Before any serious fighting could begin, the courtesies and formalities inherited from the chivalric medieval period had to be observed. Medina Sidonia acted first by hoisting to the top of his mainmast a vast banner. This flag was embroidered with religious images and had been blessed on the altar of Lisbon Cathedral in a lengthy service before the Armada had set sail. Howard chose to issue a challenge in the English fashion: a pinnace was sent to dash forward at high speed, it got between the trailing tips of the crescent, then bore about and fired its gun at the enemy fleet. The pinnace was out of range of its tiny gun, but that did not matter. Defiance had been shouted in approved fashion. The formalities over, the battle began.

As with all the battles that were to follow, the scene is confused for historians by the fact that no one observer was in a position to see everything. The distance from tip to tip of the Armada was over a mile and the hulls and sails of the ships restricted the view of any man substantially.

Once the gunfire began, the smoke obscured vision even further. Gunpowder in the sixteenth century produced great billowing clouds of grey-black smoke that clung to the ground, or sea, and would not disperse unless blown away by a wind. Some land battles became so densely covered in smoke that the sun was blotted out and men could see barely 20 yards – a situation which gave rise to the phrase 'the fog of war'. At sea things were rarely that bad as there was usually a wind blowing and in any case the guns were not so closely grouped nor as stationary as in land battles. Nevertheless, gunfire did make it very difficult to see what was going on. This situation is made worse by the fact that some of the key players in the drama left no written account, either because they were later killed or because nobody asked them to do so. From reading the various accounts, however, it is possible both to follow the general outlines of what happened and to pick out some details.

The action began on the Spanish right wing, the majority of the English force, led by Howard, came rushing down in a straggling line ahead. They stayed at long range, using their culverins to fire at the Spanish while staying out of range of the enemy cannon. As they swept past the rear of Bertondona's Squadron of the Levant, the English fired, then passed on to turn, return and fire again.

The impact of the English guns was impressive. It was not that they inflicted a huge amount of damage – when the fight was over it was found that they had not – but the psychological impact proved to be major. The men on the Spanish ships were accustomed to fighting a boarding battle, but this concentrated and prolonged gunfire was something new. Usually there would be one or two salvoes of cannon fire before the boarding took place and the cannons were replaced by the pops of musketry and the ringing of edged weapons on armour.

Now the Spanish found themselves subjected to a prolonged cannonade of ear splitting noise. It was not just the boom of the guns that deafened the ears, but the unearthly and terrifying howl of the balls as they flew through the air. Culverin balls flew fast, creating a demonic howl as they passed by. Men could be killed merely by the passing of such a ball at high speed. Men were also killed and wounded as the balls smashed home into hulls, knocked down spars and rigging and swept across the decks.

Perhaps most unnerving of all was the sight of ship after English ship coming into range, running out its guns and then firing. As if in slow motion, the Spaniards saw the death-dealing culverins coming toward them, and there was little they could do about it.

Their own ships carried very few long range culverins, most of the cannon were short range weapons to be fired just before boarding. Some of these were fired in response, but the shot was seen falling short of the English ships.

It is no wonder that some of Bertondona's ships chose to edge away from the English ships, moving inward across the arc of the crescent. They began to get muddled up with Oquendo's Squadron of Guipuzcoa. On board the *Rata Coronada*, de Leyva kept his station, and soon Oquendo was bellowing across the waters to get his ships and those of Bertondona under control.

Meanwhile, Drake had led another straggling column of English ships down to assault the left tip of the Armada crescent. He arrived some minutes after Howard, and got a very different reception.

Commanding the left wing, or rearguard, of the Armada was Don Martinez de Recalde, the premier fighting admiral of Spain. We do not know why Recalde acted as he did for he left no written acount of the Armada campaign, but it is possible to make an educated guess. He was experienced at sea fighting and, as a prominent nobleman himself, might have expected to be given command of the Armada after the death of Santa Cruz. There is no hint in any surviving documents that he resented Medina Sidonia's promotion, but he would not have been human if he had not harboured some feelings on the matter.

Recalde will have known that the leader of that first English onrush must have been Howard, for the etiquette of war at the time demanded that the commander in chief have the honour of attacking first. That meant that the second English force now bearing down on his command would almost certainly be led by the English second in command: Drake.

Recalde knew also that Medina Sidonia had lost the weather gauge, and that Philip's orders meant the Armada was likely to proceed up the Channel without attempting to regain it and so bring the English to battle. Recalde was also well aware of the design of the new English warships, and the gun fighting tactic that they were built to exploit. He was at this moment watching that tactic being put into operation as Howard closed with de Leyva's vanguard. As Recalde could see, the Spanish ships were recoiling from the English guns.

If the English were determined to use their new tactics, then Medina Sidonia's actions would play into their hands. Only by forcing the English to engage in a boarding battle could the Spanish

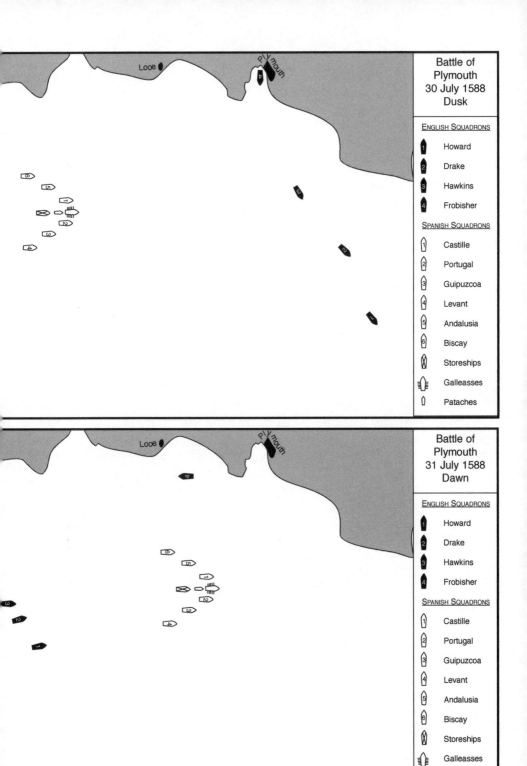

Battle of
Plymouth
30 July 1588
Dusk

ENGLISH SQUADRONS

1 Howard
2 Drake
3 Hawkins
4 Frobisher

SPANISH SQUADRONS

1 Castille
2 Portugal
3 Guipuzcoa
4 Levant
5 Andalusia
6 Biscay
Storeships
Galleasses
Pataches

Battle of
Plymouth
31 July 1588
Dawn

ENGLISH SQUADRONS

1 Howard
2 Drake
3 Hawkins
4 Frobisher

SPANISH SQUADRONS

1 Castille
2 Portugal
3 Guipuzcoa
4 Levant
5 Andalusia
6 Biscay
Storeships
Galleasses
Pataches

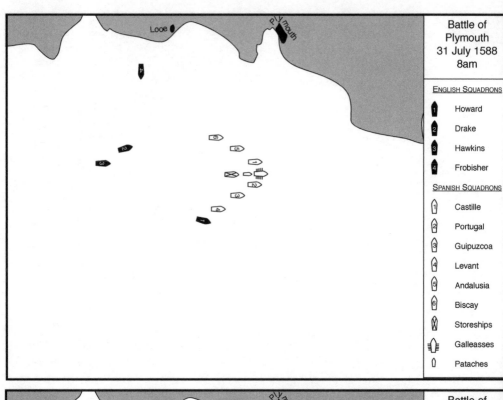

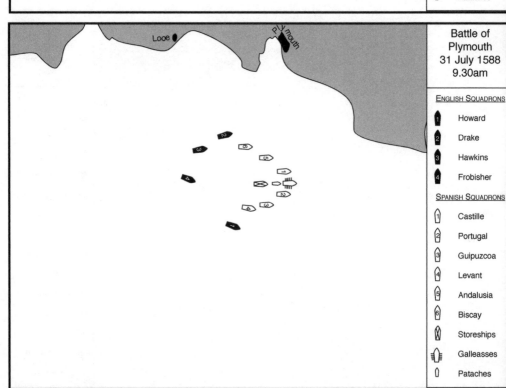

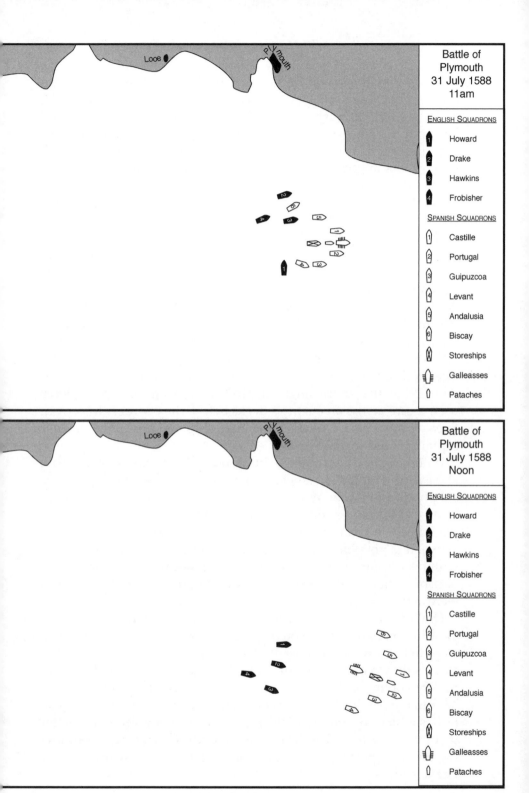

Battle of Plymouth
31 July 1588
11am

ENGLISH SQUADRONS

1 Howard
2 Drake
3 Hawkins
4 Frobisher

SPANISH SQUADRONS

1 Castille
2 Portugal
3 Guipuzcoa
4 Levant
5 Andalusia
6 Biscay
Storeships
Galleasses
Pataches

Battle of Plymouth
31 July 1588
Noon

ENGLISH SQUADRONS

1 Howard
2 Drake
3 Hawkins
4 Frobisher

SPANISH SQUADRONS

1 Castille
2 Portugal
3 Guipuzcoa
4 Levant
5 Andalusia
6 Biscay
Storeships
Galleasses
Pataches

hope to win the naval battle now beginning. The best way to achieve that was to precipitate a confused melee at close quarters. So long as the English ships had room to manoeuvre they could keep out of range of the Spanish grappling irons, but if the ships got close together then sooner or later one English ship would fall prey, others might have to try to rescue it and so the boarding battle that the Spanish needed would begin.

Recalde may have been encouraged by the fact that one of the advancing English ships was the *Triumph*. Recalde could not know, at this point, that the ship was commanded by Martin Frobisher, but he could plainly see that this great ship was very different from most of the English warships. The *Triumph* was rated at 1100 tons, which made her by a wide margin the largest ship in either fleet. At this date she had not been fully converted to the new race-built design. The flimsiest top platforms had been removed from both forecastle and sterncastle, but the towering castles still remained. Although she had been given seventeen culverins, the *Triumph* still mounted seven old fashioned cannon on her lower decks, together with 29 of the short-range, small bore fowlers and port-pieces used to fire across an enemy's decks before the boarders took over. Recalde must have looked at this huge ship and presumed that her captain would want to board.

Whether Recalde wanted to bring on such a battle, snub his nose at Medina Sidonia or fancied taking on the great *El Draque*, we simply do not know. What we do know is that as Drake's column came on, Recalde suddenly took his ship, the *San Juan*, out of it place in the formation, turned about and waited for the English to arrive. It is possible that Recalde had discussed this sort of a move with his captains beforehand. If so, what followed must have been part of a plan. If not, the captains of Recalde's Biscay Squadron were acting on their own initiative.

Drake in the *Revenge* swept down on the *San Juan*, poured his guns into her and passed on. He was followed by the other English ships in his command, most of them firing their guns into Recalde's ship as they passed. The Spaniard shot back, but the English were mostly staying out of range. Drake then turned about and came back to the *San Juan*. This was perfectly in accordance with English tactics which sought to isolate one or more enemy ships and batter them with gunfire. The rest of the Squadron of Biscay was moving away in perfect formation, and so offered no such target for Drake's guns.

As he came back, followed by the other ships in his group, Drake chose to close the range. We do not know exactly how close he got, but it was significantly closer than Howard's ships on the other flank of the Armada. The English guns inflicted much more serious damage on the *San Juan*. The ship's foremast stay was shot away, hit twice by cannonballs and her rigging crippled. All of this was of little concern to Recalde. In fact he may have welcomed it if the apparent disorder tempted the English ships to come in close.

But they did not. Drake, Frobisher and Hawkins were too wary for that. Instead they chose to circle the wounded Spaniard, firing their guns when they could, but always staying outside of the effective range of the cannon, never mind the grappling irons. It seems that only the purpose-built warships were involved in this delicate manoeuvring. The converted merchant ships in Drake's command appear to have pulled back.

It was at this point, when it had become clear that the English could not be tempted to close, that another of the great ships of the Biscay Squadron pulled out of line. The *Gran Grin* put about and began sailing back toward the *San Juan*. Firing her cannon and other heavy guns, the *Gran Grin* came pushing into the swirl of English ships. If Recalde had planned the move, he had planned well. The English captains were by this point intent on the *San Juan*, and the *Gran Grin* was able to get close to the circling English ships. If the enemy had been any navy other than the English the ruse would have worked. Grappling would have begun and a boarding battle broken out but the nimble English ships were able to dodge out of the way at the last moment.

By this point the entire Biscay Squadron had come to a halt. Some of the English ships moved forward to open fire on them, perhaps hoping to isolate the entire squadron from the Armada itself but it was not to be. Medina Sidonia had been taken by surprise by Recalde's move and was slow to react. Now, however, he brought the flagship *San Martin* to a halt and the rest of the Armada pulled to in formation. Recalde in the *San Juan* together with the *Gran Grin* turned and sailed up to join the Squadron of Biscay which in turn then got under sail to rejoin the Armada.

Drake and his captains pulled off at this point, baulked of their prey. The ships streamed back upwind to join Howard's ships some distance behind the Armada. Medina Sidonia now led some of the leading warships of the centre, including the galleasses, to the rear of the storeships. He formed his warships into a sort of screen across the rear of the Armada. As the bulk of the ships pushed east, downwind, Medina Sidonia spent some time trying to lure the English ships into close battle.

No matter what ruse the Spaniards tried, the English stayed out of range. They were happy enough to dash forward, fire their guns at a galleon and then change direction to get out of range again, but they never got really close. One thing that Medina Sidonia did notice, however, was that the English stayed well away from the galleasses: 'The English when they saw the galleasses enter, they retired and went away all that they could.' He concluded that the English were worried both by the big guns of the galleasses and by their ability to move independently of the wind.

Otherwise, Medina Sidonia was forced to conclude that his ships could do little to outmanoeuvre the English. In the Duke's official report for King Philip after the campaign was over, he wrote: 'The enemy had gained the wind and the English ships being swift and well handled, so that they could do what they liked with them.' This was the last time that the Spaniards made any concerted attempt to out sail the English. The desultory fighting came to an end around 3pm, though some isolated skirmishing seems to have continued for another hour or so.

The hours of fighting and manoeuvring had left the Armada out of formation. Medina Sidonia's first priority was to get his fleet back into formation before either the English tried something new or night fell. In the event it was neither that would cause the problems that were to follow.

As the warships of the Armada moved slowly to regain their crescent formation the *Nuestra Senora del Rosario*, flagship of Pedro de Valdes of the Squadron of Andalusia collided with another ship of the Andalusian Squadron. The *Nuestra Senora del Rosario* lost her bowsprit and a yard off her foremast in the collision. This was a serious loss for a ship of this kind as steering was carried out by balancing the pull of the sails on the foremast with the tug of the rudder on the water. Without a foremast she could only be steered poorly and with difficulty. Pedro de Valdes fired a gun – the recognised signal of distress – and edged out of his position toward the shelter of the storeships. Presumably he intended to replace the lost yard and rig up a temporary bowsprit.

As the Spaniards concentrated on the *Nuestra Senora del Rosario*, there came a sudden and deafening explosion, followed by a great pillar of flames and smoke towering up into the sky from the opposite wing of the Armada crescent. The powerful *San Salvador* of the Squadron of Guipuzcoa had blown up. Medina Sidonia ordered the Armada to come to a halt, then sailed his *San Martin* toward the stricken vessel.

Exactly what caused the great store of gunpowder kept under the sterncastle to explode with disastrous results is something of a mystery. This is understandable as anyone close to the powder store when it went up would have been killed instantly. In the absence of any more definite information, the most likely explanation would be that some crew member was careless in some way. However, it was not long before a rather different story began to circulate through the Armada as the survivors of the blast were taken off.

It was said that the explosion had been set off deliberately as an act of sabotage by a German gunner (one version said that he was a Dutchman), who had had an argument with the ship's captain. It was said the gunner had stormed off below after the argument, had reappeared on deck in great haste a few seconds later to jump over the side and the explosion had followed seconds later. A few weeks after the campaign a newssheet was published in Hamburg by a pamphleteer who claimed to have got the whole story of the tragedy from survivors.

According to this account, the gunner was not only a German but a native of Hamburg. We know that at least one ship from the city, the *Bark of Hamburg*, was in the Armada and German mercenaries served on both sides in the Netherlands war, so the presence of such a man on the *San Salvador* is not impossible. The gunner had taken his wife and teenage daughter into Spanish service with him and they made themselves useful cooking and washing clothes.

Unfortunately the gunner's wife gave into the charms of a Spanish officer and much to the gunner's resentment the two became lovers. In the cramped conditions of a warship filled with soldiers and sailors, the situation must have been difficult to say the least. Then another Spanish officer began to eye up the teenage daughter. That proved too much for the gunner, and it was this that led to the fatal argument.

Most historians do not believe this elaborate tale of sexual jealousy and parental protectiveness and it must be admitted that the story does seem very far fetched. However, after the English captured the wreck of the *San Salvador* they made a complete inventory of everything aboard and of the prisoners they captured. Among these was a 'German woman' who was subsequently released. Was she a native of Hamburg who later went home and told her story? We don't know.

Whatever the cause of the blast, its results were clear. Most of the officers and many of the crew had been killed outright or so badly injured that their deaths were only a matter of time – 200 men in all. A total of 224 men survived, but were wounded and needed medical treatment. Only 92 men were unhurt. The upper decks in the stern of the ship had been blown out, leaving only the charred and shattered hull walls. Fire had taken hold and was burning furiously. Medina Sidonia sent men over to get the fires under control. Once that was achieved, two galleasses were ordered to take the ship in tow and pull her into the centre of the Armada formation.

It was very quickly obvious that the *San Salvador* was doomed. Medina Sidonia ordered that she should be stripped of as much as possible. Most of the survivors were taken off, along with the administrative papers and the treasure chest that had survived the blast. A few of the fatally wounded were left dying on board, along with a group of mercenaries – two French and four Germans, plus the enigmatic German woman – who had presumably had enough of Spanish service. Then the wreck was cast loose and abandoned. While this evacuation was going on a new disaster struck. A fresh westerly wind had got up and the Channel waters had become choppy. Don Pedro de Valdes was still trying to repair his battered *Nuestra Senora del Rosario*. He later recorded what occurred next:

The sea did rise in such sort that my ship having struck sail and wanting her halyard of the foremast, being withal but badly built, did work so extremely as shortly after and before it could be remedied, her foremast brake close by the hatches and fell upon the mainmast, so as it was impossible to repair that hurt but in some good space of time. I did again send word thereof several times to the Duke [Medina Sidonia]; and discharged three or four great guns to the end that all the fleet might know what distress I was in, praying him either to appoint some ship or galleass to tow me or to direct me what other course I should take.

Two pataches came up to the stricken ship. One asked for news, then slipped off to the *San Martin* to explain to Medina Sidonia what was happening. A tow rope was got to the *Nuestra Senora del Rosario* by a galleon, but it quickly parted in the choppy seas. After some time and with no word from the flagship, Don Pedro ordered a senior monk, Bernado de Gongora, to get into the second patache and go to beg for help. With him he took four Englishmen who were sailing in the Armada, three more remained behind.

Brother Bernado arrived on the *San Martin* to find an argument taking place between the senior commanders. Medina Sidonia had sent orders to a galleass to go over to the *Nuestra Senora del Rosario* and take her in tow. Captain Ojeda, commanding the vice flagship of the *Andalusians San Francisco*, was hovering nearby awaiting orders how to help out.

Diego Flores, the admiral Medina Sidonia had chosen to advise him on naval matters, now took a hand. He pointed out to Medina Sidonia that the freshening wind and choppy waters were making it difficult for the ungainly storeships to keep in position. The warships too were drifting out of position. With darkness coming on, Diego Flores warned that the Armada was taking a risk staying where it was: a hostile fleet was not far away in one direction, a hostile shore not far in another. If the defensive formation broke up the Armada would be at the mercy of the English and their long range guns.

Diego Flores urged that the Armada had to get under way so that the ships could get steerage way and so keep formation. The crippled *Nuestra Senora del Rosario* could be left with the galleass, the *San Francisco* and some pataches. If she could not be saved, she could be abandoned.

Eventually Medina Sidonia agreed, and gave the necessary orders. The Armada got underway, leaving the *Nuestra Senora del Rosario* and her little cluster of helpers behind. Leaving a wounded companion to the enemy is never popular with an army or navy; it tells every man present that if he is wounded, or his ship damaged, he will be left in his turn. The decision served to demoralise the men of the Armada. Nobody was in any doubt who to blame: Diego Flores was known to have a feud with Don Pedro de Flores. The move was regarded as shameful.

Darkness closed in and the Armada moved on. Two hours later from the darkness behind the fleet, in the direction where lay the crippled *Nuestra Senora del Rosario* came the sound of heavy cannon being fired. Then there was an ominous silence.

Don Jorge Manrique noted in his diary of the *Nuestra Senora del Rosario*: 'The Armada passed on, leaving her behind in sight of the enemy. What subsequently became of her and her crew is not known.'

VIII

The Battle off Portland Bill

The main English fleet passed by the *Nuestra Senora del Rosario* and her attendant ships. Howard was intent on keeping in touch with the Armada to prevent the Spanish from landing. The crippled galleon and her companions posed no threat to England, and so could be left to be dealt with later.

Some hours later the English ship *Margaret and John* came hastening up from the west. This ship of 200 tons was a converted merchantman, but she had been equipped with culverins and had a modern rig. She was a useful ship in battle and must have been almost as much use to Howard as a race built galleon. She was commanded by Captain John Fisher, aided by Lieutenant Richard Thomson, who later wrote an account of what happened. Thomson did not record why the *Margaret and John* was so far behind the main English fleet, perhaps she had been on a mission for Howard or had been later getting out of Plymouth.

Thomson's account begins at about 8.30pm as the *Margaret and John* is hastening to catch up with the main English fleet. The lookout sights the *Nuestra Senora del Rosario* wallowing in the waves. He wrote this some days later when the identity of the ship's commander was known.

At our approach, we found left by her for her safeguard a great galleon, a galleass and a pinnace ... all three which upon the sudden approach of our ship, forsook the ship. About 9 of the clock the same evening we came hard under the sides of the ship of *Don Pedro*, which by reason of her greatness and the sea being very much grown, we could not lay aboard without spoiling our own ship. And therefore, seeing not one man show himself, nor any light appearing in her, we imagined that most of the people had been taken out. And to try whether any were aboard or not we discharged 25 or 30 muskets into her cagework, at one volley with arrows and bullet.

And presently they gave us two great shot, whereupon we let fly our broadside through her, doing them some hurt, as themselves have and can testify.

After this we cast about our ship and kept ourselves close by the he Spaniard until midnight, sometimes hearing a voice in Spanish calling us, but the wind being very great and we in the weather the voice was carried away, that we could not well understand it, but were persuaded by our mariners, to be the voice of one swimming in the sea, whereupon we put off our ship boat with 8 oars to seek, call and taken up; but found nobody.

Captain Fisher was in a tricky position. He was incapable of capturing the Spanish galleon since his own ship was equipped for gun fighting, not for boarding. Yet he did not want to let such a valuable prize slip through his fingers. If he left the galleon she might manage to complete some temporary repairs and limp off to a neutral French port, or even head back to Spain. In the end, about 1am, he decided to go after the English fleet to report the matter to Howard.

The night was cloudy and visibility poor. As the *Margaret and John* sailed off eastward, the *Nuestra Senora del Rosario* fell behind and disappeared into the darkness. Don Pedro de Valdes was showing no lights. Fisher must have despaired of ever finding her again before dawn. In the event he was not even able to find the English fleet that night. Something very odd had happened.

As the squally evening winds got up, Howard had issued his orders for the night. He wanted to keep his fleet together, following close behind the Armada so that the English ships would be in a position to engage the Spaniards should they seek to enter Torbay, which they were likely to reach next day. At the same time Howard did not want his ships to push on so that they got so close to the Spanish ships that a boarding battle became likely. It was going to take a fair degree of seamanship. He sent for Drake. The *Revenge* was to show a bright light in her huge stern lantern, all other ships were to keep that light in sight and ahead of them.

As dusk came down Drake's lantern shone out clear and bright. There were occasional patches of mist and the clouds obscured the moon. Sometimes Drake's lantern slipped out of sight, but it soon came back into view again. The English ships cruised slowly east following the light. Then suddenly the light was gone, never to return. The English captains did their best to keep close together, but inevitably they became scattered.

According to Drake's account given to Howard the next day, all had been going well until about 1am or so. Drake's lookout had then sighted sails to the south-east. Drake had himself peered into the darkness and seen the outlines of six or more large ships. The mystery ships were heading west several miles to the south of the English fleet.

Drake feared that they might be a squadron of Spanish warships hoping to get around the southern flank of the English fleet unseen. If Medina Sidonia had managed to get a number of his big war galleons upwind of the English then he would have put himself into a battle-winning position. Drake said that he was worried enough that he believed that he should go after the unrecognised ships. If they turned out to be Spaniards he would need to attack quickly and without warning.

To enable him to creep up on the silent ships unseen, and so that the entire English fleet did not follow, Drake put out his lantern. He turned the *Revenge* south, then west to follow in the wake of the mysterious ships. Two pinnaces followed Drake, as did a converted merchantman, the *Roebuck* commanded by Captain Whiddon.

Drake reported that he got close to the ships around 3am and recognised them as German merchant ships. However, it was known that some German ships were in the Armada, so to make sure Drake overhauled them and hailed them. Satisfied that the ships were harmless, Drake had then put his helm about and headed east to catch up with the English fleet. But when the sun came up, Drake found the *Nuestra Senora del Rosario* only half a mile off his bows – helpless before his guns. That magic mirror of his must have been working well that night.

Drake had an English merchant named Nic Oseley on board his ship. Oseley was a fluent Spanish speaker and had spent much time doing business in Spain. Indeed, he was the last Englishman out of Spain before the war began. It was typical of Drake that he should have got such a useful man to sail with him. Oseley was put into a rowing boat and sent off to talk to the Spanish captain. Don Pedro de Valdes was impressed to learn that he was dealing with Drake, and clambered down into Oseley's boat to be rowed over to the *Revenge* to discuss surrender terms.

Drake's offer was both courteous and brutal. If Don Pedro surrendered his ship without a fight then the lives of all his men would be spared, everyone would be decently housed and fed until such time as King Philip would arrange for them to be returned to Spain. If he did not surrender than every man on the *Nuestra Senora del Rosario* would be killed before sunset.

Even without her foremast – and it has never been really explained why Don Pedro had not managed to rig up a temporary mast over night – the *Nuestra Senora del Rosario* was a powerful warship. She could probably have held off the *Revenge* and the *Roebuck* without too much trouble, though if other English ships appeared she would have been doomed. However, Don Pedro knew Drake by reputation, and must have known that he was perfectly capable of carrying out both his promise and his threat. Moreover, Don Pedro reasoned, there was no shame in surrendering to the great *El Draque*, so he did.

Drake ordered that the Spanish ship should be immediately plundered of all cannonballs and gunpowder, as this would be of use to the English warships. The Spaniards were allowed to keep their personal belongings, though they had to give up all weapons and were locked below. The rest of the ship's contents – food, drink, paychest and the ship itself – were sent to Torquay, escorted by Whiddon and the *Roebuck*. The captured men were marched through what was then a mere village to a large barn that stood in the grounds of the local manor. There they were locked up while the campaign continued. The Devon locals later had many tales to tell about the Spaniards locked in the barn. One of the most widespread was that one of the 'cabin boys' was actually a young woman who had disguised herself so as to be able to accompany her lover to the wars.

One man who was not imprisoned in the Spanish Barn – as it is known to this day – was Don Pedro de Valdes himself. Drake invited the Spaniard to be his guest on board the *Revenge* and Don Pedro accepted. He moved into Drake's cabin along with his wardrobe of clothes and fine table silver and stayed on the *Revenge* for the rest of the campaign. This was not an unusual tactic of Drake's for he had often taken enemy officers into his ship as guests before. Perhaps he used his charm to get information out of them, or maybe he was simply interested in learning more about the enemy. Whatever his motives, they did not go down well with Walsingham who ordered Don Pedro to be sent ashore to a secure prison – but that was not until after the fighting was over. Meanwhile, Drake with Don Pedro aboard was hurrying east to catch up with the English fleet. Much had happened while he had been gone.

While most of the English fleet shortened sail and pushed slowly east, Howard in the *Ark Royal* and two other royal warships, the *Bear* and *Mary Rose* had pushed on fast through the night. He had sighted a lantern far ahead and thought that it might be the *Revenge* that had somehow got ahead. It was not. When the cold grey light of dawn came up, Howard found his three ships alone and only 300 yards from the Spanish Armada.

Howard hurriedly put his ships about and began to claw up to windward, both to escape the Spanish ships and to get back in contact with his own. How Medina Sidonia reacted to finding the English flagship within gun range has not been properly recorded. We know that Moncada, the commander of the galleasses, believed that he could catch the English ship with his oared warships rowing into the wind. He was not allowed even to try.

As Howard set about reuniting his scattered fleet, the *Margaret and John* arrived to report that the *Nuestra Senora del Rosario* was alone and abandoned. Barely had Fisher got his story out than Drake arrived to announce his tale of mysterious German merchant ships and his fortuitous capture of the abandoned galleon. Howard himself, seems to have accepted Drake's story and put his capture of Don Pedro's ship down to his proverbial luck.

Others were less kind. Frobisher believed that there had never been any German ships, but that Drake had gone back solely to capture the galleon. He was furious both that Drake had abandoned his post and that he had got first pick of the loot to be had. Several weeks later he was still denouncing Drake as 'a cowardly knave' to anyone who would listen to him.

Meanwhile, the other crippled Spanish ship was in trouble, the *San Salvador* had been taking on water all night. The ship towing her, the *Santa Maria de la Rosa* was having trouble keeping her underway. At 11am Medina Sidonia received a note telling him that the *San Salvador* was sinking and could not be managed. He ordered that the surviving crew should be taken off her, everything of value removed and then the ship scuttled.

Pedro Coco Calderon, the Armada's chief accountant, recorded in tactful fashion what happened next: 'The captain, however, was badly wounded and the men in a hurry to abandon the ship so that there was no one to sink her; besides which she had many wounded and burnt men on board who could not be rescued as the enemy was approaching.' Howard was not very close at all at this time, and in any case had less than half the English fleet close about him. It seems the men detailed to strip and sink the wreck simply panicked and fled.

It was Hawkins on board the *Victory* which got to the *San Salvador* first. He was appalled by the stench of burnt flesh, the sight of the dying wounded and the terrible condition of the ship. Hawkins was, however, pleased to see that the forward magazine was still crammed full of gunpowder and cannonballs. He ordered the wreck to be taken in tow by *Bark Fleming*, the same ship that had first brought news of the Armada into Plymouth. Like the *Nuestra Senora del Rosario*, the *San Salvador* was soon stripped of anything of use to the fighting ships. Not much of value was left on her by the time the official government agents went on board at Weymouth to make an inventory.

Later that day the westerly breeze died away and the two fleets were becalmed. Both commanders took the opportunity to call a meeting of their senior officers. We know rather more about what happened on board the *San Martin* than on board the *Ark Royal* as Medina Sidonia kept more complete records of such events.

The sailing abilities of the English ships seem to have taken the Spaniards by surprise. Certainly the number of longer range culverins being mounted by even the smaller English warships had come as a bit of a shock. Medina Sidonia's orders had not been to engage in a naval battle unless he had no choice, and Spanish intelligence had kept the Spanish admirals well aware of the preferred English tactics of gun fighting. Even so, the ability of the English to inflict damage from a distance seems to have been unexpected. The most vulnerable ships in the Armada were the store ships and transports that would be essential for getting Parma's army across the North Sea. Medina Sidonia knew that he had to protect these ships come what may.

Another unexpected setback in the fighting up until then had been the ease with which the English had managed to drive the Spanish ships out of formation. This had apparently been achieved by the psychological shock of the English cannonballs ploughing at high speed and from a long range into the hulls and masts of the Spanish vessels. The actual damage done does not appear to have been very heavy, but it was much worse than the Spaniards would have expected to suffer in a boarding battle. The Spanish captains had borne away from the guns, disrupting the formation. The most obvious casualty of this had been the loss of the *Nuestra Senora del Rosario*.

Medina Sidonia had apparently decided both to ensure the safety of his storeships and to enforce strict formation keeping on his fleet. To that end he reorganised the command structure of the fleet. The Vanguard and Rearguard were combined under the command of Don Alonso de Leyva. The veteran Recalde was still repairing the damage his *San Juan* had sustained in the heavy fighting of the previous day and was unable to assume command of the new squadron. De Leyva had not only his own ships, but also four galleons transferred from Medina Sidonia's squadron: *San Mateo*, *San Luis*, *Florencia* and *Santiago*. He was also given three of the four galleasses. De Leyva therefore had the bulk of the fighting power of the Armada under his command. Medina records de Leyva's task as 'to withstand the enemy'. In other words he was to keep station at the rear of the Armada and drive off any English attacks.

Medina Sidonia kept command of the remaining ships of the Centre, plus one galleass, as his fighting force. The storeships and pataches would seem from later events to have come under his immediate command, though this is not clearly stated. Medina Sidonia was expecting that within the next day or two he would meet the English ships stationed in the Dover Straits and North Sea coming up the Channel toward him. He thought that these ships were under Hawkins, though in fact they were under Seymour and Winter. It was for this reason that he kept a sizeable force of fighting ships at the front of the Armada. As events would show, however, he was quite willing to move his ships to where they could do the most good. Presumably this flexibility on his part was agreed at this council of war.

If Medina Sidonia, or perhaps his sailing adviser Don Diego Flores, kept a degree of flexibility for his own ships, he was determined to allow none to other captains. In his later account of the campaign Medina Sidonia made clear what his views were.

The Duke summoned the whole of the *sergentos mayores* [military police] and ordered each one to go in a patache and take his instructions round to every ship in the Armada specifying in writing the position which they should respectively occupy. Orders were also given to them, in writing, to immediately hang any captain whose ship left her place. And they took with them the Provost Marshals and the hangmen necessary for carrying out the order. Three *sargentos mayores* were assigned to each of the squadrons, whose duty was to execute the aforesaid order.

Clearly Medina Sidonia meant to keep order. It must be said that in the fighting that took place over the next few days the Armada did show admirable discipline and formation keeping.

There has been some dispute over exactly what formation the Armada kept during these actions. Medina Sidonia does not explain, and the English accounts are contradictory. Some talk of a round formation for the Armada in place of the crescent that the Spanish had adopted to that date. Other accounts continue to refer to a crescent. It may be that the Armada still adopted the crescent, but that with the two wings of the formation now under one command they were more inclined to cooperate in action than they had been.

The council of war that took place on board the *Ark Royal* was not described in any surviving account, nor were its decisions noted down by anyone. We know that in the battles that followed the English followed a set plan, so presumably that plan was discussed and agreed. Frobisher in the towering *Triumph* and with some of the slower ships would take the coastal position. They would seek to drive the Spaniards past any potential landing places, fire into the enemy when possible and generally keep things moving along. The more manoeuvrable ships were given to Drake and Hawkins to command. They were stationed out to sea where they could use their nimbleness to launch darting attacks at the seaward wing of the Armada. Howard himself had a fourth squadron which he kept between the forces of his subordinates, ready to intervene when he saw an advantage.

Unlike Medina Sidonia, Howard encouraged his captains to use their initiative and to move as they saw fit. Fast sailing and hard shooting were the English advantages and these could best be exploited by captains who were free to fight their ships as they thought best as the battle unfolded. It seems to have been decided that to get closer to the enemy, certainly this is what would happen. The fighting off Plymouth had shown that the English ships were nimble enough to get out of the way of the ungainly

Spanish galleons with some ease. At the same time, the English were finding it difficult to estimate how much damage their guns were doing. Certainly sails and rigging were seen to be shredded, and holes were punched into hulls. How much structural damage was being done to the ships was unclear. No Spanish masts had fallen due to gunfire and no Spanish ships had been sunk. It seems to have been decided that the English needed to get in close to be certain that they were hitting the enemy and that each hit caused damage.

That night, Monday 1 August, the galleass commander, Moncada, decided to try his hand. While the sailing ships of both sides were becalmed, he led his four powerful ships out from the Armada toward the English. Howard recorded that 'The four galleasses singled themselves out from the fleet, whereupon some doubt was had lest in the night they might have distressed some our smaller ships which were short of our fleet. But their courage failed them for they attempted nothing.' Whether it was a lack of courage or some other reason is unknown, but Moncada led his oared warships back to the Armada before dawn.

When the dawn came it brought a surprise. The wind was blowing from the northeast, which gave the Spaniards the vital weather gauge. The fleets were now off Portland Bill, which meant that Weymouth was only a few miles to the northeast. This was one of the possible landing places already identified by Howard. The English plan was to hustle the Spanish fleet to the east so that they could not land an army here to fortify a base. Howard put his plan into operation.

First Howard and Frobisher steered for the shore, close-hauled against the wind. We are not entirely certain where Hawkins and Drake were, but they must have been either out to sea to the south or heading that way. Medina Sidonia and de Leyva, however, had their eyes fixed on Howard and on Frobisher's great ship. It seemed to Medina Sidonia that with the wind as it was he stood a real chance of trapping these two squadrons between the Armada and the coast, enabling him to force a boarding battle on the English.

The straggling column of English ships was getting closer to both the shore and de Leyva's warships which were now shadowing them. Suddenly the English ships opened fire, then put about and fired again. Medina Sidonia sighted the *Ark Royal* in the midst of this group of ships. To his great delight Howard's flagship was not now making off at high speed as had been the usual English tactic until then. Instead Howard and his ships were staying hauled up close as if awaiting the oncoming Spaniards.

De Leyva led his ships down toward the waiting English. No doubt Howard's men were reloading their guns, but this time it really did look as if the English were going to stand and fight. Medina Sidonia recorded his ships as they swooped down to attack: *San Marcos, San Luis, San Mateo, La Rata, San Felipe, San Juan de Sicilia, Florencia, Santiago, San Juan* and *Valencera*.

But the actions of Howard were only a diversion. As Howard put it in his report, Frobisher and his ships had slipped past the Spaniards and were now in position off Portland Bill. If the Spanish were to try to land at Weymouth, Frobisher was in an ideal position to intercept them. And, as the Spaniards were to discover, he had another trick up his sleeve.

Frobisher had with him not only his own big *Triumph*, but also the *Margaret and John* which had encountered the *Nuestra Senora del Rosario* the night before, *Mary Rose, Merchant Royal, Centurion* and the *Golden Lion*. Of these *Mary Rose* and the *Golden Lion* were older royal warships, the *Merchant Royal* was a converted merchant ship belonging to Elizabeth, and the *Margaret and John* a modern ship with culverins.

The *Mary Rose* had four demi cannon, eleven culverins, ten demi culverins and four sakers. The *Golden Lion* had four demi cannon, eight culverins, fourteen demi culverins and nine sakers. With the exception of the *Margaret and John* and perhaps the *Centurion*, about which little is known, these were wide-bodied, old-style galleons. Their castles were higher than was normal for English ships, but they did not have the towering cageworks of the Spanish galleons. They were well suited to the task that they now performed.

Frobisher's squadron was spotted by Medina Sidonia who sent Moncada and his galleasses to the attack. 'The Duke sent orders to them to make every effort to close using both sail and oars', as Medina Sidonia recorded it, but Moncada was in for a frustrating time.

What Frobisher knew, but Moncada did not, was that the notoriously strong and treacherous Portland Race was in full flow. The way that the English Channel is shaped means that large quantities of water have to move up and down it with each turn

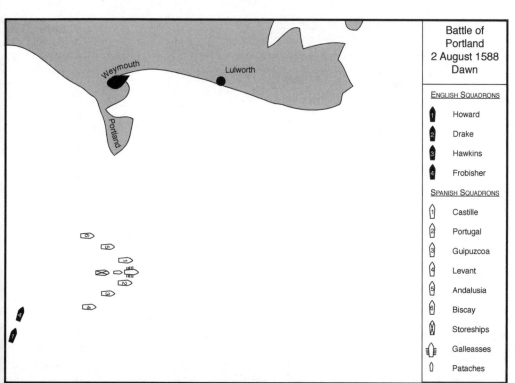

Battle of
Portland
2 August 1588
Dawn

ENGLISH SQUADRONS

1 Howard
2 Drake
3 Hawkins
4 Frobisher

SPANISH SQUADRONS

1 Castille
2 Portugal
3 Guipuzcoa
4 Levant
5 Andalusia
6 Biscay
Storeships
Galleasses
Pataches

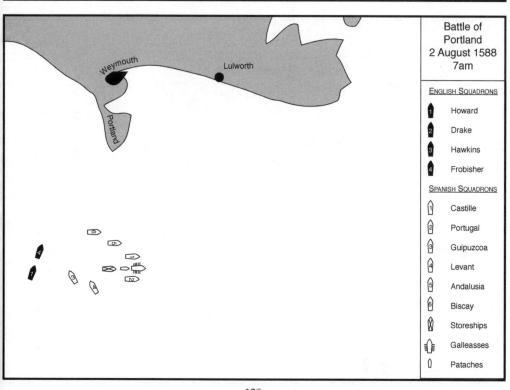

Battle of
Portland
2 August 1588
7am

ENGLISH SQUADRONS

1 Howard
2 Drake
3 Hawkins
4 Frobisher

SPANISH SQUADRONS

1 Castille
2 Portugal
3 Guipuzcoa
4 Levant
5 Andalusia
6 Biscay
Storeships
Galleasses
Pataches

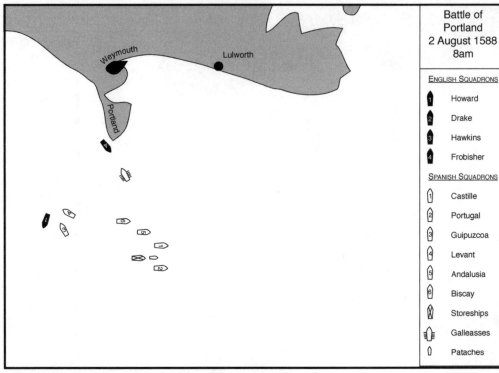

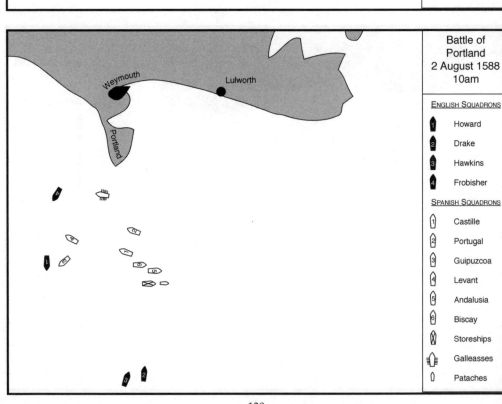

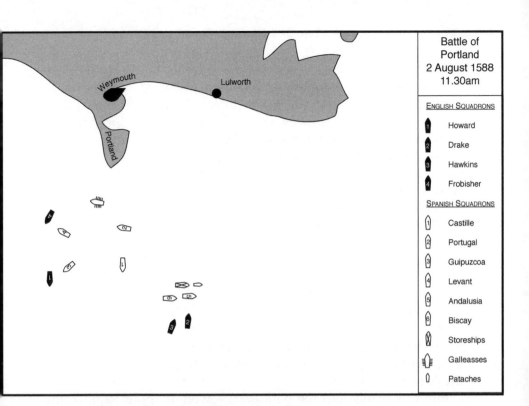

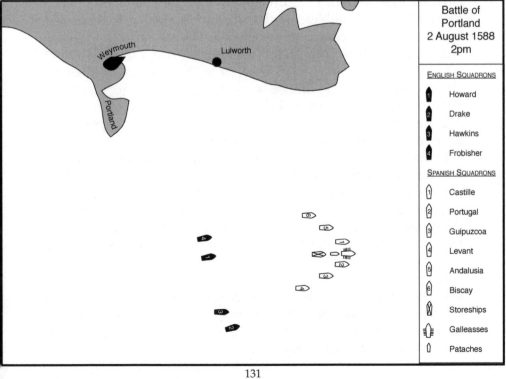

of the tide. The seabed is not flat and smooth, but is cut by deep gullies, broken by submerged hills and fractured by sheer rock faces. The moving tide takes many different courses, the most dangerous of which are the races where the tide builds up speed to pass between underwater obstructions. On the surface there is little to be seen. For a seaman such as Moncada who had spent nearly his entire adult life sailing the tideless Mediterranean, races and eddies were something new, and the Portland Race was the most dangerous and deceptive of them all.

When flowing at full speed, as it was now, the Portland Race consisted of three parallel flows of water. That closest to the shore was flowing at about two knots toward the east. The central flow was heading east at about seven knots. That furthest from the shore was going west at one knot. Between and interspersed with each flow were 'boilings', the opposite of a whirlpool in that the water welled up in the centre and flowed outward in a spiral of sometimes dizzying speed. And only two miles east lay the Shambles, a long shallow bank of sand and shell that could wreck any ship in the Armada with ease.

Into this maelstrom the galleasses rowed at about 8am. In the circumstances Moncada did relatively well. He managed to keep his craft off the Shambles, but the race and its attendant eddies and boilings had him completely confused. He was unable to get to within 300 yards of Frobisher. Whenever he tried, Moncada found his ships whirled away to the east, or to the west, faster than his slaves could row back. Moncada tried repeatedly to get across the Portland Race so that he was close enough to use his cannon with effect but he failed; whilst all the time Frobisher was pounding away with his culverins and demi culverins.

In the centre, Howard was meanwhile edging away. As the Spanish warships came down to board, Howard and his ships slipped away downwind. They never went so far that the Spaniards lost all hope of closing and boarding, so the Spanish ships followed them east. Howard was putting his plan into action, firing his guns from closer range than before and yet not getting so close that he risked being boarded.

For two hours the gun fight went on. The Spanish were unable to close and the English were firing as fast as they could. There was no sign of Drake and his forty or so ships which must have worried Medina Sidonia and perhaps this was why he was leaving the fighting up to de Leyva and Moncada.

Then, just before 10am, the wind shifted round to the south. This was what Drake and Hawkins had been waiting for; now they had the weather gauge. They piled canvas on to their ships and led a furious charge up from the south toward the seaward edge of the Armada. All Spanish eyes had been on the fighting closer to shore, and most of de Leyva's warships had gone to join in. The seaward edge of the Armada was thinly guarded with only Recalde's battered *San Juan* being of any real fighting worth.

Back close to shore, the Portland Race was beginning to lose its force as the tidal flow weakened. It was time for Frobisher to go before the galleasses could get close to him. Howard, however, now had the weather gauge of de Leyva and was determined to use it. He does not say so, but he probably wanted to keep de Leyva and Medina Sidonia distracted while Drake and Hawkins got in among the vulnerable storeships. Howard says that he 'called unto certain of her Majesty's ships then near at hand and charged them straitly to follow him, and to set freshly upon the Spaniards, and to go within musket shot of the enemy before they should discharge any one piece of ordnance.'

Medina Sidonia saw the move and realised that this was his best chance to date to get to grips with Howard, the enemy commander, in true chivalric fashion. He turned about and led sixteen galleons of his squadron back past the shoreward flank of the storeships to attack Howard. Soon the ships of Howard's squadron and those led by Medina Sidonia were within culverin range. The Spanish fired the few long range guns that they had, though to little effect. The English held their fire, or battered away those ships of de Leyva's that were close enough to hit with certainty.

That was when Drake and Hawkins struck. Their straggling column of warships and converted merchantmen, some 45 ships in all, cruised up to the seaward flank of the storeships and opened fire. Cannonballs tore through the sails and rigging, or crashed into the hulls. Damage was being done on a large scale, but the Armada storeships had a saviour that day. Just as off Plymouth, Juan Martinez de Recalde brought his ship to attack Drake.

The *San Juan* had completed repairs during the night, but had not yet been passed fit for full duty by Medina Sidonia. Now Recalde manoeuvred to get his big ship between Drake and the storeships.

His heavy guns boomed out, which attracted the attention of somebody on the *San Martin*. Recalde's actions were pointed out to Medina Sidonia, who sent a messenger in a boat to order the galleons of his squadron to turn about and go to help Recalde. He himself kept on course to intercept Howard.

As the two fleet flagships closed, Medina Sidonia struck the top-sails of the *San Martin*. This was the recognised invitation to board and fight it out in traditional fashion, but Medina Sidonia was to be disappointed. Howard was not going to get bogged down in a boarding battle. He fired his guns into the Spanish admiral's ship, then swept on. He was followed by his squadron, each of which fired at Medina Sidonia's ship as it passed by. Then the battle became confused as de Leyva's ships sought to close with Howard's, which slipped out of grappling range and the *San Martin* sought to chase Howard.

Seaward, the arrival of the galleons sent by Medina Sidonia tipped the scales. They formed up in a tight formation between the English and the storeships. Drake and Hawkins engaged the Spanish warships for some time, but they could no longer get at their prey. At about 2pm, Howard turned about and began to beat up wind away from the Spaniards. Seeing the move, Drake and Hawkins also bore off and broke off the action. The Spaniards rejoiced. 'We watched the enemy's flagship retreat,' wrote Medina Sidonia, 'and she seemed to have suffered much damage.' Most Spaniards thought that they had driven off a determined English attack, proving themselves to be the equal of the English in even the gun fighting that the English favoured. Maybe next time boarding would be possible.

In fact the English 'retreat' was the pre-planned end to the battle. The Armada had been hustled past Weymouth and were now so downwind of that anchorage that they had little chance of getting back again, certainly not with the English warships in position to attack. The English congratulated themselves on having driven the Armada away from a landing place where Medina Sidonia had never intended to land.

Thus the battle of 2 August off Portland Bill ended with both sides thinking that they had won a victory when, in fact, neither had done so. Now both fleets were continuing east toward the Isle of Wight. This was the point where the English felt most threatened. The Privy Council, Howard and Drake had all identified it as the most likely target for a Spanish landing.

Philip's orders to Medina Sidonia had been precise. He was to head for Cape Margate and cooperate with Parma in invading England. But now Medina Sidonia had made a dramatic decision. He was going to disobey his King and instead listen to the advice of his admirals and soldiers. The Armada was going to capture the Isle of Wight.

IX

The Battle of the Isle of Wight

For a man to disobey a direct order from King Philip of Spain was extremely unusual, not to mention risky. In fact there were probably less than half a dozen men in Spain who would have dared to do so. The Duke of Medina Sidonia – with his family's distinguished history, extensive contacts and astonishing wealth – was one of the very few who could even consider refusing Philip's will. Even then it was a step to be taken only in an emergency.

Medina Sidonia had made his decision to assault the Isle of Wight several days before the Armada came in sight of that island. On 30 July he wrote a letter to King Philip telling him of his decision and explaining the reasons for it:

> The object of the present letter is to say that I am obliged to proceed slowly with all the Armada together in squadrons as far as the Isle of Wight, and no further. All along the coast of Flanders there is no harbour or shelter for our ships. If I were to go from the Isle of Wight thither with the Armada our vessels might be driven on to the shoals, where they would certainly be lost. In order to avoid so obvious a peril, I have decided to stay off the Isle of Wight until I learn what the Duke of Parma is doing, as the plan is that at the moment of my arrival he should sally with his fleet, without causing me to wait a minute.

The timing of the decision can be pinpointed, for Medina Sidonia had written another letter to Philip earlier that day in which he makes no mention of this change of plan. The decision must have been made at the council of war held that day and it is not difficult to determine how the decision was reached. Medina Sidonia was no sailor, yet the reasons he gives for attacking the Isle of Wight are all sailors' opinions. It is likely he had been persuaded by his admirals, and most likely by Diego Flores. These men must have known all this before the Armada set sail, but had not dared question the orders of King Philip directly. Once at sea, however, they had been pestering Medina Sidonia, and now he had given into their pleas.

Defending the Isle of Wight was Sir George Carey, Baron Hunsdon, governor of Carisbrooke Castle. Aged 41 he had held his post since 1582 after an eventful career as a diplomat and soldier. He had begun fortifying the island in the spring of 1587, and now was confident that he could 'impeach a landing'. Whether or not he could actually drive off a determined Spanish assault was unclear, despite his optimism. The soldiers on the Armada outnumbered his, and were better trained. Nevertheless he had strong emplacements overlooking the landing beaches and Carisbrooke was ready to withstand a siege. He could probably hold out for some weeks in the castle, remaining a nuisance to the Spanish.

Ever since the beacons had warned him that the Armada was in sight Carey had had men posted on the cliffs keeping look out night and day for the coming onslaught. He had marched his men out of barracks and they were now camped around the island close to the most likely landing sites. If the Spaniards came, the Isle of Wight was ready to receive them.

Incidentally, the letter sent by Medina Sidonia announcing the change of plan was the last message that got through directly from the Armada to Philip in Spain. Once the English fleet had taken up its position just behind the Armada it was impossible for pataches to slip past them. Philip had to rely on messages passed on second hand through Parma or Don Bernadino de Mendoza, his ambassador in France. Much of the news they passed on came from merchants, fishermen and the like rather than from Medina Sidonia. Without firm news, rumours were to run rife.

Dawn came on Wednesday 3 August and opened with gunfire. Once again it was Admiral Juan Martinez de Recalde who seems to have brought on the engagement. His ship had been repaired once again and was ready to resume its place. First, however, he decided to drive off a few English ships that had got close to the rear of the Armada in the night. He did not drop out of his position, thus respecting Medina Sidonia's hangmen, but he did put about to fire his cannon at the cheeky English ships. The three galleasses with the rearguard came back to support him, and de Leyva fired such guns as he could get to bear without turning out of formation. It was all over very quickly: 'The enemy then retired without attempting anything further' noted Medina Sidonia. A galleass captain claimed to have brought down the mainsail boom of a large English ship. We do not know which ships these were, for nobody on the English side mentions the short action. Howard's official report states only: 'The next day being Wednesday there was little done.'

Howard, in fact, had some serious problems that he needed to sort out. Many of his captains had reported to him that they were almost out of gunpowder and cannonballs. He noted that 'much of our munition had been spent in the great fight, and therefore the Lord Admiral [himself] sent divers barks and pinnaces unto the shore for a new supply of such provisions.' He sent a request for help to Henry Ratcliff, Earl of Sussex, who was Constable of Portchester Castle and Warden of Portsmouth. His appointed task was to defend Hampshire from a Spanish landing. Although he must have been worried about a possible Spanish landing, he loyally sent large quantities of gunpowder and cannonballs to Howard. 'I have altogether unfurnished myself', he wrote to London in his report on the campaign.

While Howard's men spent much of the day loading Ratcliff's ammunition into their ships, Howard himself carried out a reorganisation of the English fleet. Over the previous few days several ships had joined the fleet. These were mostly privately owned merchant ships, hurriedly converted to war work by having guns of various sorts loaded on to their decks. Neither the crews nor the ship owners were paid by the state, they came to defend England from Spain, and if possible, to pick up any booty that might be had. The ships were not as useful in battle as were the royal galleons or the properly converted ships, but they could add firepower and an intimidating presence to any assault.

Howard actually had a very specific task in mind for these ships. They were to harass and pester the Armada at night: 'In the night the merchant ships should set upon the Spanish fleet in sundry places to keep the enemy waking.' It was a task that did not call for great fighting ability, but did demand loud guns, personal courage and the skill required to sail at night. The merchant captains and their crews could provide all this.

Howard decided to divide his fleet formally into four squadrons. Previously, the fleet had been led by the four admirals: Howard, Drake, Hawkins and Frobisher. The royal ships had been assigned to the admirals, but the captains of the private ships remained free agents. Howard seems to have asked some of them to serve in particular places, but most were free to choose their own station. Now Howard took the opportunity of a day on which no fighting was expected to bring some improved order to things.

During the course of the afternoon, Howard sent messengers to every ship in the fleet ordering their captains that they had been attached to the squadron of one of the admirals. There was still no attempt at a official formation, but the captains were expected to follow the lead and orders of their squadron commander. So far as we know the reorganisation proved to be successful and the captains stayed in their assigned squadrons.

Medina Sidonia also carried out a minor reorganisation. Recalde's ship was now ready to reassume its role as a flagship. He was made joint commander of the rearguard with de Leyva. Each of the admirals was given his own squadron to command directly, but Medina Sidonia made it clear that they were cooperate. It was a diplomatic move on Medina Sidonia's part. Recalde had the greater fighting experience, and had shown himself to be very able in the fighting to date. De Leyva on the other hand was better connected socially and had the sons of many of Spain's leading noblemen in his ship.

Light westerly winds dominated all that Wednesday. The two fleets moved slowly eastward at about two knots, slower than a man could walk along the cliff tops of Dorset and Hampshire. The English thought that it was unlikely that the Armada would try to get into the Solent by the narrow western entrance past the Needles; the wider eastern entrance was much more suited to the use of a large fleet, and offered better landing beaches on the Isle of Wight. Given the fitful winds, the Armada would not reach that point until mid-morning on the Thursday. It is most likely that Howard timed his attack for that time, and that he intended to follow the same basic battle plan that had worked at Portland.

For his part, Medina Sidonia did not record his plan for assaulting the Isle of Wight. It seems most likely that he did intend to enter the Solent by the eastern entrance since he sailed past the Needles without making any effort to get in past them. He had with him pilots who had sailed to England in merchant ships many times, and at least some of them must have called at Portsmouth before. It cannot be proven, but it seems that Medina Sidonia intended to anchor in the Solent between Cowes and Ryde, landing soldiers on the gently sloping coastline there and so securing the island. He must have known that the island would be defended, but had no idea how strongly. He probably intended to get around Foreland in the morning, hustling his ungainly storeships in past Ryde while his warships formed a screen against English efforts to intervene.

In the event, the day did not turn out as either commander envisaged. The cause of the disruption to both Howard's and Medina Sidonia's plans was the fact that a dead calm fell that night. Howard was thus unable to send his merchant men to keep the Spaniard's awake, while Medina Sidonia was nowhere near Foreland when dawn came.

What the dawn did reveal was that during the night the tidal currents had separated two Spanish ships from the Armada. These were the 900-ton converted merchant ship *Duquesa Santa Anna* and the royal galleon *San Luis de Portugal*. The ships were isolated and offered tempting targets, but there was a dead calm with no wind to fill the sails.

Hawkins had the answer. He put down his boats and had his men row hard to tow *Victory* toward the drifting Spanish ships. The other captains of Hawkins's squadron followed suit and soon some thirty ships were being hauled slowly over the glassy sea toward the enemy. Hawkins was clearly determined to get to close quarters before he opened fire. The Spanish soldiers in the *Santa Anna* were firing their muskets at the rowers before Hawkins ordered them to change direction, thus turning the *Victory* so that its broadside culverins could be brought to bear. The *Victory* opened fire, followed by the other English ships as they slowly came up.

The Spaniards were not going to let the English get away with this. De Leyva ordered the three galleasses of the rearguard into action. The *Zuniga*, *San Lorenzo* and *Girona* got underway, their oars thrashing the still sea as they pushed forward. One of them got de Leyva's ship the *Rata Encoronada* under tow so that her battery of cannon could be added to the battle.

To reach the developing skirmish, the galleasses would have to pass in front of Howard's idle ships. Howard at once put down his boats and the men began rowing in an effort to get the flagship and its escorts into a position to open fire on the galleasses as they passed. The *Ark Royal* and *Golden Lion* were leading Howard's squadron and managed to get into position in time.

'There were many good shots made at the galleasses by the *Ark* and *Lion* in sight of both fleets, which could not approach it being calm,' recorded Howard. 'They fought a long time and much damaged the galleasses, that one of them was fain to be carried away upon the careen [meaning it developed a list]; and another by a shot from the *Ark* lost her lantern which came swimming by, and the third lost his nose.'

The galleasses did not stop to trade shots with Howard's ships. Instead they swept on, firing as they passed but not inflicting much damage. Their main task was to rescue the *Duquesa Santa Anna* and the *San Luis de Portugal* from Hawkins. This they did with admirable efficiency, taking the two isolated ships in tow and hauling them back to the shelter of the Armada.

Although the two fleets were becalmed, they were not stationary. The tide had been moving them eastward, then northeast until they now lay off Dunnose. Sir George Carey was astride his horse on the cliff top there, anxiously watching the Armada for any sign that a landing was going to take place. It was the tides that would be the key to whether or not the Spaniards got ashore.

When the tide was going in, as it was due to do around dawn and for some hours thereafter, the flows of water around the Isle of Wight were relatively straightforward and would favour the Spaniards. As along any coast line with numerous headlands and bays, and with submerged shoals and depths, the tide was nowhere straightforward, but the overall pattern was quite simple. As the tide waters surged up the Channel from the west, they were divided by the Isle of Wight. The southern branch swept around the southern tip at St Catherine's Point, then north to round Foreland and turn northwest into the Solent. Just past Ryde the incoming tide met the northern surge that had been pushing past the Needles and Cowes. There then formed a mass of eddies and boilings as the colliding masses of water flowed past each other to get into the deep inlets of Southampton Water, Portsmouth Harbour, Chichester Harbour and Longstone Harbour. This tidal flow would have worked for the Armada. It would have pushed the ships round the eastern end of the Isle of Wight and into the Solent, just where they wanted to be.

However, as the tide went out the flow of waters changed dramatically. It was not just a matter of the water flowing in the opposite direction – things were not that simple. The huge mass of water coming out of Southampton Water, Portsmouth Harbour, Chichester Harbour and Longstone Harbour would be diverted east by the coast of the Isle of Wight, as it swept past Foreland it continued east, not turning south until diverted by the great headland of Selsey Bill, and the waters off Selsey Bill were a maze of treacherous shoals and sandbanks. At the time of greatest tide flow,

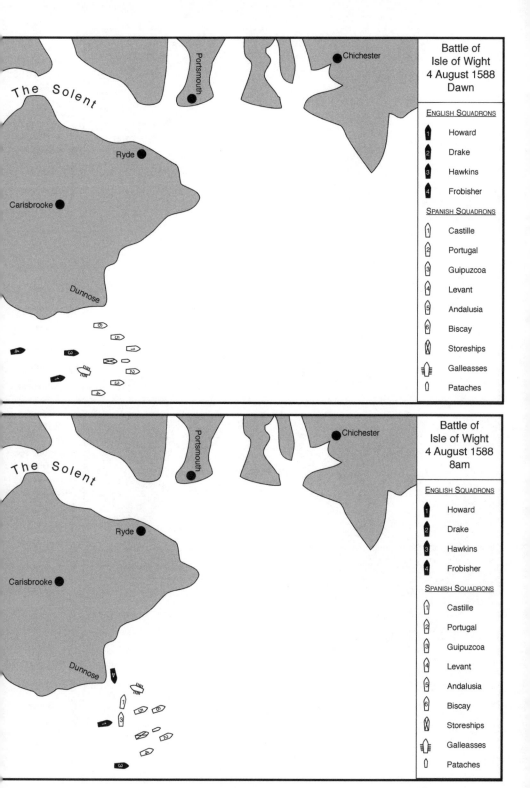

Battle of Isle of Wight 4 August 1588 Dawn

ENGLISH SQUADRONS

1	Howard
2	Drake
3	Hawkins
4	Frobisher

SPANISH SQUADRONS

1	Castille
2	Portugal
3	Guipuzcoa
4	Levant
5	Andalusia
6	Biscay
	Storeships
	Galleasses
	Pataches

The Solent

Portsmouth

Chichester

Ryde

Carisbrooke

Dunnose

Battle of Isle of Wight 4 August 1588 8am

ENGLISH SQUADRONS

1	Howard
2	Drake
3	Hawkins
4	Frobisher

SPANISH SQUADRONS

1	Castille
2	Portugal
3	Guipuzcoa
4	Levant
5	Andalusia
6	Biscay
	Storeships
	Galleasses
	Pataches

The Solent

Portsmouth

Chichester

Ryde

Carisbrooke

Dunnose

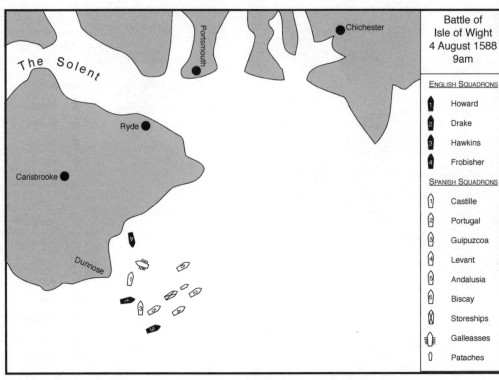

Battle of Isle of Wight 4 August 1588 9am

ENGLISH SQUADRONS
1 Howard
2 Drake
3 Hawkins
4 Frobisher

SPANISH SQUADRONS
1 Castille
2 Portugal
3 Guipuzcoa
4 Levant
5 Andalusia
6 Biscay
Storeships
Galleasses
Pataches

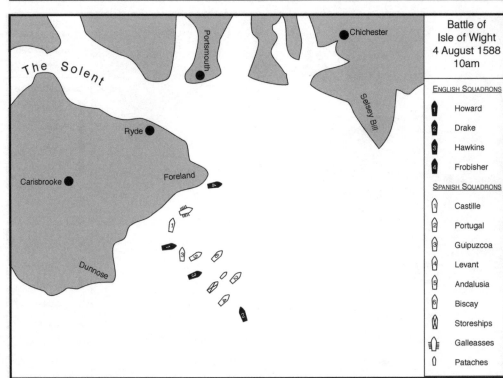

Battle of Isle of Wight 4 August 1588 10am

ENGLISH SQUADRONS
1 Howard
2 Drake
3 Hawkins
4 Frobisher

SPANISH SQUADRONS
1 Castille
2 Portugal
3 Guipuzcoa
4 Levant
5 Andalusia
6 Biscay
Storeships
Galleasses
Pataches

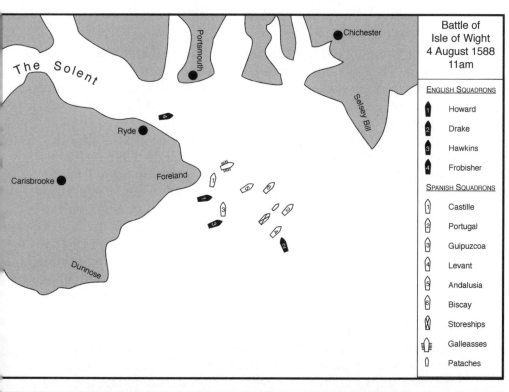

Battle of Isle of Wight 4 August 1588 11am

ENGLISH SQUADRONS
1 Howard
2 Drake
3 Hawkins
4 Frobisher

SPANISH SQUADRONS
1 Castille
2 Portugal
3 Guipuzcoa
4 Levant
5 Andalusia
6 Biscay
⋈ Storeships
⚓ Galleasses
◊ Pataches

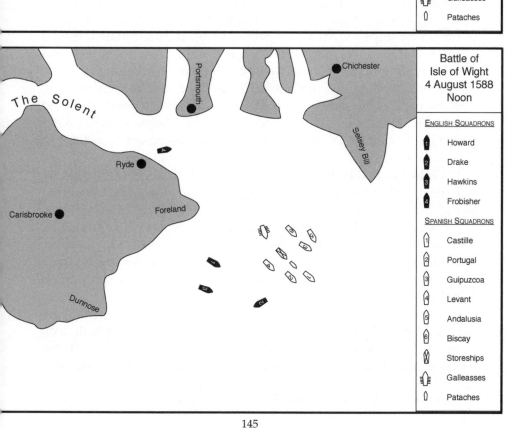

Battle of Isle of Wight 4 August 1588 Noon

ENGLISH SQUADRONS
1 Howard
2 Drake
3 Hawkins
4 Frobisher

SPANISH SQUADRONS
1 Castille
2 Portugal
3 Guipuzcoa
4 Levant
5 Andalusia
6 Biscay
⋈ Storeships
⚓ Galleasses
◊ Pataches

the waters coming out past Foreland ran at about four knots, faster in places. This was faster than the unwieldy storeships could be expected to make even with a good wind behind them. If the wind was anything other than favourable, they would be swept away completely.

Howard's aim must have been to deny the Spanish the opportunity to land on the Isle of Wight by using the tide. First, he had to delay them so that they could not use the incoming tides. Then he had to push them on so that the outgoing tides would carry them eastward. With luck he might wreck some Spanish ships on the Selsey shoals, but at the least he could expect to push them well past Selsey Bill by nightfall. Then the Spaniards would be faced by the choice of either having to work against the prevailing winds and fight past the English fleet to get back to the Isle of Wight or of continuing east toward the Netherlands and Parma's army.

Not only that but the complex flows of waters off Foreland sets up numerous races, eddies and counterflows that change and shift dramatically as the tide grows and slackens. No matter how many times the Spanish pilots might have gone into Portsmouth on board merchant ships they would never have tried to negotiate the tidal races. But the local men on the English ships knew them well and were willing to use them as they had done off Portland.

Soon after the galleasses hauled the isolated, and by then battered, ships back to the safety of the Armada formation a southerly wind got up. This was ideal for the Armada, giving them a perfect wind to take advantage of the tide flowing into the Solent. The English would have to move fast if they were to stop the Spanish.

Frobisher had been working since nightfall to get into position. It seems that he had been using the tidal flows, manoeuvring his ships in and out of them by being towed by his rowboats. However he did it, Frobisher had his squadron off Dunnose by dawn. That put him both inshore of the Armada and, when the southerly breeze got up, downwind of them. The nearest Spanish ships were Medina Sidonia's own *San Martin* and its companion galleass the *Patrona*.

The accounts of what happened in the fighting that morning are inconsistent. Both Medina Sidonia and Howard concentrated on what they themselves were doing. Several other Spanish officers likewise left accounts of what they saw, but they recorded only what was happening in the immediate vicinity of their own ships. Neither Drake nor Frobisher left an account that has survived.

The version left by Hawkins is concerned mostly with the need for the London government to send enough powder and ball to make up for the amounts shot off in the battle.

Although some details are lost, and others are confused, the overall picture of the Battle of the Isle of Wight is clear. The English fleet was arranged in what an officer on the Zuniga called 'a half moon formation'. Frobisher's squadron formed the eastern tip on the left of the fleet, pushed forward close along the coast of the Isle of Wight. Howard's squadron was in the centre about two miles or so off Dunnose. Hawkins was southeast of Howard, some four miles off the island coast. The whereabouts of Drake's squadron at this point is less clear. He was certainly further out to sea than Hawkins, but nobody mentions him or his ships until later in the battle. Presumably they did not join the early stages of the engagement.

Medina Sidonia's attention was at first fixed on Frobisher's squadron. From the decks of the *San Martin*, Frobisher looked to be in trouble. The southerly breeze seemed set to blow his ships on to the shore of the Isle of Wight, as it would have done were it not for the tidal flows. He also appeared to be dangerously isolated from the rest of the English fleet. Moreover, the *Triumph* was behaving strangely. Calderon thought that her rudder was broken, while another Spaniard recorded that it 'had suffered much damage'. Medina Sidonia decided to attack.

'They came closer than on the previous day,' wrote Medina Sidonia, 'firing off their heaviest guns from the lowest deck, cutting the trice of our mainmast and killing some of our soldiers.' These ships of Frobisher's were the older ones in the English fleet and were equipped with cannon as well as culverins. Medina Sidonia almost certainly means cannon when he talks of 'heaviest guns'. It would seem that this was the first time that the English had let fly with these potentially damaging weapons, showing that Medina Sidonia was right, the fighting was taking place at much closer quarters.

But if the Spaniards thought that they would be able to board, they were mistaken. They soon discovered that the reason why the *Triumph* was behaving oddly was not because she was damaged but because she was riding the tidal races. Medina Sidonia himself makes this clear. After explaining that Miguel de Oquendo brought his ship up to join the fight, he continues: 'Oquendo placed his ship before our flagship, as the current makes it impossible for him to stand alongside.' Clearly the ships involved in this section of the battle were being moved about by the tidal flows in a way that the Spaniards could neither predict nor understand.

Seeing other Spanish ships moving up to join the battle around Frobisher's squadron, Howard came up to lend his support. He brought with him only the five most powerful ships in his squadron: the *Ark Royal*, *Bear*, *Elizabeth Jonas*, *Golden Lion* and one other he does not name. Of these the *Bear* and *Elizabeth Jonas* joined Frobisher in working the tidal races, slipped past the Spanish ships and came up with the *Triumph*. The rest of Howard's squadron followed up behind their admiral, but do not seem to have closed immediately with the Spanish. The purpose seems still to have been to delay the Armada.

Recalde, as so often during the campaign, spotted what was going on and moved to help. He came down in his *San Juan* leading the other ships of his squadron to engage Howard and his ships in gunfight. While this was going on, Hawkins was getting into action. That he was moving against de Leyva's ships we know, but we do not know much about the course of the fighting. De Leyva had with him some of the ships from Medina Sidonia's squadron, which will have strengthened his force. Most likely, Hawkins was seeking to keep the Spanish tied up in a fight to stop them heading into the Solent while the tide and wind were right for such a move. Of Drake at this time there is no word.

Back under Dunnose, the fighting around Frobisher continued at very close quarters. Howard estimated that at times the enemy ships got to within 60 paces of Frobisher's *Triumph*. Frobisher and his local pilots were up to the task of keeping out of boarding range. *Triumph* certainly, and probably other English ships were not manoeuvring under sail, but were being towed by boats in and out of the tidal flows.

Calderon thought that the Spanish ships had Frobisher and his ships at their mercy. So did Medina Sidonia who wrote: 'We were sure that at least we should be able to succeed in boarding them, which was our only way to victory.' They were both wrong. Whatever they tried, the Spanish ships could not get to grips with the currents as they pulled the ships apart.

The wind freshened and moved around from south to south-west. High tide was approaching and with it a slackening of the eddies and races that Frobisher was using. It was time to go. Calderon describes what happened next: 'Our ships were sailing toward her [the *Triumph*], but she moved out so swiftly that the galleon *San Juan* and another quick sailing ship – the fastest in the Armada – although they gave chase seemed in comparison to her to be standing still.' Presumably Frobisher was using the last of the flows to whip his ships away to safety.

Given the direction of the wind it seems most likely that Frobisher headed north-east to round Foreland. Slack water was approaching, so he may have pushed up the Solent. This would make sense; as the shoreward guard, Frobisher's principal task was to threaten to intervene in any attempted Spanish landing. The best places to land an army on the Isle of Wight would have been around Ryde, so Frobisher probably took his ships to lie at anchor off Ryde. But if Frobisher had got away, Howard and his ships were still in action. Recalde and Medina Sidonia turned on these ships. The fighting continued as fiercely as ever. That was when Drake struck.

Drake must have been hovering somewhere nearby during the action thus far, but now he crowded on sail and bore down on the extreme right, or eastward wing of the Armada crescent. He closed rapidly with de Leyva's ships, battering them with furious gunfire at close range. It is easy to imagine his purpose, though nobody wrote down precisely what it was. The eastern point of the Spanish formation was some eight miles or so east of Dunnose, perhaps a little further. The wind was in the south-west, and the slack water of high tide was upon them. Drake must have been trying to chivvy the Spaniards to the north, to get them past the Foreland.

To the Spaniards, such a direction would have been natural. They were, after all, trying to get into the Solent. Given that the flow of the tide is faster inshore than offshore, the ships of Recalde and Medina Sidonia may well have been further north than those offshore. They may even have been not far from Foreland by this point.

What Drake knew, but the Spanish captains did not, was that within a couple of hours the outgoing tidal race would be flowing at full speed. If that struck the ungainly Spanish transports when they were in the mouth of the Solent they would be swept east toward Selsey Bill. And just off the Bill lay the Owers, an horrific area of shoal water, jagged rocks and murderous hazards. Once on the Owers, the Armada would be doomed.

Drake very quickly achieved his goal. The great *San Mateo*, one of the premier fighting galleons of Portugal was pounded so badly that she began to drift to leeward, into the huddled masses of the Armada's storeships. They broke formation to get out of the way and in turn edged north and east. The *Florencia* moved up to hold off Drake's ships to give the storeships time to reform, but Drake knew his business and came in even closer to pound the Spanish with his guns.

Medina Sidonia suddenly realised the danger that he and the Armada were in. Most likely it was a pilot with knowledge of the coast that managed to tear his interest away from the battle with Howard's squadron and get him to concentrate on what was happening to the east. Medina Sidonia suddenly broke off his action with Howard and led the fighting ships off toward Drake's squadron. He fired a signal gun, the usual method of calling attention to an imperative order, and signalled the Armada to head south.

One of the Spanish storeship captains left behind sketchy and unsigned account of the campaign. His view of this engagement shows that with hindsight the Spanish understood the danger they had been in: 'The enemy charged upon the said wing [de Leyva's] in such wise that we who were there were driven into a corner so that if the Duke and not gone about with his flagship we should have come out vanquished that day.'

Faced by the oncoming Armada, Drake's squadron could do little but fall back. The ruse had failed, but it had been close. The Armada might have been within less than half an hour of total ruin. As it was, the Spanish ships headed out to clear Selsey Bill by several miles.

Still, the English seemed content with their day's work. They had got the Armada to move on beyond the Isle of Wight. Moreover they had shown that they could get very close to the Spanish ships and still manoeuvre away to avoid boarding. Howard and his captains were convinced that they were doing damage to the enemy, both in terms of men killed and ships damaged, but they had no way of knowing for certain. They could see that some of the enemy warships fell away from the fighting and were kept out of the front line for a day or two, but they always came back. Despite their hopes, the English were not sinking enemy ships nor forcing them to be abandoned or even to stay out of the fighting for long. Of course, the Spanish were taking punishment, some of it serious, but it was not enough to break the iron discipline and determination of what were arguably the best trained fighting men in Europe.

If Howard remained uncertain how much damage his gunfire was doing to the Spanish, he knew very well the damage it was doing to his stores. In his official despatch he wrote of this moment and his decision to call off the battle.

> No, forasmuch as our powder and shot was well wasted, the Lord Admiral thought it was not good in policy to assail them anymore until their coming near unto Dover, where he should find the ships which he had left under the conduction of Lord Henry Seymour and Sir William Wynter [sic], ready to join with his Lordship, whereby our fleet should be much strengthened and in the meantime better store of munition might be provided from the shore.

The lack of gunpowder and shot was clearly a great worry. Howard again sent messages ashore to ask for ammunition and we know of two men who responded: Sir George Carey had watched the Armada sailing off eastward from the shore of the Isle of Wight that it was his duty to defend. He gave orders for his men to return to barracks and for much of his gunpowder to be sent off to Howard. He reported all this to Walsingham in a letter that he dashed off on his desk at Carisbrooke Castle at 8pm that evening.

Richard Pitt, Mayor of Melcombe Regis, also sent Howard his stores of powder and shot once the Armada was safely out of sight. He reported this to the Privy Council and emphasised the need to keep the fleet supplied with ammunition by ending his letter saying 'powder and shot be sent unto his Lordship with all possible expedition, for that the state of the realm dependeth upon the present supply of such wants.'

Howard's appeals for powder and shot travelled a surprisingly long way. The Sussex town of Lewes had 42 barrels of gunpowder stored in the castle for the use of the local militia who manned the town walls and the served the artillery that stood on them. This powder belonged to the town, not to the Queen or the navy. Nevertheless, Lewes responded to the appeal and sent twenty barrels of powder by wagon to Newhaven where a ship was waiting to take it out to the fleet. Another barrel was given to 'Patrick Hacket of Brighthelmston' (now Brighton). This Hacket seems to have been a fisherman, but at any rate he promised to get the barrel of precious powder into a boat and out to Lord Howard.

Also doing their bit were the men of the Sussex villages that have since grown into the holiday resorts of Bognor Regis, Selsey and Littlehampton. Together with neighbouring villages, they had formed a regiment of infantry militia. Every Sunday from early in

1587 the local farmers and shepherds had mustered at Sidlesham to drill and practice with weapons. For one farmer the regiment proved a fortuitous move for he met and fell in love with the daughter of one of the men chosen to be an officer. The wedding was set for the bride's birthday, 4 August 1588.

That morning, the entire regiment of volunteers turned up at Sidlesham for the wedding. The service had just begun when the ominous sound of distant gunfire was heard. The officer, eager not to interrupt the wedding of his daughter, ordered the men to stay in the church. Just as the service ended, a horseman came clattering up; it was the lookout who had been stationed on Selsey Bill. Breathlessly he reported that the Armada was in battle with the English fleet off the Bill. The men grabbed their weapons, fell in and marched off for Bognor. The groom went with them. All were grateful when he great Armada stood out to sea, heading southwest. The young groom could return to his new wife.

The two fleets headed gently east past the coast of Sussex. The Armada stayed some miles off shore. This came as a relief to the locals. Although it had not featured much in discussions at a national level, the Sussex men had thought that the port and town of Rye might be a target for the Spanish. The town had been burned by the French in 1377 and attacked several times since. In 1520 a new gun bastion was built to guard the harbour, but the locals were still nervous at the town's vulnerability to attack. In 1587 they hired the aptly named Captain Shute to advise them how best to modernise the town's defences and how to train their local militia. The town also hired a merchantman and paid for her to be converted to war use. Sent off under the command of a local seaman named John Conny, the *Anne Bonaventure* was even then sailing in the English fleet.

The local archives of Chichester record an event not logged by any of the sea officers. As the Armada sailed east off Sussex one of the Spanish ships fell out of position, having suffered serious damage to her rigging during the fighting off the Isle of Wight. The mizzen mast of this vessel, the *Carthagena*, fell overboard and she wallowed helplessly. Seeing the Spaniards' predicament, the local Susssex men grabbed whatever weapons came to hand, clambered on to fishing boats and put out to do battle.

Ever since they entered the Channel, the Spaniards had been thirsting for a boarding battle. Now they got one, but it was not what they had envisaged. The English hung back out of gun range until enough fishing boats overloaded with armed men were present. Then they rushed the ship. The captain, Don Antonio Lorenzo Miguel de Xararte, knew he was hopelessly outnumbered and surrendered at once. The jubilant Englishmen towed the Spanish ship into Chichester Harbour where it was promptly stripped of anything of value.

What happened to the *Carthagena* next is disputed. One account says that she was impounded by royal agents, taken to Portsmouth and hurriedly repaired to join Howard's fleet. A second version has it that she was so badly damaged that she was scrapped and her timbers used to build a farm, dubbed Carthagena Farm in her honour, that stood near Earnley.

The affair of the *Carthagena* is something of a mystery. None of the ships in the Armada had that name. Howard does not mention the capture of a ship off Sussex, nor does Medina Sidonia mention such a loss. Perhaps she was a tiny patache that might have escaped the notice of the admirals, in which case the local men must have exaggerated the importance of their prize.

If Howard was bothered by a lack of ammunition, Medina Sidonia was deeply troubled. He had not been in communication with King Philip since the English fleet closed behind him off Plymouth. His casualties and the damage to his ships had been mounting steadily, though not overly seriously. His real worry was the Duke of Parma.

The whole point of the Armada was that it would link up with Parma's army to stage a victorious invasion of England. And yet Medina Sidonia had received no news from Parma at all. He now began to ponder one question more than any other: where was the Duke of Parma?

X

Into Calais

If Medina Sidonia was beginning to worry about where Parma and his army was and what they were doing, Parma himself was even more worried about what the Armada was up to. In the sixteenth century communications relied upon men carrying messages. They might carry written letters or verbal messages in their heads, but however they did so they had to physically go from one place to the other. This inevitably meant long delays and, in times of war, the constant danger that messengers might be captured by the enemy.

Parma was, in fact, at his central headquarters at Bruges, where he had been all along, not as Medina Sidonia had hoped down on the coast getting his troops ready to embark into boats. Historians have long argued over Parma's behaviour during these crucial days in late July and early August. On the face of it his actions were quite bizarre.

This was recognised at the time and rumours abounded to try to explain things. Some whispered that Parma had fallen out with King Philip and was dragging his feet accordingly. It was said that some years earlier Philip had promised Parma that in the event of a Spanish conquest of England he would marry Mary Queen of Scots and so become Philip's regent in England. Others said that Philip had gone so far as to promise the English crown to Parma in his own right. Now that Philip was going to give the crown to his daughter instead, it was rumoured that Parma was angry and saw no point in making much effort over the invasion.

Others thought that Parma had been bought off by Elizabeth. It was rumoured that Elizabeth and the Dutch rebels had suggested to Parma that he should become independent Duke of the Netherlands – a throne to which he would have had a claim if his mother had not been illegitimate. The price demanded, men gossiped, was that Parma would have to allow freedom of worship to his subjects.

So far as we know neither of these scenarios had any foundation in fact at all. There is nothing in the records to indicate that Parma was anything other than unswervingly loyal to his uncle, Philip II of Spain. Nor is there much to show that he was less than a competent general, indeed one of the best of the sixteenth century. In fact it was probably this fact that explains Parma's behaviour.

What was not widely known at the time, but which has come to light since, is that Parma had written several times to Philip explaining the practical difficulties that he would have getting his army across to England. They key difficulty was to do with the ports available to Parma. Given the current state of play between Parma, the Dutch rebels and the English army operating in the Netherlands, Parma had secure access to Gravelines, Dunkirk, and Nieuport. The rest of the Netherlands was either in the hands of the rebels or was too close to their territory for comfort. The problem with the ports that Parma had in his hands was that none of them were deep water harbours. Each was a relatively small port that, because of the shoals and sandbanks offshore, were accessible only to shallow-draft craft. The big ships of the Armada would be unable to get into them, but would have to anchor four or five miles offshore in areas where they would be vulnerable to storms.

That gap of from port to anchorage was not usually a problem. Any big ship that had a cargo to unload would anchor in deep water, then move the cargo to local coastal craft which would take the goods into port. For the Armada, things would be very different. Parma would have to get his unarmed barges out across the shoals and sandbanks before they could be protected by the Armada's guns. All well and good if the only enemy to consider was the English navy – for their warships were no more able to operate over the shoals than were the Spaniards.

But the English were not the only enemy. The Dutch rebels had a fleet of around 100 flyboats just a few miles to the northeast. Armed with culverins and with a shallow draft, these boats would be able to get in among the shoals, smashing Parma's barges to matchwood and drowning his men wholesale. It was quite impossible for Parma to get his barges out to the Armada if the Dutch flyboats were in a position to intervene.

Parma had written as much to King Philip II several times. He received no firm reply one way or the other. He was neither told to abandon the attempt, nor given reassurance as to how things could be managed. So far as Parma was concerned, the invasion plan was to go ahead despite the fact that he thought it was impossible.

By the early spring of 1588, Parma had begun to get seriously worried. In and around Bruges he had some 30,000 men – all of them crack troops with years of experience behind them and the finest military equipment available in their hands. These were expensive men to keep idly in camp, and many of them were mercenaries who would be getting lucrative offers of employment from other princes. Parma had his plans for the campaigning season of 1588, including an assault northwest into the heart of the rebel territory. But he could do nothing as King Philip's orders were to keep the peace negotiations going while awaiting the arrival of the Armada.

In April, Parma lost patience and decided that he had to do something. He sent a new message to King Philip at his palace-monastery-office complex at El Escorial. The message itself was simply yet another query about proposed actions and requests for instructions. It was, however, carried by a high ranking Spanish nobleman who was not only a key diplomat of King Philip but one of Parma's most trusted advisers. Parma gave this man, Don Luis Cabrera de Cordoba, a top secret verbal message that he was to deliver personally to King Philip and to nobody else.

Writing some years later, Cordoba recalled that the message had been:

It is going to be impossible for the Duke of Parma's craft ever to meet the Armada. The Spanish galleons draw 25 or 30 feet of water, and around Dunkirk and Nieuport they won't find that much water for at least 5 miles off the coast. The enemy's ships draw so much less that they can safely place themselves to prevent anything coming out of Dunkirk. So, since the junction of the barges from Flanders with the Armada is the whole point of the enterprise, and it is impossible, why not give it up now and save much time and money?

It is doubtful if Cordoba was quite that blunt with Philip, but there can be no doubt that Parma's clear analysis was delivered to Philip by the end of April in terms as forceful as anyone dared make to him.

All Parma got in reply was a bland assurance that everything would be all right and that he was not to worry. Parma seems to have concluded from this that Philip had something up his sleeve. Perhaps the Armada was bringing with it a fleet of small craft able to get across the shoals? Perhaps the Armada was going to invade England by itself, or go to Ireland, or land troops in Scotland and get at England that way?

Perhaps the most inexplicable part of this whole episode is that Philip did not pass Parma's messages or worries on to Medina Sidonia. In all the long pages of instructions, encouragement and orders that the King sent to the Duke there is not a word about Parma's insistence that his barges could not get out to the Armada. It is true that Philip several times warned Medina Sidonia to beware of the shoals off the coast of Flanders, but there is not even a hint that Parma would have any problems getting his fleet of transports out to where the Armada was anchored.

In Flanders, Parma seems to have shrugged his shoulders and given up on the idea. As instructed he kept the peace talks rambling on. He made a half-hearted effort to get some barges gathered at Dunkirk and Nieuport. He even began building a couple of dozen armed flyboats of his own to counter the Dutch craft, but when money ran short he cut back on the numbers of workmen.

As the weeks ticked by and Parma had no firm news from Spain, he must surely have begun to agree with the merchants whose livelihoods depended on knowing which trade routes would be open and which closed by wars. By June 1588 they were openly trading as if the expected Spanish war with England would not take place. One leading Paris merchant declared that there was not one chance in six that the Armada would come to the English Channel.

On 18 July Parma sent a message to Philip giving an account of the negotiations, the state of the army and other details. He then added:

> I am greatly grieved at receiving no news of the Duke of Medina Sidonia and the Armada, although vague rumours of all kinds continue to reach us. I pray God fervently to bless the enterprise, which is undertaken in His cause and which I cannot persuade myself He will allow to fail.

It therefore came as something of a shock to Parma when a hot, dusty and dirty Don Rodrigo Tello arrived at Bruges on 30 July. Tello had come in a patache from the Armada, having left the fleet as it came around Brittany and prepared to enter the English Channel. He told Parma that the Armada should be arriving off Flanders on or about 5 August. Parma told Tello that he was not ready to embark his troops as he had had no messages from Spain informing him that the Armada had sailed. Nevertheless, Parma said, everything should be ready within a week, ten days at the most. Tello was given rooms and staff to help him recover from his arduous voyage up the Channel, then he was packed off back to Medina Sidonia with a reassuring message from Parma. Out at sea, events were moving forward in a way that was going to give Parma an even greater shock.

Thursday 4 August was a day of fitful, light winds that saw the Armada progress only as far as Hastings. Then a dead calm fell and lasted throughout 5 August. Once again the two commanders made use of the enforced inactivity.

Howard sent off more messengers demanding gunpowder and cannonballs from any source he that he could think of. He also held a ceremony that was traditionally staged to mark a military victory. Clearly he was treating the Battle of the Isle of Wight as a victory. The decks of the fleet flagship *Ark Royal* were decorated with flags and banners. Lord Howard used the power invested in him by Elizabeth to knight those men who had most distinguished themselves in the fighting. Hawkins and Frobisher were both knights, so were Thomas Howard, captain of the *Golden Lion*, Lord Sheffield, Roger Townshend and George Beeston. Drake, of course, was already a knight having received that honour from Queen Elizabeth herself. In any case somebody had to keep an eye on the Armada while the elaborate ceremony went on.

Medina Sidonia for his part called a council of war. Before doing so he sent a patache off to carry a message to Parma. After giving a brief account of events to date, the letter continued:

> The Duke has tried to induce one of the enemy's ships to grapple and so begin the fight, but all to no purpose as his ships are very light and mine very heavy, and he has plenty of men and stores. My stores are running short with these constant skirmishes, and if the enemy continues his tactics, it will be advisable for your Excellency to load speedily a couple of ships with powder and balls of the size noted in the enclosed memorandum, and to despatch them to me with the least delay.

The memorandum specified that he needed shot of four, six and ten pounds. These are balls for demi culverins, bastard culverins and sakers. That the Spanish were so low on these shot, but not others, shows beyond doubt that the fighting had been taking place at a much greater range than they had expected.

At the council of war several decisions were taken. Although no record of the meeting itself has survived, the subsequent orders have. Some of these were purely practical and almost routine. Men were sent to search the storeships for any cannonballs of the needed size, for example. However there were two decisions which stand out as being crucial.

The first was that the Armada was to head not for Cape Margate but for Calais. The reasons for this change of plan are not given, but are not too difficult to deduce. At this date Medina Sidonia had received no word at all from Parma. He did not know if Parma was ready to join him, if he would need to wait for Parma or even if Parma's army had suffered some crushing defeat by the Dutch rebels. In the circumstances heading for the anchorage of the Downs would have been foolhardy.

As with so much during the Armada campaign, it was winds and tides that drove Medina Sidonia's decision. The prevailing winds in the Channel were westerly, and the Armada had encountered mostly westerlies in its voyage so far. Any ship in the Armada could have made its way back down the Channel even in the face of westerly winds, but only if it were sailing individually and without the threat of hostile warships in the offing. To manoeuvre a fleet of 120 or so ships against the wind was an altogether more difficult operation, and with the nimble, heavily gunned English warships on hand it became even more so.

The Straits of Dover were a crucial turning point. It was here that the tides rushing up the Channel from the west met those coming down the North Sea from the north. Once through the bottleneck of the straits, the tidal flows made getting back again difficult. Again a lone ship unmolested by an enemy would have little trouble, but a large fleet harassed by the enemy would be in difficulties.

Once past the Straits of Dover the Spanish Armada was going to find it very difficult to work its way through them to the west again, and the North Sea was not a friendly place to be. The coasts of Germany and Scandinavia were in the hands of Protestant monarchs who although not directly involved in the war were hardly going to be kindly disposed to Philip's fleet. England, of course, was hostile and armed. Scotland was neutral and in truth nobody really knew how to take the attitude of its king, James VI.

Once in the North Sea, Medina Sidonia would be committed to the invasion plan. He would have to get Parma's men over to England to ensure a successful invasion after which the English harbours would be available to him and his ships. It therefore made sense to stay to the west of the tidal confluence off Dover. From there the Armada would be enabled to head back to the west. Medina Sidonia could have another attempt on the Isle of Wight if he found he would have to wait for Parma to be ready. In the worst case scenario he could cruise back down the Channel and head for Spain. Until he had definite word from Parma, Medina Sidonia decided to anchor in the sea off Calais where the seabed gave a secure hold for heavy anchors.

Calais was part of France, and the King of France was neutral. The Armada would probably not be welcome, but so long as the ships stayed out of French waters – and the reach of the guns of Calais – they would be safe enough. The French might even be induced to sell supplies to the Spanish.

The other main topic of discussion between Medina Sidonia and his senior officers seems to have been the conduct of sea fighting against the English. Since the last council of war, the Armada had enjoyed the weather gauge against the English, and had used galleasses in a dead calm but neither had proved to be particularly useful. Even when the Spanish ships had the advantage of being upwind, they had not been able to close with the English ships and force them into a boarding battle. They had been too nimble and had been able to dart away at the last minute.

What was needed, the Spanish officers seem to have agreed, was smaller craft that could outmanoeuvre the English. These smaller craft could grapple the English ships, slowing them down so that the larger Spanish ships could catch them and board them. The smaller ships would need to be not only fast but armed, which ruled out the pataches and zabras that had come with the Armada. Medina Sidonia had no such craft with him, but he knew a man who did – Parma.

Thus it was that after the council of war broke up, Medina Sidonia sent a second patache racing eastward toward Flanders. This craft carried the pilot Domingo Ochoa with orders to arrange the rendezvous and decide exactly where the Armada should anchor off Flanders. He was told to find a few local pilots who knew the coastal waters and to send them back to the Armada. The craft also carried a message which repeated the request for cannonballs and then added: 'The Duke [Medina Sidonia] praying him [Parma] as soon as possible to send 40 flyboats to join with this Armada that he might be able with them to close with the enemy, because it had been impossible to come to hand-stroke with them.'

When he got this letter a couple of days later, Parma must have finally realised that disaster was staring them all in the face. He had been warning for months that he could not get his barges out unless he had protection against the Dutch flyboats. He had received no reply and had assumed that Philip had a plan. Now it was plain that there was no plan at all, just hope. That Medina Sidonia was asking Parma to send the very craft that Parma hoped the Armada had with it was proof that the rendezvous was not going to take place. After all, Parma only had a dozen flyboats, and he needed all of those to patrol the entrances to Dunkirk and Nieuport to keep them free of the Dutch vessels. He had nothing to spare.

All that was left for Parma to do was to keep his troops safe and try to ensure that he did not get the blame for what was about to happen. Parma gave orders for the embarkation of the troops into the barges to begin. On the evening of Monday 7 August Parma left Bruges to ride to Dunkirk to personally supervise the embarkation – knowing that it was all a charade.

Although Parma did not know it, he was already too late. The climax of the campaign was underway. The final battle was about to begin.

XI

Fireships

The Armada came to anchor off Calais on the afternoon of 6 August. The English fleet dropped anchor only about a mile away to the west. The arrival of the two hostile fleets so close to his town came as a nasty surprise to the French Governor of Calais, the one-legged veteran soldier Giraud de Mauleon, the Seigneur de Gourdon. He had known the Armada was coming, as did everyone else by this date, but had assumed it would pass by to link up with Parma. But now he had the two most powerful warfleets in the world sitting on his doorstep. Battle might break out at any moment. He and his officers must have wondered what to do.

The problem was solved by Madame de Gourdon, who put on her best frock and declared that she wanted to watch the battle at close quarters. So she and her husband climbed into the governor's coach and drove down to the shore. What happened next must have been something of a disappointment to Madame de Gourdon. There was no fighting, only a messenger rowed ashore from Medina Sidonia in the *San Martin*.

The visitor brought with him the conventional pleasantries expected of a foreign duke visiting a French town for the first time. Once those were out of the way, the Spaniard asked if ship's officers could come ashore to buy goods in Calais. Gourdon was no friend of the English – it had been an English cannonball that had taken his leg off some 30 years earlier – and although his monarch was officially neutral he was known to favour the Catholic cause. Gourdon agreed, stipulating only that the Spaniards could not buy any weapons or ammunition.

Then, with nothing much else going on, the Gourdons went back to their residence. Gourdon subsequently sent a basket of fresh fruit off to the *San Martin* for Medina Sidonia's own table. With it went a message from the chief pilot of Calais warning the Spanish admiral that his anchorage was fit only for good weather and that it should be occupied if a strong wind got up. No doubt Medina Sidonia's own pilots had already told him this, but there was not really much choice – at least not until he heard definite news from Parma. It is noticeable that Gourdon sent no messengers to Howard.

About 7pm there was a flurry of excitement. Over the northern horizon came a smaller fleet of warships. As they drew closer the people of Calais recognised them as the English squadron of William Winter which had been patrolling the area all summer. An hour later more ships came into view, it was the squadron of Lord Seymour. The English were gathering in strength. They now had about as many ships present as were in the Armada. The daunting sight was too much for some – several men from the Armada deserted that night.

News from Parma was of paramount importance for Medina Sidonia. It would tell him if the promised rendezvous would take place soon or not – if the Armada should stay where it was, move on to the Downs or head back for the Isle of Wight. Almost as soon as the anchor was down, Medina Sidonia sent a fast rider off toward Bruges to find Parma. He took a message that repeated the contents of the earlier letters, but added a rebuke about not hearing any news these long weeks. The letter finished:

> I am anchored here, two leagues from Calais, with the enemy's fleet on my flank. They can cannonade me whenever they like and I shall be unable to do them much harm in return. If you can send me forty or fifty flyboats of your fleet I can, with their help, defend myself here until you are ready to come out.

Even as that messenger was galloping east, Tello was heading back the other way. He left Bruges and took ship at Dunkirk. He arrived with Medina Sidonia early on the morning of Sunday 7 August. Tello brought with him Parma's polite note that all would be ready soon, but he also told Medina Sidonia what he had seen. At Dunkirk the barges were weak and unarmed – as Parma had repeatedly told Philip was the case – and the troops were not even at Dunkirk but still in their camps inland. Tello estimated it would be at least two weeks before the troops and barges were ready to put to sea, and even then there were no flyboats to protect them still less to come to aid the Armada.

The news startled Medina Sidonia, and seems to have worried his naval adviser Diego Flores. Medina Sidonia decided that a normal messenger was no longer enough. He sent his own private secretary, Arceo, to carry a secret verbal message to Parma. Medina Sidonia demanded a firm date for the rendezvous, a definite number of flyboats that were ready for action and a dire warning that the Armada could not stay off Calais for more than a couple of days. When he arrived in Dunkirk, Arceo sent back a hurriedly scribbled note giving his own assessment of preparations. He said that he thought at least fourteen days would be needed before Parma could put to sea. Then he raced on toward Bruges to confront Parma. His message got back to Medina Sidonia on the Sunday evening.

The harassed duke responded by sending no less a personage than Don Jorge Manrique, the Inspector General of the Armada, off in a patache to head for Dunkirk. Manrique carried a blunt note from Medina Sidonia.

> I represent to you the urgent need of providing a port for the Armada, without which it will doubtless be lost as the ships are so large. Besides that, it is impossible to continue cruising with this Armada as its great weight causes it always to be to leeward of the enemy and it is impossible to do any damage to him, had as we may try.

If the written message was blunt, the verbal message was harsher still. And Manrique was a senior nobleman of Spain who had the social rank to talk to Parma in no uncertain terms.

By the Sunday evening Medina Sidonia was deeply worried. If he had known what was going on in the English fleet he would have been more worried still. Early on the Sunday morning Howard called a council of war. For the first time he had all his squadron commanders with him: Drake, Hawkins, Frobisher, Seymour and Winter. No doubt he wanted to listen to the reports of Seymour and Winter, then ask the advice of all his commanders as to what to do next.

The great unknown for the English that day was Parma. It was now clear that the Armada was going to combine with Parma to transport his army over to England, this being the only realistic option left to them. The English were totally ignorant of how many warships Parma had ready for action. For all they knew he had more than enough to destroy the Dutch flyboats of Justin of Nassau, which were now patrolling off Dunkirk having taken over when Seymour's ships left their station. If Parma could fight his way past the Dutch to rendezvous with the Armada there seemed to be little the English could do to stop an invasion. All the way up the Channel the English had tried to break up the Spanish formation so that they could get in amongst them, isolate ships and blast them to pieces. They had failed every time. Spanish ships had been damaged and men killed – they knew that – but the fleet was intact. It was clearly necessary to break up the Armada's formation and get in among them before a rendezvous with Parma could take place.

Drake and Winter were the first to speak up for the option of fireships, but the others probably already knew that this was the best option. At their most basic, fireships were vessels that were set on fire and sent toward an enemy ship or fleet in the hope of setting fire to their ships. Wooden ships of this era were incredibly vulnerable to fire. Not only were the wooden hulls, masts and spars flammable, but so were the sails and rigging. To make things even worse, much of the rigging was soaked in tar to make it water and weatherproof, but this also made it liable to go up like tinder. Fire was always dreaded at sea, and especially so in wartime.

Although the prime purpose of fireships was to try set the enemy vessels on fire, their uses went well beyond that. When used against a fleet, fireships could cause the enemy formation to break up as the individual ships manoeuvred to avoid the oncoming danger. They could also drive a ship out of a safe anchorage. On that Sunday the English were keen to do both to the Armada: both to drive it out of Calais and to break up its formation.

Fireships were such a useful weapon that Howard had ordered that some should be prepared days before when he did not know if he would want to use them or not. The ships selected were a collection of fishing boats from the ports of south-eastern England that had been gathered in Dover. They had been stuffed with straw, smeared with tar and fitted with fuses. Richard Barry, governor of Dover, had nineteen such vessels ready by the Sunday morning and was merely awaiting Howard's orders of what to do with them.

The debate in the English council of war very soon agreed that fireships were needed, but arguments raged about how and when they should be used. It would take until the next day to get the fireships over from Dover, and when they arrived they would almost certainly be seen by the Spaniards who could then take countermeasures. It seems to have been Drake and Hawkins who argued forcefully for the alternative.

They pointed out that an especially strong tide was expected that night, and that it would be running directly from the English anchorage toward the Spanish one. The next night the tidal flow would not be so strong. Not only that but the squally, westerly wind that was blowing was ideal for sending fireships down on the Armada and could not be relied upon to stay in the westerly quarter. By the time the Dover fireships arrived it might have shifted round to the east. Speed was necessary if the Armada was to be blocked from joining up with Parma. For all these reasons, Drake and Hawkins argued, the fireships should be launched that night.

But there was a problem, there were no fireships with the fleet. Drake took the lead in solving that issue. He offered to consign one of his own ships to the flames: the 200-ton converted merchantman *Thomas*. Hawkins promptly offered one of his own ships as well. Others joined in and Howard agreed; eight ships would be prepared to be fireships. The task was assigned to Captain Yonge and Captain Prowse, whose own ships were among those selected for the task. Presumably these craft were the older and deemed the least useful in the English fleet, but we cannot be certain.

The two officers went to work with a will. The ships were manoeuvred round to be out of sight of the enemy and the French, then conversion began. As much of value as could be removed was transferred to other ships: stores, gunpowder, cannonballs and the like. These were replaced with anything flammable that could be spared. Then the guns were doubleloaded so that they would go off when the flames heated them enough. Finally fuses were laid and skeleton crews handpicked to man the ships as they began their voyage toward the Spaniards. The crews would need to wait until the ships were clearly heading at the Armada, then they would light the fuses and clamber down into rowboats to make their escape.

Although Medina Sidonia could not see the preparations underway, he will have guessed that the English were up to something. At about 4pm a small English pinnace came scooting across the blustery waters. It cruised along the front of the anchored Armada until it found the *San Martin*. Four blasts came from the puny guns on board the pinnace. All the shots missed, but one ball from the Spanish flagship tore a sail on the English vessel. Then the pinnace put about and headed back to the English fleet. The Spanish took it for an act of bold impertinence to relieve the boredom of the Sunday at anchor, but in fact it had been a trip to check the tide flows. Soon afterward a group of 26 English ships lifted their anchors and sailed a few hundred yards toward the shore before dropping anchor again.

In response to these moves, Medina Sidonia prepared for trouble. He called for Captain Antonio Serrano, a man who he had known personally for some time and knew to remain cool even in the thick of battle. He put Serrano in charge of about eighteen pataches and zabras. His task was that as soon as darkness fell he was to move forward in these small craft to patrol the area between the two fleets. If he saw any English ships moving forward to launch a night assault Serrano was to fire his guns in warning. If the English tried to launch fireships he was given the delicate task of getting hold of them with grappling hooks and towing them away from the Armada. No wonder Medina Sidonia needed somebody with a cool head.

Medina Sidonia then sent an order through the Armada to every captain warning them that a night attack or fireship assault might be expected. If the English warships came on, he said, the Spanish were to remain anchored and shoot back as best they could. If fireships came then the pataches were to deal with them. No ship was to move unless a fireship got past the pataches. Even then it was to move only so far as necessary to avoid the fireship, then anchor again. Above all the Spanish captains must not panic, as that was what the English wanted.

It is not often that a man entirely unconnected with a battle has a profound and decisive impact on a campaign, but that is exactly what was about to happen off Calais. Just before the Spanish had sailed they had received news that the Italian engineer Federigo Giambelli had left the Netherlands to work for Queen Elizabeth. Giambelli had been hired to improve the defences along the Thames below London where the English expected to Parma to land. He was not with Howard, nor had he lent any advice to the English mariners. Elizabeth trusted her seamen to know their jobs.

However, Giambelli had used his talents alongside the Dutch sea beggars a couple of years earlier, and had done so with such dramatic effect that his fame spread across Europe. When Parma had been laying siege to Antwerp he had tried to starve the Dutch rebel garrison into surrender by blockading the Scheldt Estuary. In order to break that blockade, Giambelli had come up with a device that became known as the Antwerp Hellburner.

This consisted of an apparently harmless merchant ship, but the lower hold had been packed with a huge quantity of gunpowder, on top of which were laid several tons of heavy stones. Unlike modern explosives, gunpowder explodes upwards. The stones served a dual purpose, not only would they be thrown up when the gunpowder went off, but they would direct some of the blast sideways. The barrels of gunpowder were then fitted with, what were at the time, complicated timed detonators in the form of modified pistols operated by a clockwork device. The adapted ship was then sent out as if to run the blockade. As soon as the Spaniards moved to intercept, the crew had put on a show of panic and had fled. The Spaniards then towed the abandoned ship into port. This was, of course, exactly what Giambelli had wanted.

When the explosion came it was devastating, taking place as it did in the heart of the Spanish camp. More than a thousand men were killed outright and more than twice as many were wounded, the Duke of Parma among them. From that moment on every soldier and sailor in Europe knew and feared the name of Giambelli, and dreaded what terrible inventions he would come up with next. The men in the Armada were no exception.

Just after midnight movement was seen in the English fleet. Some ships were nosing forward. Serrano moved forward to investigate. A light showed on one of the English ships, then on a second. Flames appeared next, licking along the decks and up the rigging. Within a few minutes it could be seen that eight fireships were advancing. The Spaniards noted anxiously that these were not the usual type of fireship: small fishing smacks and the like. They were proper ships. Was Giambelli up to something?

Then one of the ships began to fire its guns, then a second joined in. Serrano's boats fled, and the fireships came on through the screen. Then the upper deck of one of the English fireships collapsed inward. A vast sheet of flames leapt up to engulf the masts and riggings. In the utter darkness of the night the huge rush of fire illuminated the sea for miles about. Mixed with the exploding cannon and relentless onrush of the fireships it was terrifying. Every Spaniard who left an account of that night was convinced that this was some fiendish hellburner-style device. It is safe to assume that every Spaniard thought the same. These were not ordinary fireships, but destructive works of diabolical genius and frightful power.

Panic spread through the Armada. Captains ordered their anchor cables to be cut, not even waiting to get the anchors lifted out of the sand. Even Medina Sidonia on board the *San Martin* had his anchor

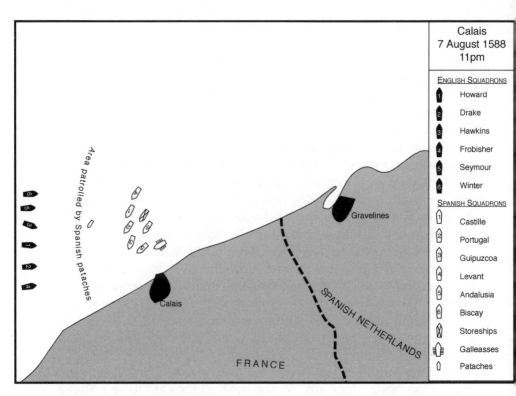

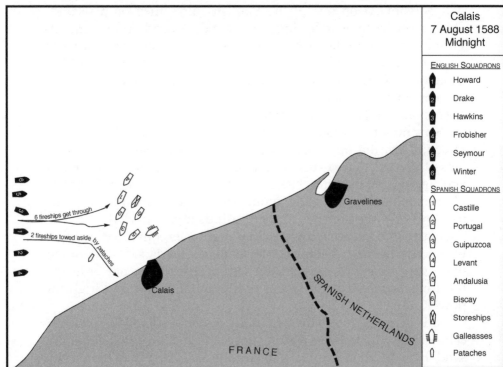

cable let go. In the darkness a fleet of 130 ships was blundering around in unfamiliar seas with a blustery wind blowing squalls of rain down while a powerful current was sweeping to the west. It is no wonder that the panic-stricken crews got into a terrible mess. Several ships collided with each other, wrecking rigging and tearing loose spars. Even the great galleon *Rata Encoronada* of de Leyva got tangled up with another ship and suffered critical damage. The confusion was terrible and far greater than the English could possibly have hoped.

When dawn came, it revealed an astonishing sight to the English sailors. The Armada was scattered across hundreds of square miles of sea, many of them were not even in sight. Drake gave a grin of delight and loosed his sails, leading the English ships down like a pack of wolves on to a scattered flock of sheep.

XII

The Battle of Gravelines

Merchant ship. This illustration is based on merchant ships operating between England and the Bay of Biscay, but most other ships of this date would have followed a broadly similar external pattern. They did, however, vary greatly in their interior arrangements. Ships from the Baltic, for instance, were arranged to carry long planks and tree trunks while those operating out of Bordeaux were compartmentalised to carry large barrels of wine. The rig is a simplified form of that used by warships, having only one mizzen mast and less elaborate detaling on the remaining sails. The 'ship rig' shown here would soon become standard, and would remain so for a century or more. The ship is built with a high stern and forecastle, though these were used mainly for crew quarters and not for fighting. The ship has a few guns mounted on the upper deck as a deterrent against pirates or harbour thieves. They were not up to major actions and would not have been used in battle. If a merchant ship were to be converted for war use the lower deck would be cleared of any obstructions, such as barrel racks, and gunports cut in the side. Heavier guns could be mounted on the lower deck without making the ship top heavy. The converted ship would also need to have a fireproof gunpowder store added, plus extra crew quarters and additional storage space for canonballs and food supples.

Having got over his initial panic, Medina Sidonia realised within less than an hour that what he and his Armada faced were not hellburners, but simply normal fireships. With admirable presence of mind he dropped anchor at once, having gone less than a mile from his initial position. Not trusting his fellow captains to do the same, he sent off a number of boats and pataches to try to find the scattered ships and bring them back to the Calais anchorage.

When the sun came up on Monday 8 August he realised that the task of reassembling the Armada was going to be a lot more difficult than he had imagined. Only five other ships were within signalling range. A number more were far to the east, but most were completely out of sight. Medina Sidonia was nothing if not brave, and he knew his duty. He ordered the *San Martin* to stand out to sea so that it was in the path of the charging English ships. There he would fight it out with the enemy, delaying them and so giving his scattered fleet time to get back into order. He was followed into action by Recalde's *San Juan*, and three other great Portuguese galleons, probably the *San Marcos*, *San Felipe* and *San Mateo*.

If Medina Sidonia was acting with courage, honour and skill, Howard was not. The previous day it had been agreed that the English fleet would attack in three great columns or squadrons. The first would be led by Howard himself and would consist of most of the English royal galleons. Drake would lead the second, having under his command Hawkins and Frobisher with their squadrons. The third would be led by Seymour and would include Winter's ships. Assuming the Armada had been scattered by the fireships, the English attack would be aimed at isolating ships so that they could be battered into surrender, or driven on to the dangerous shoals that lay off the Dutch coast. Howard's column was to be closest to the shore, Drake's next out to sea, with Seymour's running up the centre of the Straits.

Howard had a problem, which was to affect his judgement for the worse that day. His constant requests for more gunpowder and cannonballs had been met with some resistance from the officials at court whose duty it was to arrange payment for such munitions. They had sent Howard everything he had asked for, but had been demanding to know why he was not capturing more Spanish ships. Howard pointed out in vain that they were engaged in a new form of naval warfare: one that involved battering the enemy with guns not boarding his ships. The courtiers did not understand and still envisaged battles fought in the old style and thought that a lack of captured ships meant a lack of victory.

Howard was under pressure. So when he saw the *San Lorenzo*, flagship of the galleass squadron, crippled and alone it proved to be too much for him. As a squadron flagship the *San Lorenzo* could be counted upon to have noblemen on board who would make important prisoners, a pay chest that would make good booty and her capture would bring prestige enough to silence those courtiers who had never fought at sea.

No doubt the galleass had to be taken, but in her crippled condition – her rudder was gone and she had sustained some damage to her hull in a collision during the night – she could not have put up much of a fight. Howard should have left her to others, but he did not. Desperate to capture a rich prize, he went for her himself. It was one of the few mistakes that Howard was to make in his long and successful career, but it turned out to be a serious one.

By turning the *Ark Royal* away from the general chase, Howard took his entire squadron out of the battle. Not only that, but the *San Lorenzo* soon headed for the shallows where she could slip over the sands, but Howard's warships could not. The English guns could not be brought to bear and fell silent just at the moment when they would have been most use among the scattered ships of the Armada.

Instead of using his big guns, Howard loaded his men into rowing boats and sent them off to tackle the *San Lorenzo* by boarding. In charge of the operation was Amyas Preston, Howard's lieutenant. Soon other captains in Howard's squadron were following his lead, as was their duty. They put down their boats full of armed men and sent them off toward the galleass. The *Margaret and John* tried to get close enough to use her culverins to support the boarding parties, but she ran aground. The tide was going out, so much to her crew's disgust they were stuck where they were for the next few hours.

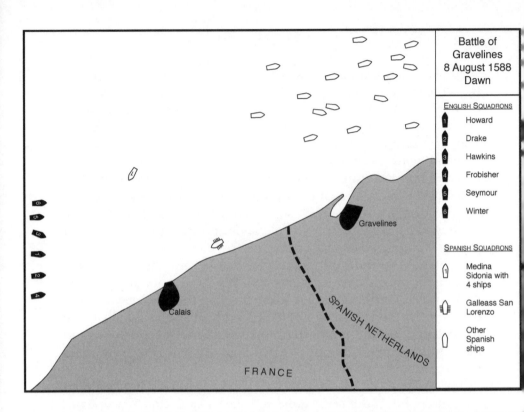

Battle of Gravelines 8 August 1588 Dawn

ENGLISH SQUADRONS
- 1 Howard
- 2 Drake
- 3 Hawkins
- 4 Frobisher
- 5 Seymour
- 6 Winter

SPANISH SQUADRONS
- 1 Medina Sidonia with 4 ships
- Galleass San Lorenzo
- Other Spanish ships

Gravelines

Calais

FRANCE

SPANISH NETHERLANDS

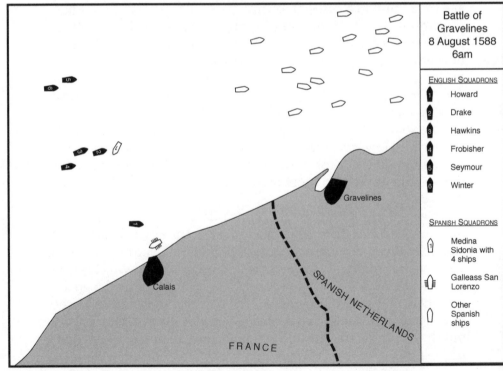

Battle of Gravelines 8 August 1588 6am

ENGLISH SQUADRONS
- 1 Howard
- 2 Drake
- 3 Hawkins
- 4 Frobisher
- 5 Seymour
- 6 Winter

SPANISH SQUADRONS
- 1 Medina Sidonia with 4 ships
- Galleass San Lorenzo
- Other Spanish ships

Gravelines

Calais

FRANCE

SPANISH NETHERLANDS

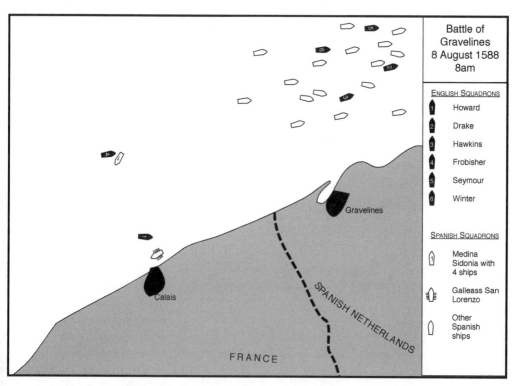

Battle of
Gravelines
8 August 1588
8am

ENGLISH SQUADRONS

1 Howard
2 Drake
3 Hawkins
4 Frobisher
5 Seymour
6 Winter

SPANISH SQUADRONS

1 Medina
   Sidonia with
   4 ships

   Galleass San
   Lorenzo

   Other
   Spanish
   ships

Gravelines

Calais

SPANISH NETHERLANDS

FRANCE

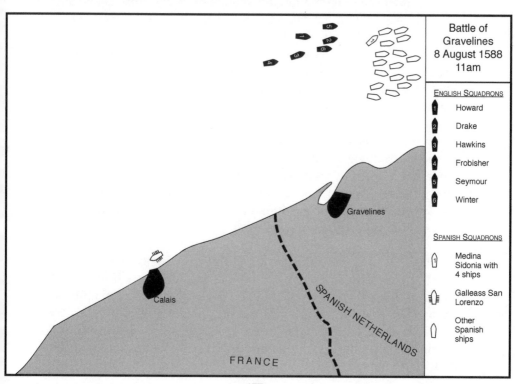

Battle of
Gravelines
8 August 1588
11am

ENGLISH SQUADRONS

1 Howard
2 Drake
3 Hawkins
4 Frobisher
5 Seymour
6 Winter

SPANISH SQUADRONS

1 Medina
   Sidonia with
   4 ships

   Galleass San
   Lorenzo

   Other
   Spanish
   ships

Gravelines

Calais

SPANISH NETHERLANDS

FRANCE

By this time the *San Lorenzo* had also run aground. As the sea retreated she heeled over on to one side. On her seaward side the heavy guns pointed helplessly into the sky, while on her landward side the cannon pointed with equal futility into the muddy waters. Several English pinnaces began to close in to aid the men in row boats. The craft were armed with small guns, which they fired at the galleass, but without much effect.

The first of the boats to get within musket shot of the galleass was the longboat from the *Margaret and John* packed with 40 men under the command of Richard Tomson. The boats from the *Ark Royal* came up next with about 60 men in her. Thomson takes up the story:

> These two boats came hard under the galleass sides, being aground; where we continued a pretty skirmish with our small shot against theirs, they being ensconced within their ship and very high over us, we in our open boats and far under them, having nothing to shroud and cover us; they being 300 soldiers, besides 450 slaves and we not, at the instant, 100 persons, Within one half hour it pleased God, by killing the captain with a musket shot, to give us victory above all hope or expectation; for the soldiers leaped overboard by heaps on the other side and fled with the shore, swimming and wading. Some escaped with being wet; some, and that very many, were drowned. The captain of her was called Don Hugo de Moncada, son to the Viceroy of Valencia. He being slain, and the seeing our English boats under her sides and more of ours coming rowing towards her some with ten and some with eight men in them, for all the smallest shipping were the nearest the shore, put up two handkerchers upon two rapiers, signifying that they desired truce. Hereupon we entered her, with much difficulty, by reason of her height over us, and possessed us of her. For the space of an hour and a half, as I judge, each man seeking his benefit of pillage until the flood came that we might haul her off the ground and bring her away.

It is only fair to point out that not all the witnesses agree with one aspect of Thomson's version. Thomson states that only his boat and that from the *Ark Royal* were engaged in the fight with the galleass, and implies that they were still the only boats engaged when the Spaniards surrendered. The other boats were, he says, 'coming rowing towards her'. Others stated that they were alongside the *San Lorenzo* when her crew surrendered. It is likely that the reasons for this was that the men were vying for a share of the loot. At this date only those who took part in the actual capture were entitled to a share of any prize money on offer – it would be some decades before the navy adopted the rule that anyone engaged in the battle would get a share.

An account by a Spanish prisoner has survived, though it is scanty. 'The Italian sailors and artillerymen, with some others, were the first to escape and fly to shore. And so many went that not more than 50 men stood by the captain to defend the ship.' He also gives the detail that Moncada was killed by a musket ball that penetrated his brain through his eye.

Such minor discrepancies apart, the general picture is clear. The capture of the *San Lorenzo* took over an hour to accomplish, and the subsequent events on board up to two more hours. About 50 Englishmen had been killed or badly wounded, and some 30 Spaniards were casualties as well.

Thomson's claims notwithstanding, the first Englishman on board the galleass after she surrendered was William Coxe of the pinnace *Delight*. In addition to any freelance looting of cabins and persons that went on, the English found 22,000 gold coins and four-teen chests of 'very noble spoil'. Being the property of the Spanish Crown this was official booty that was taken away for Howard to divide up later.

It was at this point that two French gentlemen were rowed out from the shore. They scrambled up into *San Lorenzo* and looked around for whoever was in charge of the captured ship. This was Amyas Preston, but he had been wounded. Thomson could speak French so Thomson was brought forward to speak to the visi-tors. The Frenchmen announced that they were the messengers of Monsieur Gourdan, who had been watching the gallant fight and who rejoiced in the English victory, saying that the English prow-ess and manhood had been exceptional. It is unlikely that any Englishmen listening to Thomson's translations took this statement very seriously.

The Frenchmen went on to explain that Gourdon recognised that the English fully deserved the spoil and pillage of the galleass as their due for having captured her with such gallantry. But, and here came the nub of the message, since the galleass had run aground before she had been captured she was officially a wreck. And since she had been wrecked in French waters she was the property of the French crown, not the English. There was obviously a matter of annoyance from the English at this point for the Frenchman doing the talking waved his arm toward Calais castle and pointed out that the ship lay within range of the town's guns 'and therefore did of right appertain to him'.

Preston and Thomson were equal to the task. The French claims were open to question. A wreck did belong to the shore on which it ended up, but the ship had run aground only because the English were chasing it. In any case, it was not obvious that the ship was wrecked at all. When the high tide returned she would probably float free, and she did not seem to be too badly damaged in the hull.

Thomson recalls that 'I answered unto them that, for our parts, we thanked Monsieur Gourdan for granting the pillage to the mariners and soldiers that had fought for the same, acknowledging that without his leave and good will we could not carry away anything of that we had gotten considering it lay on ground hard under guns.' He then suggested a compromise regarding the ship itself. 'As concerning the ship, we prayed it would please him to send a pinnace aboard my Lord Admiral [Howard], who was here in person hard by from whom he should have an honourable and friendly answer which we all are to obey and give place unto.'

The French seemed content to let Gourdan and Howard sort out the legalities of the matter and turned to leave. Thomson and the other officers turned back to organising the last of the looting. That was when things went wrong. As the Frenchmen were climbing over the side, one group of English sailors jostled and scuffled with them, snatching away their jewelled brooches and purses. When the outraged Frenchmen reported back to Gourdan, he ordered a gun from Calais to open fire on the galleass. The English abandoned the ship. They had got the loot and the prisoners, but not the ship or its guns.

Lord Seymour was scathing about the episode in his report. 'It being resolved the day before that my Lord Admiral should give the first charge, Sir Francis Drake the next and myself the third, it fell out that the galleass distressed altered my Lord's former determination, as I suppose, by prosecuting the destruction of her.'

While Howard was spending some three hours or so failing to capture the *San Lorenzo*, the rest of the English fleet was getting on with the prearranged plan to attack the Armada.

Had they but known it, there was a prize almost as great as the *San Lorenzo* for the taking. A solitary patache had been spotted hanging around the *San Lorenzo*, now that the galleass was lost to

Spain the little craft turned tail and fled eastward in the wake of the Armada. In the excitement none of the English thought it worth the effort to chase, except for one pinnace which followed for a while and then bore off to rejoin Howard's squadron.

In that patache was a lost and worried man: the Prince of Ascoli. This was no ordinary young Spanish nobleman, but the illegitimate son of King Philip himself. As befitted his parentage, Ascoli had been travelling with Medina Sidonia in the *San Martin*. The previous night he had been one of the officers sent off in boats to try to find and regroup the ships of the Armada. He had failed to find any ships and as dawn approached had returned to the original anchorage to find even the *San Martin* gone.

When dawn came, young Ascoli had been troubled to see the entire English fleet bearing down on him. He had headed for the shoals to escape the warships, and waited to see the outcome of the *San Lorenzo* fight before fleeing. For some hours Ascoli coasted eastward, carefully keeping to the shallows. Most of the ships he saw out to sea were English, the few Spanish vessels he spotted were beset by English ships and being badly battered. In the circumstance, his progress was painfully slow for he had to dodge any ship that approached and stay out of the way of the Dutch flyboats that were patrolling the shoals looking for victims. It was to be the following morning before he got to the safety of Dunkirk.

Out at sea, Howard's actions had kept a quarter of the English fleet standing idle, but the rest were in furious action. For the most part the battle was ragged, strung out and confused. The ships of the Armada were scattered, and many captains had only the haziest notion of where they were. The English pursuit was fragmented and disordered as each captain was under orders both to follow the flagship of his squadron and to act as he saw best in the circumstances. In practice the Battle of Gravelines, as the day's fighting has become known, was a confused succession of small actions as individual ships or small groups of vessels came across each other and began fighting. It is impossible to pick out much of an overall picture from the accounts that have survived, as each deals mostly with the author's experiences in the small fights in which he was himself involved.

Certainly the first fight to get underway began when Drake in the *Revenge* came up with the four Portuguese galleons led by Medina Sidonia in the *San Martin*. This time Drake was determined to inflict real damage on the Spanish ship, and not leave any doubt as had been the case in earlier fights. He kept the bows of the *Revenge* pointing straight towards the *San Martin* as the distance closed between the two ships. Closer and closer came Drake. When he was only 80 yards from the Spanish ship he fired his bowchasers, then at once turned aside to pour a broadside into Medina Sidonia's ship before passing on.

Drake was followed by Captain Fenner in the *Nonpareil*. This was one of the earlier ships built during Hawkins' time. She was not fully race-built like the *Revenge* but was sleek enough. She mounted 7 culverins, 8 demi culverins and 12 sakers, but also had 2 cannon and 3 demi cannon. She also had a number of small anti-personnel guns, so she must have been built at a time when it was thought that boarding would be involved in a battle. Like Drake, however, Fenner did not wait to see the results of his broadside but raced away downwind. Ship after ship of Drake's squadron followed in their turn, pounding the four great galleons before racing on with the wind behind them to find other victims.

The only account that Drake left of that day's fighting that has survived is a brief letter that he dashed off that evening to Sir Francis Walsingham.

> God hath given us so good a day in forcing the enemy so far to leeward as I hope in God the Prince of Parma and the Duke of Sidonia shall not shake hands this few days; and whensoever they shall meet, I believe neither of them will greatly rejoice of this day's service. I assure your Honour this day's service hath much appalled the enemy and no doubt but encouraged our army. From aboard her Majesty's good ship the *Revenge*.

After the signature and seal, Drake added a postscript: 'There must be great care taken to send us munitions and victual whitherosever the enemy goeth. Drake.'

Although the note does not say where Drake went after blasting the *San Martin* nor what he did, the contents speak volumes. Unlike Howard, Drake had been keeping in the forefront of his mind that the primary aim of the day's action was to break up the Armada, push it eastward and stop the rendezvous with Parma from taking place. He had clearly been heavily engaged, as his plea for more ammunition shows. His final remark 'whithersoever the enemy goeth' shows that the question of where the Armada was bound was still an open one.

Hawkins, like Drake, pushed on downwind to get in amongst the Armada before it could reform. He also wrote to Walsingham that evening:

All this day we had with them a long and great fight, wherein there was great valour showed generally of our company. In this battle there was spent very much of our powder and shot and there was hurt done among the Spaniards. I doubt not but that all these things are written more at large to your Lordship than I can do.

While Drake and Hawkins dashed ahead, Frobisher pulled up to fight Medina Sidonia. His *Triumph* was big and old, ideal to take on the four great galleons. He was, however, careful not to get so close that boarding took place. After a while, Medina Sidonia realised that his fleet was not coming to him, so he decided to go in search of them. With Frobisher and his squadron circling them and firing cannon, the four galleons eased off downwind. About 2pm other ships came into sight and at 3pm Frobisher gave up the assault.

The *San Martin* was in a terrible state. Calderon recorded:

So tremendous was the fire that over 200 balls struck the sails and hull on the starboard side, killing and wounding many men, disabling and dismounting three guns and destroying much rigging. The holes made in the hull between wind and water caused so great a leakage that two divers had as much as they could do to stop them up with tow and lead plates, working all day. The crew were much exhausted by nightfall with their heavy labours at the guns, without food.

The other galleons must have been similarly damaged.

By mid-morning Drake and Hawkins were in amongst the mass of the Spanish ships, battering at them with all guns. At one point Captain Fenton of the *Mary Rose* was racing east to catch up with Hawkins when it passed a Spanish galleon, name unknown, heading west toward the battle raging around the *San Martin*. The *Mary Rose* was an older ship, but she had been recently converted and mounted 39 guns, most of them of the culverin family. The two ships passed each other at pistol range, probably only 20 yards or so. The English fired a broadside at this point blank range, inflicting considerable damage on the enemy. One gunner was certain that he saw his shot not only enter the Spanish hull, but blast out the far side as well. Fenton was delighted and noted the claim.

The English did not get it all their own way in this battle. They were getting so close to the enemy that the Spanish cannon and demi cannon could inflict damage. Drake's ship was, we know from a later dock repair report, hit by more than three dozen balls of large size. She must have suffered casualties.

Throughout this running fight the wind was in the north-west. The Armada was being driven before it, and before the English guns. Few of the ships had anchors, having cut their anchors free when escaping the fireships the night before. Some ships put out sheet anchors, small anchors for use in an emergency, but not all carried them. The main danger to the Armada lay to the south-east, where the extensive shoals and sandbanks of the Dutch coast were being exposed by the outgoing tide. This whole area had been dry land used as cattle pasture during Roman times, so there was little enough depth of water over them at the best of times. With an extra low tide expected that day, they were especially dangerous.

Somewhere amid the confusion a group of five powerful galleons got together. These were de Leyva's *Rata Encoronada*, Martin de Bertondona's *La Reganzona*, the *San Juan de Sicilia*, *San Christobal* and *San Juan of Castile*. Behind the group a number of the storeships and smaller warships began to get together. The group was assaulted by a squadron of English warships around 11am. The fight went on for some time, then the English went off to search for scattered and more vulnerable victims. Which squadron this was we do not know. It may have been Seymour's, for his account of the battle mentions that he came across a formation of enemy ships at one point.

Winter, meanwhile, had sailed rapidly past all these actions to seek out scattered Spaniards to attack. He spotted a confused and disorganised group of ships, among which were two of the galleasses. Winter raced into the attack. His gunfire had the desired effect of not only inflicting damage, but also causing confusion among the enemy as they turned this way and that to escape. Four of the Spanish ships collided with each other.

One huge galleon valiantly pushed forward to try to get between the English and the less well armed Spanish ships. Winter and other ships closed on her and inflicted such damage that some Spanish sailors leapt into the sea. They were picked up by Winter and held prisoner so that they could be questioned later. The lone galleon fought on until at one point she was surrounded by seventeen English ships. Finally the ships she was protecting got themselves into order and the galleon hurried to find shelter among them.

Almost certainly this was the *San Felipe* commanded by Don Francisco de Toledo. A Spanish account of her battle has survived and it sounds almost identical to that recorded by Winter. The *San Felipe* sustained 100 hits by cannonballs, fired at a range so close that her soldiers were firing muskets at the enemy, and being shot at in reply. The ship's foremast came down and went overboard. More than 200 men were killed, and many more injured.

Calderon spoke to an officer from the *San Felipe* later and recorded:

> She had five of her starboard guns dismounted. In view of this, and that his upper deck was destroyed, both his pumps broken, his rigging in shreds and his ship almost a wreck, Don Francisco de Toledo ordered the grappling hooks to be got out and shouted to the enemy to come to close quarters. They replied summoning him to surrender in fair fight. And one Englishman standing in the maintop with his sword and buckler called out: 'Good soldiers that ye are, surrender to the fair terms we offer'. But the only answer he got was a bullet which brought him down in sight of everyone. The infantry officer then ordered the muskets and harquebuses to be brought into action. Thereupon the enemy retired while our men shouted out to them that they were cowards, with foul words reproached them for their want of spirit calling them Lutheran hens and daring them to return to the fight.

Nobody could say that the Spanish did not fight well, nor that they lacked courage. The Italians in the fleet did as well. One Spanish officer recorded that at one point he saw three Italian ships which were so battered by shot that they looked as if they were sinking, yet still their guns were blazing at the English. Another said he saw 'an Italian ship all full of blood, which yet retained her fight.' When Bertondona's *La Reganzona* put about late in the day she heeled over and a horrified onlooker from the *San Martin* saw blood gush out of her scuppers.

In the late morning Howard led his squadron into the fight, adding his guns to those of Drake, Frobisher, Hawkins, Seymour and Winter. By this time the Spanish ships were getting themselves organised. Recalde was reforming his squadron and using it to guard the stricken ships already battered by the English guns. Medina Sidonia came down from the west with his group of galleons. As he approached he at first could not make out what was going on.

He later wrote:

> The Duke heard the sound of small arms fire but was unable to distinguish what was going on even from the maintop in consequence of the smoke. But he saw that two of our ships were amongst the enemy and that the latter, leaving our flagship concentrate all his fleet in that direction, so the Duke ordered the flagship to put about to assist them. The Duke's ship was so much damaged with cannon shots between wind and water that the inflow could not be stopped and her rigging was almost cut to shreds.

Between four and five o'clock the fighting petered out. The Spanish had reformed their crescent formation and the English could no longer get in amongst them to isolate and batter individual ships. As the last few guns were fired, Drake's ship suffered a hit that quickly became famous. Sir Charles Blount was exhausted by the day's fighting and sent down to rest in his small bed that was set up in Drake's own cabin. A stray Spanish cannonball came plunging through the stern windows, struck the bed and smashed it to pieces. The startled Blount was thrown violently to the floor, but was quite uninjured.

The English fleet hung around the edges of the Spanish, darting in now and then to fire their guns. Howard was still hoping to drive the Spanish on to the shoals. But at 6pm a sudden violent squall heralded a change in the wind. The breeze strengthened and swung around to the south. The Armada turned north, away from the shoals.

If most Spanish ships were able to get away from the deadly shallows, not all of them made it. First to go was the *Maria Juan* of the Biscay Squadron. She had lost her mizzen mast and rudder in the fighting and had been wallowing badly for some time. She fired off a distress gun and began to settle deeper in the water. Her crew swarmed up into the masts as the water rushed into her hull. Boats put off from the nearest ships to take off the men. About 80 had been rescued when the ship went down, taking the rest of her crew of 92 sailors and 183 soldiers with her.

A few minutes later the heroic Francisco de Toledo ordered a gun to be fired from the *San Felipe* to signal that she was in distress. The galleass *Zuniga* closed in to try to get a tow rope aboard, but failed. The old hulk *Doncella* then came alongside and the crew of the stricken galleon began to transfer across. Toledo was with his infantry commander, Juan Posa de Santiso, supervising the transfer when the merchant ship gave a sudden lurch.

'I think that I had rather be drowned in a galleon than a hulk,' jested Toledo in grim fashion. He and Posa climbed back to the *San Felipe* as the two ships drifted apart. With only the wounded and dying left on board, the galleon was helpless. She was last seen by the men of the Armada being swept eastward by the currents. In fact the *San Felipe* did not go to the immediate watery grave that all those who saw her being swept away assumed. During the night she ran aground on a sandbank three miles or so off Nieuport. The Spanish forces in that port saw her at dawn and sent out boats to rescue the crew. Toledo and Posa managed to get all but the most badly wounded men ashore before the Dutch flyboats arrived and made further rescue efforts impossible.

The *San Mateo* which had fought alongside the *San Martin* all day was also in trouble. She was wallowing heavily in the waves and had obviously taken in a lot of water. Her captain, Don Diego Pimental, sent a message to Medina Sidonia asking if he would send across a diver skilled at patching underwater leaks. The commander responded by sending boats to rescue the crew from the sinking ship. Some men were taken off, but Pimental refused to leave his ship and again requested a diver. This time Medina Sidonia did send off a diver and a pilot in a boat but, as he wrote later to King Philip by way of explanation, 'because it was no late and the sea grown very heavy they could not reach the *San Mateo*, and watched her afar off going towards Zealand.'

As evening came both Howard and Medina Sidonia tried to sort out what had happened during the day. Before Howard could attend to his fleet he had to deal with an annoying letter that he had received from Sir Francis Walsingham. The letter has not survived, but Howard's blistering reply has. Clearly the letter from Walsingham was a request for more information on the amount of gunpowder and cannonballs used by the English fleet to date. Howard received it that evening after the Battle of Gravelines. He was in no mood for hair-splitting requests for information from shore-bound bureaucrats.

I have received you letter wherein you desire a proportion of shot and powder to be set down by me and sent unto you. By reason of the uncertainty of the service, no man can do. Therefore I pray you to send with all speed as much as you can. And because some of our ships are victualled for a very short time and my Lord Henry Seymour with his company not for one day, in like to pray you to dispatch away our victuals with all possible speed, because we know not whether we shall be driven to pursue the Spanish fleet.

Having got that out of the way, Howard could turn to the campaign itself. After reviewing some of the action, Howard wrote:

Ever since we have chased them in fight until this evening late, and distressed them much; but their fleet consisteth of mighty ships and great strength; yet we doubt not by God's good assistance to oppress them and so I bid you heartily farewell. From aboard her Majesty's good ship the Ark.
Your very loving friend, Howard

He added a scribbled postscript before the letter left by pinnace.

I will not write unto her Majesty before more be done. Their force is wonderful great and strong; and yet we pluck their feathers by little and little. I pray to God that the forces on the land be strong enough to answer so present a force. There is not one Flushinger nor Hollander at the seas. I have taken the chief galleass this day before Calais, with the loss of divers of my men but Monsieur Gourdan doth detain her, as I hear say. I could not send unto him because I was in fight, therefore I pray you to write to him either to deliver her or at leastwise to promise upon hi his honour that he will not yield her up again unto the enemy.

Howard's letter is interesting from a number of points of view. Firstly, He had clearly not yet given up hope of securing the *San Lorenzo* and was still thinking of that rich prize. He hoped in vain; the French held on to her.

Second, Howard was uncertain how much damage had been done to the Armada that day. He emphasises their strength, while his evocative comment 'we pluck their feathers by little and little' would seem to minimise their damage. He must have seen the loss of the three galleons that evening, but seems not to have been aware of the carnage that his ships' guns had been inflicting on the enemy. Perhaps he was being cautious. Certainly he was worried about where the Armada might be heading for next. The east coast of England offered several possible anchorages and landing points, and they could not all be guarded.

One thing of which Howard was very much aware was the shortage of ammunition and food in his fleet. Seymour's ships had just put into Dover to restock with food and drink after yet another long patrol when they received news that the Armada was at Calais. Seymour put to sea at once, although his ships were down to two days' worth of food at the time. They were now out of supplies completely and were being kept going by food sent over from other ships.

The state of ammunition was just as bad. The English had enough gunpowder and cannonballs left on board for only about one hour's worth of fighting, some ships did not even have that much. It was probably this that explains Howard's concern both for the strength of the Armada and for the preparations that Walsingham was making on land. With so little ammunition left the English ships would be powerless to stop the Spanish landing in England if they chose to do so. All he could do was to follow the Armada making a show of being ready to fight and hope that the bluff worked.

In terms of actual damage and losses sustained, the English had got out of the day's fighting relatively lightly. They had lost about 300 men killed or seriously wounded. It is impossible to be certain as only the royal ships kept detailed records; the private ships had no need to tell anyone of their losses.

Medina Sidonia, however, was only too well aware of the losses his ships had suffered. One of the reasons why Spanish losses in men were so many times higher than the English was that the Spanish decks were crowded with soldiers waiting for the opportunity to board the enemy. That opportunity never came, but the packed ranks of soldiers made ideal targets for the high-velocity cannonballs shot by the English culverins. An iron ball weighing 17 pounds and travelling at hundreds of miles per hour will kill a man in an instant, then pass on to kill the man behind him, the third man in line and right through an entire squad of infantry. It was these mass casualties among the soldiers that had accounted for most deaths. By contrast the English decks were almost empty as they had only gun crews on them.

Medina Sidonia later wrote: 'Nearly all of our trustworthy ships were so damaged as to be unfit to resist attack, both on account of the cannon fire to which they had been exposed and their own lack of projectiles.' The Armada was not short of gunpowder, it should be noted, but only of the cannonballs of the correct size to fire the big guns. The anti-personnel guns had hardly been used as no boarding had taken place.

Medina Sidonia ordered the fleet to heave to and stay more or less where it was, so far as the battered ships were able to do so. We know that as the sun set Medina Sidonia was hoping that he would be able to re-enter the English Channel, but we do not know for what purpose. Perhaps he was still hoping that he could link up with Parma, though this seems doubtful at this point. More likely he was hoping to salvage something from the campaign, perhaps by landing on the Isle of Wight or by landing soldiers to raid and burn coastal villages and towns. At any rate he does not seem to have been ready to give up the fight.

At 2am the already worried Spanish commander suddenly had another and much more serious problem to think about: the wind changed back to north-west. Medina Sidonia noted that the *San Martin* 'began to fall off to leeward towards the Zeeland coast'. She was not alone, the entire Armada was being driven downwind back toward the deadly shoals and sandbanks. Any ship that ran ashore would make an easy victim for the Dutch flyboats which, contrary to Howard's belief, were shadowing the Spanish close to shore. Even if the crew of a ship could hold off the Dutch they would still be doomed. The surf would soon pound their ship to pieces on the sands, and they would be drowned. Caught in such a position most ships would have anchored, the wind was not strong after all. But the Spanish anchors were lying on the seabed off Calais and were no longer to hand.

When dawn came on Tuesday 9 August it revealed a terrible scene to the eyes of Medina Sidonia. His fleet was still together, though rather more scattered than it had been the night before. In the distance could be seen the fatal surf and, darting among the breakers, the sails of the Dutch flyboats. The wind was still brisk and from the north-west.

Upwind of the *San Martin* was a large ship, one of the Squadron of Castile, which was wallowing heavily. She put up a signal of distress, but it was the English ship *Hope* that got to her first. Of 600 tons and mounting 30 big guns, the *Hope* was a powerful royal warship. The *Hope* pulled up within shouting distance of the stricken Spanish ship and a crew member who spoke some Spanish shouted out a demand for surrender. The Spanish captain called back something about terms of surrender, but what exactly nobody recorded. There then came a sickening grinding crack from deep within the hull of the Spanish ship, which almost at once went down like a stone. There were no survivors. It was hardly an encouraging start to the day for Medina Sidonia and it was soon to get worse.

Howard began to manoeuvre his fleet as if he meant to attack, though in truth he was bluffing and hoping to hustle the Spanish fleet toward the shoals. The threat was taken seriously by Medina Sidonia who signalled for any ships still able to fight to come to join him. Pataches and boats were sent out to go around the rest of the Armada with the advice that they were 'to keep their heads close to the wind as they were almost on the Zeeland shoals'. The advice was superfluous, for every captain could see the surf for himself and more than one captain must have cursed the Duke for his pointless advice and for getting them into this deathtrap in the first place.

Meanwhile the warships still able to get into the wind were closing on the flagship. Recalde was there, as ever, and so was de Leyva. The three surviving galleasses came up with their oars thrashing the water. A few other warships bore up, though they were all desperately short of ammunition. It seems that Medina Sidonia hoped to delay the coming English attack on his more vulnerable ships.

Then up came the great *Santa Ana*, flagship of the Squadron of Guipuzcoa, with the admiral Miguel de Oquendo on board. This ship came within hailing distance of the *San Martin* and the figure of Oquendo was clearly visible on the sterncastle. Medina grabbed a speaking trumpet and bellowed across the waves to his subordinate admiral.

'Senor Oquendo, what shall we do?' demanded the hapless commander.

'Ask Diego Flores,' snarled back Oquendo his anger boiling over. 'As for me, I am going to fight the English and die like a man. Give me your shot.'

It was an extraordinary and calculated insult. That a man, even a fighting admiral as experienced as Oquendo, could feel able to talk to his commanding officer and a premier grandee of Spain in such a fashion was astonishing and showed the feelings in the Armada. That he should blame Diego Flores, Medina Sidonia's naval adviser, for the mess was natural enough. Few of the naval commanders had forgiven Diego Flores for persuading Medina Sidonia to abandon the crippled ships – the *Rosario* and *San Salvador* – earlier in the campaign. But his furious insult to Medina Sidonia himself was unparalleled. By asking for the flagship's cannonballs, Oquendo was openly implying that Medina Sidonia would not need them himself as he was too cowardly to fight the English. Of all the events in the Armada campaign this brief exchange was surely the most amazing. Medina Sidonia was speechless. He put down the speaking trumpet and turned away to return to his cabin. There was not much else he could do.

The Spanish warships clustered around the *San Martin* sat hove to, waiting for the manoeuvring English ships to attack. A short while later one of the pilots felt it his duty to report the dire news to Medina Sidonia that the man heaving the lead had found bottom at seven fathoms. A galleon like the *San Martin* drew five fathoms. There was not much time left. It looked as if the entire Armada would end up on the shoals. Medina Sidonia returned to the deck about this time; it was his duty to watch the final catastrophe.

In the English fleet, Thomson of the *Margaret and John* was writing a quick despatch of things as he saw them from the deck of his ship.

> At this instant we are as far to the eastward as the Isle of Walcheren, wherein Flushing doth stand, and about 12 leagues off the shore. The wind hanging westerly we drive our enemies apace to the eastward, much marvelling if the wind continue in what port they will direct themselves. There is want of powder, shot and victual amongst us which causeth that we cannot so daily assail them as we would, but I trust her majesty may, by God's help, little fear any invasion by these ships; their power being, by battle, mortality and other accidents so decayed, and those that are left alive so weak and hurtless and they could be well content to lose all charges to be at home, both rich and poor.

On shore, a quite bizarre scene was being played out. On the previous day, Parma had marched to Nieuport to supervise the embarkation into barges of the 12,000 men there. He then moved on to Dunkirk and by dawn was busily engaged in marching troops down to the docks and loading them on to barges. He had 16,000 men in Dunkirk that afternoon, and more were marching up from camps inland.

His scouts along the coast must have seen something of the fight the day before, but most of the action had taken place miles out to sea so it was impossible for him to know the truth of what was happening. Some time after dawn a rider came in to report that the *San Felipe* was aground and that boats were going out to rescue the crew. Still Parma loaded men into barges, moving them out from the quayside to sit in mid-canal and mid-river so that other barges could come up to take their load of armoured men.

It was on the dockside at Dunkirk that Parma was found by Don Jorge Manrique, the Inspector General of the Armada who had been sent by Medina Sidonia from Calais on the Sunday evening with the blistering message for Parma. Manrique had ridden hard for Bruges, where Parma had been on the Sunday morning, arriving there on Monday afternoon to be told that the Duke had gone to Dunkirk. After a short rest and change of horses, Manrique had headed to the port. He was tired, worried and distraught when he arrived at 10.30am.

Manrique pushed through the crowds of soldiers and stalked up to Parma. He handed over Medina Sidonia's note and began to deliver himself of his commander's angry demands for instant action and assistance. When he demanded to know where Parma's fleet was hiding and why it was not at sea, Parma waved his hand at the barges loaded with troops or waiting their turn to pick up the men. Manrique was aghast.

The craft before him were flat-bottomed river craft quite unsuited to a sea voyage except in the calmest of weathers; none of them were armed. Parma had told King Philip this often enough, and Parma assumed that Medina Sidonia knew. He did not, and neither did Manrique. In a fit of temper, Manrique accused Parma of making excuses for not going to the aid of the Armada, of hiding his flyboats in another port and of other things not recorded.

Parma saw he was getting nowhere, so he called in his senior officers and got them to explain to Manrique what was going on and why. Manrique was having none of it. The discussion was getting angry and heated. That was when the Prince of Ascoli arrived. He had seen for himself something of the condition of the Armada, though not all of it. His report made it clear that the Armada would not be arriving for a rendezvous any time that day, nor probably for the next few days, but it was still unclear how much damage the Spanish fleet had sustained.

Then Captain Marolin de Juan arrived. De Juan was the chief navigator of the Armada and had been out in a patache on a similar mission to that of Ascoli. He had much the same story to tell: The Armada was scattered but there was no evidence that it was defeated. It would probably be back soon.

The dispute fizzled out quickly. Everyone knew that they would have to await news of events at sea. Meanwhile, Ascoli had no eyes for the barges, but wanted only to rejoin Medina Sidonia on the *San Martin*. He begged Parma to lend him some armed men for his pinnace and enough food and drink to keep his men working. Parma may have been making a show of getting ready to leave port, but he knew well enough that the Dutch flyboats were out at sea and, probably, that the Armada was scattered. He refused, and told Ascoli to go and have a hot meal instead. Ascoli was frustrated and furious, but he could do little other than follow orders. Parma almost certainly saved his life.

Meanwhile, Parma ordered the embarkation to halt. The men were put into camps near Dunkirk and Nieuport, while the barges were kept tied up to await events. He then retired to a desk to dictate to his secretary a letter designed to ensure that he did not get blamed. The letter rehearsed the difficulties that he had been writing about for months, then gave a brief account of events over the previous two weeks as the messengers had arrived in succession from Medina Sidonia. It is a long letter, but some excerpts give a flavour of how Parma was emphasising that he had done all he could, while attempting to blame Medina Sidonia for what had gone wrong.

On the 7th August came a pilot with news that the Armada was off Calais, whereupon the Duke of Parma left Bruges to hasten on the embarkation of his troops and to be nearer the Armada.

That day [9 August] the Duke of Parma came early to Dunkirk where everything was ready so that within that day the embarkation could be carried out at Nieuport and at Dunkirk. This operation proved to be impossible owing to the set of the wind which was such as to prevent even ships specially constructed for navigating those waters from putting out, to say nothing of the enemy ships which barred the egress from the ports.

While the preparations for the embarkation were rapidly progressing, the Prince of Ascoli and other personages arrived in Dunkirk. They reported that the enemy had sent fireships down upon our fleet and that, although they had done no mischief, the Duke of Medina Sidonia thought it fit to give the order to cut the cables so as to avoid the danger. The fleet was swept before the wind and the enemy did not miss the opportunity to give battle. It is to be hoped that the fleet will keep together and suffer no further damage. The Duke of Parma has all his men embarked and ready.

On Parma's staff was Don Juan Manriquez, a relative of Jorge Manriquez. Almost certainly knowing what his master had written, Don Juan penned a letter on 11 August to Don Juan d'Idiaquez, a leading bureaucrat at El Escorial, giving his version of events. The letter is tactful but it message is clear. He starts 'You may think it bold on my part to write', and then continues:

> The day on which we came to embark we found the vessels still unfinished, not a pound of cannon on board and nothing to eat. This was not because the Duke of Parma failed to use every possible effort, for it would be difficult to find another person in the world who works half as hard, but because both the seamen and those who had to carry out the details openly and undisguisedly directed their energies not to serve his Majesty, for that is not their aim, but to waste his money and lengthen the duration of the war; besides which the common people threw obstacles in the way.

While those on land were getting busy shifting the blame about, an astonishing turn of fortune was about to take place out at sea.

As the depth of water under the *San Martin* reached just six fathoms the wind died. For a while the ships bobbed motionless on the waters. When the breeze got up again it was from the south-west. The Armada was saved. 'We were saved by the wind shifting by God's mercy' wrote Medina Sidonia, 'and the Armada was then able to steer a northerly course without danger to any of our ships.' His first concern was to get the Armada well away from the dangerous shoals and sandbanks of the Dutch coast. That was achieved by mid-afternoon. But then he had to face a question every bit as difficult and contentious.

What was the Armada to do next?

XIII

Into Northern Waters

As the Armada gathered together and moved north, Medina Sidonia sent pataches round to summon his senior officers together on the flagship *San Martin* for a council of war. It was a gloomy meeting. The meeting was not only rather downcast, but also incomplete. Admiral Oquendo was not present, not altogether surprising after his insulting outburst the previous day. Whether Medina Sidonia did not invite him or he simply did not turn up we do not know. Nor is there any record of Recalde being present, though we cannot be certain that he was absent. Perhaps he simply did not say anything. Diego Flores must have been present, though again he is not mentioned. The only admiral who seems to have spoken up with anything of substance was de Leyva.

The council of war began with a run through of the present state of the Armada ships. The casualty lists for each ship were given, with any senior officers or noblemen struck down mentioned by name. In all 3,000 men were unfit for duty. The records do not specify why, but most of them must have been dead or wounded, though by this stage in a voyage during the sixteenth century there would be many men sick as well. Then came an assessment of the damage sustained by the fabric of the ships, which varied considerably but was generally heavy.

Finally a list of ammunition remaining was read out. Again the picture was depressing, with no large warship having any ammunition left for its longer range guns. Even the shorter range cannon were low on ammunition. Only the muskets and harquebuses had plentiful ammunition left to hand. Most of the useful cannonballs in the smaller ships had already been taken for the use of the big warships, so there was little ammunition left. If another disorganised battle like that on the Monday were to take place the Armada was in no fit state to fight it.

What the Armada needed above all was a rest so that the men had time to repair the damage to their ships. All ships go to sea with the means on board to effect minor repairs in case of accident or storm damage, and warships must have materials on board to be able to repair more substantial battle damage. The ships of the Armada were no different. They might have lost spars, sails, rigging and even masts, and suffered numerous cannon strikes to their hulls, but they mostly had the ability to repair the damage.

The priority for any ship is to stay afloat, so patching holes in the lower hull would have been tackled first. While relays of men worked the pumps to lift water out of the hull the carpenters went to work. Smaller holes could be sealed with wooden plugs hammered into position and then sealed with tar. Large holes required plates of lead sheet to be fixed into position, or planks of wood cut to size and nailed over the hole. Cannonballs did not just punch holes in wooden hulls, they also inflicted tremendous impacts as they struck home, causing planks to spring apart and caulking to work loose. Such openings would need to be recaulked with rope fibres and then sealed with tar.

In extreme cases it was the custom to run a powerful rope under the hull, then tighten it across the deck in order to literally bind the hull together and stop it splitting further apart. A similar rope might be passed around the hull lengthwise if necessary. No ship could hope to survive a long voyage if such desperate measures were resorted to, and the ship would usually head for the nearest port. Most of this work needed to be done from the outside of the hull. Sailors could be lowered down over the sides of the ship on ropes to do the work. Damage below the waterline was usually reserved for specialist divers, men trained to hold their breath for long periods and to work under water. But only a few ships carried such men, so most captains had to put down untrained crew members and hope for the best.

It would be ideal to heel the ship over. This means to shift the ballast, guns and other heavy items to one side of the ship so that the vessel develops a list to that side, exposing the first few feet of timbers below the waterline on the other side. Heeling was possible only in calm sea conditions and when the ship was stationary. With the English warships within sight and a stiff breeze blowing, heeling was impossible.

Once a ship was safe from sinking, the crew could turn their attention to other matters. Spare rigging and sails were carried in abundance, as were spars, so replacing them would be a relatively quick operation. Replacing masts was more problematic. At this date most masts were constructed in two pieces, each about 30 or 40 feet long. Each section was made from a single piece of timber, usually cut from the trunk of a fir tree. It was not practical to carry a full set of replacement masts on board, so usually only one or two mast sections were carried. These would be lashed into place around the stump of a broken mast and held in place by new rigging. This sort of 'jury rig', as it was known, was never as good as a proper mast but could be surprisingly effective in good weather conditions. All these repairs could be carried out on the move, but were better if the ship was stationary. That was a luxury that the Armada could not afford, as Howard and the English fleet was keeping station only a couple of miles behind.

Exactly how badly damaged the Armada ships were, we do not know. Subsequent events would indicate that the damage was severe in a minority of ships, moderate in most and only slight in some – with a few having escaped any battle damage at all. If the Armada could get into a port quickly then all would be well, but if faced by a long voyage then it was likely that some ships would not make it. It was with all this in mind that Medina Sidonia posed to his council of war the key question for which he had called the meeting: where should the Armada go?

There were no friendly ports in the North Sea. There was nowhere for the Armada to go to find shelter from the winds and waves and to buy fresh food and water. There were good anchorages in the Humber and elsewhere up the English east coast where the Armada would find sheltered waters where the ships could be repaired. Given the large numbers of soldiers on board the various ships, it would have been more than possible for the Spaniards to go ashore to loot food from farms and acquire fresh water. For some reason that has not been recorded, the council of war did not even consider this option. Perhaps they knew something that we, some 420 years later, do not understand. In effect, Medina Sidonia offered his council of war a choice of two options: Return to the English Channel or sail directly home to Spain by way of the north of Scotland. Neither option was particularly attractive.

Again, we do not know what Medina Sidonia's aim was in returning to the English Channel. He may have still intended to take the Isle of Wight, though given the damage sustained by his ships and men this seems unlikely. Perhaps he wanted to return home to Spain by those more gentle waters than by the bleaker northern route. The only clue we have is that immediately prior to considering this all important questions the council of war discussed the conduct of the Duke of Parma.

It is important to bear in mind that nobody in the Armada had a really clear idea of what Parma was doing, nor what resources he had to hand. Before leaving Spain, Medina Sidonia had been told that Parma had a fleet that was able to get his army across to England once the Armada had defeated the English fleet – or at least was in a position to keep the English warships away from Parma's craft. From this Medina Sidonia and his officers had formed the opinion that Parma had no large warships, but did possess a number of flyboats armed with guns of moderate calibre plus enough barges to transport 30,000 men and their equipment.

It was only after they had reached Calais that they had learned that Parma did not have such an impressive flotilla at his command. Medina Sidonia and his men were still utterly ignorant of what Parma did have. Tello had told them that Parma was unprepared, that he lacked flyboats, that his barges were not as seaworthy as they had thought, but Tello had seen only a part of Parma's forces and he had been in a hurry to get back to the Armada so his views were necessarily incomplete. The men who could have told the council of war the state of Parma's 'fleet' – Manrique, Ascoli and de Juan – were all still at Dunkirk having been unable to rejoin the Armada.

The record of the council of war records only that Medina Sidonia informed his officers that 'The Duke of Parma had not sent advice that he would be able to come out promptly'. In effect that the Armada could expect no help from him at all for the foreseeable future. Whatever they decided to do, they would have to do it on their own.

Turning back to the English Channel, for whatever purpose, would mean facing the English guns again. Experience had shown the Spanish commanders that they had remained relatively safe from the English tactics so long as the Armada had kept tight formation. All up the Channel they had stuck to their crescent formation and losses had been small. Once the Spanish formation was broken, however, losses had risen alarmingly.

To get back into the English Channel meant getting through the Straits of Dover. The winds in that area are predominantly westerly, and the currents are complex. Manoeuvring a fleet of more than

100 ships in formation through this bottleneck would be difficult at the best of times, with many of the ships under jury rig or short handed due to casualties, would have been impossible. Inevitably the formation would have broken up and the English ships could have got in amongst them again, as off Gravelines.

Going home by way of the north of Scotland was scarcely more attractive. The northern seas were notoriously difficult, and the coasts of Scotland and Ireland were rocky and inhospitable. It may have been August, but that did not guarantee good weather. The spring and summer of 1588 had been dreadful – harvests were to fail across Europe – so most expected the weather to be worse than normal.

In the circumstances, and after much discussion, the Spanish council of war made perhaps the only decision it could: 'The council unanimously resolved in favour of returning to the Channel if the weather would allow of it, but if not then that they should obey the wind and sail to Spain by the North Sea.' That particular day the wind continued to blow from the south south-west, and with increasing power. The Armada could not get back to the Channel with that wind, so they stood out further into the North Sea.

Once the council had broken up, Medina Sidonia got his secretary to add a further paragraph to the official record. Like Parma he was trying to escape the blame for what had gone wrong.

> With regard to the fighting on the flagship, taking up of position, etc, the Duke followed the advice of the Master of the Camp, Don Francisco de Bobadilla, who had many years experience of fighting on land and sea. In the management of the Armada and in maritime matters, the Duke was guided by Admiral Diego Flores, he being the oldest and most experienced of seamen.

Howard also held a council of war late that afternoon. The only senior officer absent was Winter, who had been hit by a recoiling gun during the fighting of the previous day and been so badly bruised in the hip that he could not stand, let alone clamber down into a boat and cross the tossing sea to the flagship. He sent a written report instead. Most of this was taken up by a concise summary of the light losses suffered by his ships, followed by a plea for more ammunition and more supplies. He summed up his view of the campaign so far with the sentence: 'And in my conscience, I speak it to your Honour, I think the Duke of Medina Sidonia would give his dukedom to be in Spain again.'

We know Drake's views because after the meeting ended he sent a letter to Walsingham.

> We have the army of Spain before us, and mind, with the grace of God, to wrestle a pull with him. There was never any thing pleased better than the seeing of the enemy flying with a southerly wind to the northwards. God grant we have a good eye to the Duke of Parma. For with the grace of God, if we live, I doubt it not but ere it be long so to handle the matter with the Duke of Sidonia as he shall wish himself at home among his vine trees. God give us grace to depend upon Him; so shall we no doubt victory; for our cause is good. Humbly taking my leave. Your honour's faithfully to be commanded ever, Drake

There followed a telling postscript: 'I crave pardon of your honour for my haste, for that I had the watch this last night upon the enemy.' Drake must have been awake for almost all of the previous 72 hours.

The most surprising thing about this message is how Drake chose to deliver it. He put it into the hands of none other than Don Pedro de Valdes, the Spanish admiral who had been staying in his cabin since his capture right at the start of the campaign. Of him and his fate Drake told Walsingham:

> Don Pedro is a man of great estimation with the King of Spain and thought next in this army to the Duke of Sidonia. If he should be given from me unto any other, it would be some grief to my friends. If her Majesty will have him, God defend, but I should think it happy.

Drake may have been thinking of the likely ransom to be paid for Don Pedro's release, but he was usually considerate toward his prisoners. It seems likely that Howard had ordered Drake to send Don Pedro ashore, as Drake had seemed in no rush to do so before the meeting.

As might be expected, the English council of war was a much happier affair than the Spanish – at least for most of those present. As on board the *San Martin*, the event began with a series of reports on casualties, damage relieved, estimated damage done and the like. On the whole, casualties were fairly low and the damage sustained was not serious on any ship. The main complaints were about a lack of ammunition and food.

Howard knew that his fleet could not fight another battle until they had received ammunition for their big guns. What he did not know was that the Armada was in a similar plight. Spanish galleons had been firing their cannon right up until the moment that the action was broken off the previous evening. So far as the English could tell the Spaniards lacked for nothing in the way of ammunition. It was suspected that they might be short of food, as some of the prisoners captured earlier had mentioned the rotten food and a lack of supplies.

What the English could tell was that the Armada had taken a battering the previous day. The damage to hulls, masts and sails was plain to see. In the fighting the English had seen their cannon balls mowing down enemy soldiers on deck. Seymour estimated that between 5,000 and 6,000 men had been killed, and nobody cared to disagree with him. Howard guessed that the Spaniards would not want to risk another battle. He sent off to England for more powder and shot, but in the meantime the council of war decided 'to set on a brag countenance and give them chase, as though we wanted for nothing, until we had cleared our own coast and some part of Scotland of them'. Nobody was worried that they would encounter any interference from the Scots as Scotland did not have a navy to speak of.

There was, however, some concern about Parma. The English knew even less about Parma's forces than Medina Sidonia. There was a real worry that he might take the opportunity of having the English fleet chasing the Armada north to slip over the North Sea to invade England. Howard therefore ordered Seymour and the absent Winter to turn about and return to their previous station patrolling off the Flanders' coast.

Seymour was furious. He had fought as hard as anyone and wanted to be at the kill. He protested, but it was in vain. The other squadron commanders were as concerned about Parma as Howard. Seymour stomped off back to his ship. As he sailed back south he sat down to write a letter of protest. He did not write to Howard, or Walsingham but took the unusual step of writing direct to Elizabeth herself. After giving his account of the fighting since Sunday, Seymour continued:

> I find my lord [Howard] jealous and loth to have me take part of the
> honour of the rest that is to win, using his authority to command

me to look to our English coasts, that have been long threatened by the Duke of Parma. I therein have obeyed his lordship much against my will, expecting your Majesty's further pleasure. I pray God my Lord Admiral do not find the lack of the *Rainbow* and that company. I protest before God and have witness for the same that I vowed I would be as near or nearer with my little ship to encounter our enemies as any of the greatest ships in both fleets, which I have performed to the distress of the greatest ships of the enemy, if I have my due.

This, hoping God will confound all your enemies and that right shortly, do most humbly beg leave to trouble your most excellent Majesty.

From aboard the *Rainbow*.

Your Majesty's most bounden and humble fisherman,

Seymour.

Winter and Seymour turned south after dark so that the Spaniards would not see them and would imagine that they were still being pursued by the entire English fleet. Seymour sailed straight back to patrol, but Winter put in at Harwich to take on fresh supplies. He was as angry as Seymour, but not being a lord and lacking contacts at court did not see the point in writing letters of protest.

While the fleets were heading north, a lone Spanish galleon was aground off Blankenberg. This was the *San Mateo* commanded by Pimental which had drifted off away from the Armada on the evening of 8 August. The ship ran ashore on a sandbank off Blankenberg, miles out of sight of any coasts held by Parma's men. The ship had no boats left intact, they had all been smashed by English gunfire, so she wallowed helplessly. Early on 10 August she was spotted by a prowling Dutch flyboat. The craft raced off to sound the alarm.

At 1 o'clock admiral Pieter van der Does of the sea beggars came down with six flyboats to attack the stricken galleon. With van der Does was an English liaison officer named William Borlas. When he saw the shattered state of the galleon he expected the Spaniards to ask for terms of surrender at once. However, as soon as the first Dutch flyboat came within range the Spanish guns boomed.

For two hours the battle went on. The Spanish infantry with superbly disciplined skill poured volley after volley of musket fire into the flyboats, killing numerous Dutchmen. The Dutch replied in kind, laying low many of the defenders. Eventually the Dutch managed to close with the ship and began scrambling up the sides. Even then the Spaniards did not give in.

Borlas knew that his superiors would want to question prisoners, so he climbed up into the ship. He found that the Spaniards were not surrendering, neither were the Dutch taking prisoners. With some haste and not to mention danger to himself, Borlas recruited a couple of Dutch officers and together they plunged into the fray. Grabbing anyone who looked important and bundling them to safety, Borlas managed to save the life of the captain Pimental, another nobleman and one other officer. A couple of seamen survived, but the rest were killed, the wounded being tossed over the side.

The Dutch proceeded to thoroughly loot the captured ship. One of them found some letters written in English while he was rifling the pockets of a dead gentlemen and brought them to Borlas. The letters were addressed to a brother of Lord Montagu who was a known Catholic and who had gone missing some time earlier. Borlas got a look at the body and scribbled down a quick description from which the missing renegade Englishman was identified. Pimental later told Borlas that there had been another English Catholic on board, but he had been killed by one of the very first cannonballs to hit the ship during the battle off Gravelines. Apparently Pimental had found it amusingly appropriate that the traitor had been the first to die. Piemental was bundled ashore and thrown into prison in Flushing to be questioned later.

The *San Mateo* broke up before she could be refloated. The Dutch then moved on to the abandoned *San Felipe*. They stripped her of everything of value, but she too foundered before she could be saved. The Dutch found another abandoned wreck aground off their shores. She was much smaller probably a patache or zabra.

After the council of war in the late afternoon and evening of 10 August, Medina Sidonia had stayed in his cabin alone. On the evening of 11 August he emerged in a foul temper. He called over Diego Flores and held a hurried and agitated discussion with him. Then the commander went back to his cabin and slammed the door.

Diego Flores called over an officer and told him that Medina Sidonia had decided to invoke his orders of 1 August. That was the order that had stated that any captain who took his ship out of its place in the formation was condemned to death. Two captains were to be hanged: Don Christobal de Avila of the *Santa Barbara* and Don Francisco Cuellar of the *San Pedro*. Eighteen other captains were condemned to a lifetime of slavery in the galleys while other officers were to be stripped of rank and honours. The military were summoned and troops of infantry from the *San Martin* were sent off in boats to escort the hangmen about their grim duty. They reached the *Santa Barbara* first and within seconds de Avila had been strung up from a yardarm.

When the executioners reached the *San Pedro* they found themselves in trouble. Cuellar guessed why they were coming and refused to let them on board, his men drawing their weapons to keep the squad of soldiers in their boat. Cuellar allowed a spokesman on to his ship. When told he had been sentenced to death, he demanded to see the written order signed by Medina Sidonia. There was none. Then he called forward the officers of his ship and told them to explain what had happened in the battle. He then produced the casualty list and pushed it into the hands of the executioner, telling him to take it to Medina Sidonia. Then the would-be killer was pushed back over the side into his boat and sent on his way.

Back on the *San Martin* Medina Sidonia had locked himself in his cabin and refused to see anyone. The man detailed to hang Cuellar could not get to see him to ask for a written, signed order. He gave up and never mentioned the matter again. Neither did anyone else.

The morning of the next day the two fleets came abreast of the Firth of Forth. Howard expected the Armada to put into the Firth. Frobisher was ready to slip up the coast while Drake stood out to sea to repeat the battle plan used at the Isle of Wight. There was no need, the Armada continued steadily northward.

Howard ordered his fleet to halt. A converted merchant ship owned by Drake and commanded by Captain Norreys, one of Drake's most trusted followers, was ordered to continue to shadow the Armada. The ship took with it two pinnaces with which to send messages south if the Armada turned about. Then Howard gave the order for the English fleet to go home. They put about and headed south.

On the *San Martin* Medina Sidonia again emerged from his cabin. He strode on to the sterncastle and stood gripping the sternrail and glaring out behind his ship at the English. He watched as the English fleet disappeared over the horizon and as the lone ship took up station behind the Armada. Then he went back to his cabin.

If Medina Sidonia had given up commanding the Armada, Diego Flores could not do it. Nobody was taking any orders from him. It was Don Francisco de Bobadilla who stepped into the void they had left. He undertook command of the shattered fleet as it headed north into the wild northern waters. On 18 August the Armada passed just west of the Shetlands, then turned to pass between the Orkneys and Fair Isle.

Captain Norreys reckoned that he had done his job. The Armada was not coming back to England. Thankfully he put about and headed south again. The last he saw of the Armada it was a compact fleet of over a hundred ships heading north. The wind was getting up and a storm would soon strike. It would be almost a month before anybody saw the Armada again.

XIV

The Western Coasts

Those at sea knew that the Armada had been beaten by the morning of 9 August but those on shore knew nothing of the kind. The last they had known for certain was that the Armada had fled east to escape the fireships on the night of 8 August. Next morning the English fleet had set off in pursuit. Since then there had been nothing but stray sightings and occasional reports.

In England the defences remained on full alert. Queen Elizabeth did not have much in the way of an army as we would understand it, but the country was far from defenceless. In addition to the handful of regiments under royal control, Elizabeth also had a number of fortresses and strongpoints in her ownership and garrisoned by her men. Some of these fortresses were rather old and obsolete, such as the Tower of London and Windsor Castle. Others were of the very latest design and equipped with the most modern of weapons. Berwick was probably the greatest of these modern strongholds, but smaller forts were scattered along the coasts.

While the older castles and fortified towns were of limited use in warfare, they did provide vital support services. Troops could be stationed there in comfort, and administrative staff had their headquarters offices there. Their prime purpose, however, was as arsenals. Huge quantities of swords, halberds, pikes, bills, shields, helmets and guns were stored in these castles ready for when they might be used. They also contained great chests of coin to pay for supplies, men and munitions in the event of war.

The newer forts were expected to withstand the most determined attacks made by the most modern of armies. These fortresses were very different from the old castles with their towering walls and turrets. The new style of fortification had been developed in the early sixteenth century as siege guns became more effective and easier to drag about the countryside on campaign. In effect, the anti-cannon defences were sunk down into the ground rather than standing up above it.

A typical fortress would have the entire area around it for up to a mile cleared of all buildings, trees and bushes. This was to give the defensive guns a clear field of fire against any attacker and remove any cover that an enemy might use to creep up and surprise the defences. The ground immediately around the fortress would be kept mown, often by being grazed by sheep, so that there was only grass growing there. For the final 30 yards or so the ground would be sculpted so that it formed a gentle upward slope. This slope was designed to absorb or deflect cannonballs fired by attackers.

Immediately behind the slope was a sheer drop, faced by a stone wall. This drop might be as deep as 30 or 40 feet, though most fortresses made do with 20 feet. This fell into a dry moat, often paved and lined with stone that was as much as 50 feet wide. The inner wall of the moat had set into it small holes through which defenders could shoot at any attackers who got into it.

At the top of the inner wall of the dry moat was built a tremendously thick stone wall, topped by broad platforms on which were mounted the defensive cannon. Seen from the outside, this wall rose barely three or four feet above the ground surface in order to present the smallest possible target for the gunners of a besieging army. Its defensive strength lay in its height from the base of the dry moat. Most of these walls were built with a distinctly curved face to deflect any incoming cannon balls, and often had sloping tops for the same reason. Some fortresses had an inner core which was raised just above the outer walls to provide a platform for a second tier of cannon. The vast majority of these forts in England in 1588 had been built by Henry VIII during his wars against France. They remained substantially unaltered in 1588 – as indeed some of them do to this day – though they had been regularly maintained and were kept stocked with all the provisions needed to withstand attack.

In addition to these royal defences, the kingdom was equipped with a mass of local defences paid for and maintained by local gentry, town councils and the like. The most important forces were those supplied by the counties and mustered under the Lord Lieutenant of each. Every able man aged between 16 and 60 was expected to register as being available to defend the county in an emergency. The Lord Lieutenant was then tasked with dividing the men into regiments, squadrons and teams.

In practice it was only the 'trained bands' who would be much use in wartime. These were men who trained regularly at weapons drill, usually on a Sunday after attending church. They were not as well trained as mercenaries, and were mostly entirely inexperienced in battle, but they constituted the main defence force of England. The trained bands were called out by the Lord Lieutenant only when danger was imminent. Every man had a farm to run, a shop to keep open or other business. If serving in the trained bands became too onerous they might not turn out when required. A wise Lord Lieutenant called out his men only when absolutely necessary.

The county was expected to pay for the weapons of the trained bands, and some counties provided uniforms as well. Gentlemen were expected to come as cavalrymen and to pay for their own horses and equipment. In general there was one horseman for every 50 infantrymen in a county force. The numbers of men fielded varied widely from county to county, as did the quality of the training. Sussex, for instance, had almost 4,000 men in its trained bands in 1588 and had hired a professional soldier to supervise training and inspect weapons. Not every county was so conscientious.

The trained bands were generally expected to serve only within their own county, but in wartime the monarch could demand that a set number of men should serve in the central Royal Army. This figure varied greatly and usually depended on how much money the central government wanted to spend. As soon as a man stepped foot outside his county the monarch had to pay him wages and provide him with food and drink. In theory the county was meant to send its best men to the royal muster, but in practice it was generally down to whoever was willing to volunteer to go. Serving in a Royal Army might take a man away from home for months on end, so it was usually a task for the young unmarried men not those with responsibilities.

The trained bands were not expected only to fight in battles; they were responsible for all round defence of their home county. Each local squad was expected to have 'road bars' – great tree trunks set with spikes that could be used to block any main roads in their area. They were responsible for erecting fences across open common land to impede enemy cavalry and had to keep huge iron chains that could be slung across rivers to stop invading ships getting inland. They were also tasked with acting as lookouts and scouts across the county, and as guides for any royal force that came into the area.

Towns and cities were responsible for their own defences. Most towns had been surrounded by walls during the medieval period, but once the Wars of the Roses ended in the 1490s they had generally been allowed to deteriorate. These old walls were designed for another era and were not proof against cannon fire. Most towns could not face the expense of building modern defences, especially in times of peace, and by 1588 few towns could be considered well defended. Some towns, however, had made the effort of erecting earthen cannon platforms alongside their old walls or had dug deep ditches in front of the old walls to make them of some use in the modern era. They might not be able to hold out for months in a proper siege, but could hold off enemy scouts and might delay an army for a few days.

Other city defences were of more use. Most of the larger towns and cities had internal divisions across which it was illegal to build houses, and most town councils seem to have rigidly enforced these rules. In times of war these divisions were filled with barricades and bastions so that even if the enemy got through the town walls they did not have free run of the town. If the exterior defences were not much good against artillery, these internal defences were as useful against men with muskets as against men with swords. Each parish in a town had a stretch of wall assigned to it, and an internal division to defend. Capturing a town could be an arduous and time consuming business for even the most professional of armies.

In 1587, as war approached, the government had imposed a new duty on the counties; the erection of a series of beacons. These consisted of an iron basket filled with kindling and wood mounted on top of a stout wooden pole. Each beacon had to be within sight of two others, so most of them were located on hilltops. The beacons had to be manned constantly by at least two men and if they saw enemy troops, or if they saw another beacon lit, they were to light their own. The flames at night or column of smoke by day would alert the next beacon in the chain. In theory this system would allow news of an invasion to be carried from one end of England to the other in less than a day. It did not always work, of course, but it was the best available and was still in use during the Napoleonic wars more than 230 years later.

The local systems of defence worked well in 1588. The trained bands of Cornwall and Devon were first out, manning the coastal defences along the southern shores of their county within a day of the Armada first being sighted. When the Armada moved east, those trained bands were stood down, while those of Dorset, Hampshire, Sussex and Kent came out in their turn, only to go home again as the enemy ships moved on.

The central royal muster did not go so well. The Captain General of England in 1588 was Robert Dudley, Earl of Leicester. He had been a childhood friend of Elizabeth's and at one time there had been talk of the two marrying. This did not happen, but Leicester remained a favourite of Elizabeth's and was among her most loyal noblemen. In 1585 he led a force of English 'volunteers' to the Netherlands to help the rebels, and fought the Battle of Zutphen. He again campaigned in the Netherlands in 1587, but was called home when the peace negotiations with Parma began.

That Leicester was a superb administrator was never in doubt. He could muster men, train them and ensure that they were kept well fed better than any other commander of his age. He was not, however, rated very highly when it came to actual fighting. The successes that he had were due more to the hard fighting of his men than the skill with which he manoeuvred them. Still, getting a royal muster together was a job demanding more administrative skill than generalship, and so Leicester was chosen.

Leicester's task was made more difficult by the fact that Elizabeth did not want to call upon the counties to send their men until she was certain that the Armada was on its way. Money was short and men in arms cost money. Thus it was that Leicester did not get his firm orders until the beacons flared to announce the arrival of the Spanish off Cornwall. The muster point was fixed at Tilbury in Essex, from where Leicester could move to protect London if the Spanish landed in the Thames estuary, or march to the north if they landed elsewhere up the east coast.

In the emergency of an invasion, the Tilbury muster was to include not only the men summoned from other counties, but also the entire trained bands of Essex, less those involved in coastal defence. Leicester marched to Tilbury with 4,000 royal troops to set up the camp, mark out where different units were to pitch their tents, find an adequate water supply, dig latrines and carry out all the other necessary preparatory work. Leicester also ordered the construction of a pontoon bridge over the Thames to Gravesend so that he could march his army to Kent if the Spaniards landed there.

The day of the muster was fixed for 1 August. At noon that day, Leicester was disappointed to find that the only men who had turned up were his own retinue and a couple of dozen local gentlemen with their armed estate workers. It was a disappointing start, but Leicester need not have worried; Everyone was on their way.

The first units came in that evening, more the next day and they formed a positive flood on armed men by the day after. Leicester eventually had 23,000 men at Tilbury. They were not as numerous as Parma's army, nor as well trained or well equipped. But they were an army, and combined with the defence in depth of fortified towns, modern fortresses and the trained bands they could well have defeated a Spanish invasion. We shall never know, for the invasion never came.

By 19 August Elizabeth knew that the Armada had taken heavy losses in the Battle of Gravelines and that it had fled north. But she did not know where it was going nor whether or not it would come back. It was even possible that Parma might yet cross the North Sea. Her troops at Tilbury had been parading, training and marching for the past two weeks. Thanks to Leicester's indefatigable work they were well fed, few were ill and all were fully armed. It was time for a morale-boosting visit.

Elizabeth went down the Thames by barge, accompanied by her personal bodyguard and court gentlemen. She had dressed herself in a suit of ornamental armour and carried a small sword. When she arrived at Tilbury, she greeted Leicester then mounted a white horse that he had brought for her use. The army was on parade in its units with its officers. Elizabeth waved off her bodyguard, which surprised and alarmed Walsingham who was with her, and then set off with only Leicester, two pages in white velvet and the Earl of Ormonde who carried her sword for her. She rode among the units, chatting to officers and gentlemen as she passed.

Every now and then she would stop and deliver to everyone within hearing a short speech which has since become recognised as one of the classics of English history.

My loving people, we have been persuaded by some that are careful of our safety to take heed how we commit ourselves to armed multitudes for fear of treachery. But I assure you, I do not desire to live to distrust my faithful and loving people. Let tyrants fear. I have always so behaved myself that, under God, I have placed my chiefest strength and safeguard in the loyal hearts and good will of my subjects; and therefore I am come amongst you, as you see, at this time not for my recreation and disport, but being resolved in the midst and heat of the battle to live or die amongst you all, to lay down for my God and for my kingdom and for my people my honour and my blood even in the dust. I know I have the body of a weak and feeble woman, but I have the heart and stomach of a king – and of a king of England too – and think foul scorn that Parma or Spain or any prince of Europe should dare to invade the borders of my realm; to which rather than any dishonour shall grow by me, I myself will take up arms, I myself will be your general, judge and rewarder of every one of your virtues in the field. I know, already for your forwardness and you have deserved rewards and crowns; and we do assure you, in the word of a prince, they shall be duly paid you.

The cheers were deafening. Elizabeth was supposed to go back to London that evening, but the tour of the camp had taken so long that it was getting dark by the time she finished. She spent the night at a nearby manor house and came back next morning so that Leicester could organise a splendid march past and put some of his units through battlefield manoeuvres for her.

That afternoon Elizabeth ate a meal in Leicester's tent, along with the senior officers of the army. A messenger came into report that a fisherman from Kent had gone out to find both the English fleet and Armada nowhere in sight. But he had seen some flyboats off the Flander's coast where Parma was known to be boarding his army. The tides were exactly right for an invasion, Leicester was convinced that Parma was coming. He sent out riders to put scouts and lookouts on full alert, then he asked Elizabeth to return to London. She was having none of it. She grabbed her sword and made an impromptu speech which has sadly not survived. It was only as the day wore on and the lookouts reported sighting no invasion fleet that she agreed to go back to her fortified capital.

Over on the continent nobody had any idea what had happened at sea. The Spanish ambassador in France, Don Bernadino de Mendoza, was sending off letters almost daily to Philip reporting what he had heard. On 7 August he got a report from Rouen; French fishermen returning from Newfoundland had passed a mighty naval battle taking place off the Isle of Wight. The fishermen reported accurately the position of the fleets in mid-morning, with one part of the English fleet, Frobisher's, apparently isolated and doomed while the rest were out at sea not engaged with the Spaniards. Again accurately, they said that the galleasses were heavily engaged and fighting hard.

The fishermen then added other details. Given that they prudently stayed some miles away from the battle it is not clear how they could have seen such detail but Mendoza chose to believe it anyway. They reported that Drake's ship had been attacked by a galleass. The first broadside from the Spanish ship had dismasted the ship, a second broadside sent it to the bottom. Drake was last seen fleeing in a small rowboat amid the smoke and flame. A total of fifteen English ships had been sunk in the fighting, and several more captured. Mendoza hurried off to see the French King to give him the good news – and to try to persuade him to sign into law several Catholic demands over which he had been prevaricating.

On 8 August, Mendoza got detailed and accurate reports from Calais that the Armada had arrived there with the English fleet in its wake. It did not sound like a victorious Armada, but Mendoza reasoned that Medina Sidonia had come to rendezvous with Parma. He also heard that a great Spanish warship had arrived in La Hogue. This was the *Santa Ana* which had got separated from the Armada in the Bay of Biscay.

On 10 August the news arrived that the Armada had left Calais after fireships had been sent down. The fate of the *San Lorenzo* was accurately reported, and that men along the coast had been hearing the distant sounds of heavy guns all day. The wreck of the *San Mateo* was reported by Parma, but after that there was nothing but an eerie silence from the North Sea.

On 17 August came the first definite news, but nobody knew what it meant. The captain of a German merchant ship put into Calais from Scotland. He reported that as he had passed along the east coast of northern England he had seen a commotion in the sea and gone to investigate. To his utter bewilderment he had seen more than 1,000 horses and mules swimming in the open sea. The animals were clearly doomed as they were miles from land. He could not imagine how they got there. They were, in fact, the animals carried in the Armada who were intended to drag the cannon and supplies of the invading army. Medina Sidonia had ordered them thrown overboard once he realised he would not need them. Next day, another merchant ship came in to report that they had seen a ship sinking off the English coast and the crew getting into rowboats. They did not know which ship it was nor to which fleet it belonged.

Parma, meanwhile, had sent off the few flyboats he had to try to find the Armada. They found no Spanish ships, but one of them did encounter a squadron of battered English ships heading south in haste. These were Seymour's ships coming back to patrol, but the Spaniards thought that they were fleeing and concluded that a battle had been fought somewhere to the north. A merchant came in from Harwich to report that as he had been leaving that port some two dozen English warships – all that remained of the entire English fleet he said – had come in short of food and out of ammunition. All the ships were badly battered and showed obvious signs of having been in battle. These were Winter's ships putting in to take on supplies.

Antwerp was suddenly swept by gossip on 21 August. Nobody knew where the news came from, but they were all assured that it was from the most reliable of sources – a trader in London had got a secret message out. A great battle had been fought off the Firth of Forth on 13 August and the Armada had crushed the English fleet. The climax had come when Drake boarded the *San Martin*. His leg had been shot off by a cannonball and he had bled to death. Nieuport heard a different version of the same story. This time the battle had ended when Drake had boarded the *San Martin*, but he had been captured not killed. Fifteen English ships had been sunk.

By 22 August the events up to the fireship attack had become fairly well established on both sides of the Channel. In England the court had the terse messages from Howard, Drake and others to go on. These announced heavy enemy losses, but expressed concern for the great strength left in the Armada. On the continent there was only rumour.

But that rumour was widely believed. What is most interesting about the stories and gossip sweeping across Europe is in one way or another they all concern one man: Drake. Drake was said to be killed or captured in a dozen different ways. He had fled the battle in a rowing boat not only off the Isle of Wight, but also off the Wash, off Scotland and somewhere in the northern seas. Mendoza lit a great bonfire in the street outside his house in Paris to celebrate the end of the great *El Draque*. In Prague the Spanish ambassador, Don Guillen de San Clemente, had a mass sung and invited the local nobles to help him celebrate the news.

The Spanish ambassador in Rome, Count Olivarez, sought and obtained an audience with Pope Sixtus. Olivarez announced the news of Drake's death and of the Armada's victory. He asked the Pope to have a special service held in St Peter's. The Pope agreed, but said he would rather wait until the news was confirmed by his own agents. William Allen, the priest who was to be appointed

Cardinal of England if the invasion was successful, was not so cautious. He packed his bags and got ready to leave.

On 18 August the English Privy Council ordered what was known to be printed in the form of a booklet. It was printed in English and French, and by 21 August copies of the French edition were on the streets of Paris. But they came from England and few people believed the tales of an English victory. A few days later the Dutch printed their version of events, complete with reports from the captains of flyboats who had seen the Battle of Gravelines or seen the Spanish wrecks come ashore. Even the staunchest Catholic began to fear defeat.

But it was still impossible to be certain. Even if the Armada had suffered losses and headed north, everyone, even the English, accepted that the Spanish fleet was still in being and sailing in strict formation. A new rumour swept Europe: the Armada had anchored in the Orkneys and was finishing repairs before sailing back south to rendezvous with Parma and his army. The English fleet, meanwhile, had been caught by a great storm while waiting off the Orkneys and had been destroyed. This was the version heard by Giovanni Mocenigo, Venetian ambassador in Paris. He wrote it down and sent it off to Venice in a letter dated 9 September. But he added dolefully: 'Nobody here believed that the Armada will return.' He also stated that Parma had broken up his camps at Nieuport and Dunkirk. The soldiers were being employed in a few autumn raids into rebel Dutch lands, then going into barracks for the winter.

As the rumours were sweeping across Europe, and men in England were wondering where the Armada had gone after sailing up the east coast of Scotland, the final nightmare was beginning to unfold. The storm that had hit the Armada off the Shetlands lasted for five days. By the time it ended, Medina Sidonia had resumed his place in command, but his fleet had been sorely reduced. Only about 80 ships were still in sight of the flagship, the rest were gone, scattered across the northern seas by the storm. Some had sunk with all hands, others were limping along alone or in small groups. The indefatigable Recalde had gathered some fourteen stray ships around his galleon and was heading south-west to get around Ireland and head home.

Medina Sidonia had the war diary of the Armada copied out and handed to Don Baltasar de Zuniga who set off in a patache to head for Spain. He carried a message asking the King to prepare the ports of Spain for the return of a battered fleet carrying sick and injured men who would be in need of medical attention. Then the wind shifted to the south-west and stayed there until 3 September. The battered Armada ships could not make headway toward Spain, but lay hove to awaiting a better wind. Some ships foundered, others turned and headed for Scotland when they were in danger of sinking.

On 8 September the first Armada ship was sighted from the coast of Ireland. Most of these ships were the more badly damaged ships that had been unable to stay out to sea. By this date the English had questioned their prisoners and had a fairly clear idea of the orders under which the Armada had sailed. They knew in particular that Ireland was a secondary objective. They feared that Medina Sidonia was going to land an army in Ireland both to organise a Catholic uprising and to secure an extensive bridgehead to serve as a base for a fresh Spanish invasion the following year. The soldiers on the Armada outnumbered English troops in Ireland by about four to one, so this was no idle threat. Orders went out from London that any attempted landing by the Spanish was to be ruthlessly dealt with.

There is no way of knowing the identity of many of the ships that were driven on to the coast of Ireland. One ship was seen to be wrecked on rocks off Cape Clear, but there were no survivors. At least two unknown ships were wrecked on Donegal, two more on Kerry and two on Clare. A ship was wrecked in the Bay of Tralee and 25 men got ashore alive. They were captured by English troops who took them to Lady Denny, wife of the garrison commander who was elsewhere at the time. She had them all hanged, explaining in her report to London that she did not have a secure prison in which to keep so many men.

Other ships are known by name. The *Trinidad* of the Squadron of Castile was wrecked in Brandon Bay. She broke up fairly close to the shore and 131 men, including a friar and a priest, struggled ashore through the surf. The men were exhausted, starving and helpless. First on the scene was McLaughlan MacCabe, a galloglass or Irish mercenary working for the English. He drew his two-handed, six foot long sword – the distinctive weapon of the galloglass and in less than an hour personally killed 80 of the bedraggled survivors. William Bourke of Ardnerie then arrived with some of his men. He stopped the slaughter, dragged aside 30 men who looked like they might be worth a ransom, then ordered his men to kill the rest.

So it went on for weeks. Ship after ship was wrecked, sometimes the crew went down with her, sometimes a few survivors got ashore only to be butchered by the local Irish or the nearest English garrison. It was a mournful and dreadful tale.

The English were right to be worried, though their tactics were brutal even in that age. Some of the Armada vessels got into Irish waters in good order and ready to fight. Recalde and his little group of ships put into Blasket Sound on 15 September. They could see on shore a force of about 100 men carrying an English flag. The small troop was commanded by James Trant, who was responsible to Sir Edward Denny in Tralee. There was not much Trant and his men could do against such a powerful force, so they sat down to watch developments.

Recalde was intent only on getting off the coast and back home as soon as possible. He sent men ashore to gather fresh water and food, and to talk to the local Irish to see if any English ships were off the coast. On 21 September a gale got up, snapping the anchor rope of *Nuestra Senora de la Rosa*. The ship was dashed against rocks at the foot of a towering cliff and there was only one survivor. Recalde's men watched the wretched man clamber slowly up the cliffs, but they could not reach him. The man waved, then turned and walked off.

Another ship, the *San Juan* commanded by Fernando Horra, began to break up. The crew were taken off and distributed among the other ships. Eventually Recalde decided it was time to go. He guessed that the English troops ashore must have reported his presence and worried that warships would soon appear – though in fact there were no English warships off Ireland that autumn. The most serious repairs had been completed, so the ships put out to sea.

They left behind them the teenage Don Antonio de Monana, the sole survivor of the wrecked *Nuestra Senora de la Rosa*. He was captured and questioned by Trant; the boy must have been terrified. He told the English that the ship had gone down with 100,000 ducats in gold and silver on board, which is not impossible, and that she had 25 big guns as armament, plus another 25 cannon in the hold that were to have been given to Parma to use in the invasion. Again this was accurate, but the boy also said that the ship had had the Prince of Ascoli on board, which was not true. When the bloated corpses came ashore, as they usually do from coastal wrecks, they were hurriedly buried by the local Irish in a field that to this day is called *Uaigmhic Ri na Spainne* – the Grave of the Son of the King of Spain.

Another group of seven ships came into the mouth of the Shannon. They too put armed men ashore to gather fresh water while repairs were undertaken. One of the ships was too battered to be repaired and was scuttled, then the rest left.

The *Falcon Blanco Mediano* went down in Galway Bay. The *Concepcion* came ashore at Ards and about 350 men got ashore. The gentlemen were saved for ransom, the other 300 were killed. The *Gran Grin* fetched up at Clew Bay. About 100 men came ashore to seek food, water and news. They were set upon by the local Irish Lord Dubhdara Rua O'Malley and butchered. The ship tried to put back to sea but was wrecked. There were just sixteen survivors, and they did not survive long. Another unidentified ship was driven on to the cliffs of Kid Island, but left no survivors.

Three big ships of the Squadron of the Levant got into Sligo Bay. These were the *Lavia*, *Juliana* and the *Santa Maria de Vision*. For five days they stayed at anchor while repairs were carried out and teams of armed men went ashore to get water and food. Then a westerly gale got up; the main anchors of all three ships were at Calais, and the smaller secondary anchors could not hold them. One by one the ships were flung ashore on to the sandy beach of Streedagh Strand – the fireships were still claiming victims.

On board the *Lavia* was Francisco de Cuellar, who had been condemned to death by Medina Sidonia, he managed to survive the wreck and eventually got back to Spain. He later wrote an account of his adventures. The *Lavia* had on board a boat with a half deck at one end and it was decided to try to use it to get ashore. Don Diego Enriquez, the Count of Villafranca and other gentlemen had themselves sealed under the deck along with the ship's treasure while seamen crowded in to row the boat ashore. It overturned in the surf and everyone on board was drowned. The boat was thrown onto the beach. The next day the local Irish arrived; they broke open the sealed deck and found Enriquez still alive. He was stripped of his clothes and jewels, but ignored when the Irish saw the money. He died of exposure.

Meanwhile, the *Juliana* and the *Santa Maria de Vision* were driven ashore. From the decks of the *Lavia*, Cuellar watched as the survivors were stripped and robbed. By the time the *Lavia* reached the shore some 200 Irish were on the beach 'jumping and dancing with delight at our misfortunes' as Cuellar put it. When the *Lavia* grounded, the crew jumped into the surf and Cuellar went with them. Cuellar got ashore and managed to run off the beach to hide in some bushes before the pillagers got to him.

Next morning a troop of English cavalry arrived and Cuellar watched from hiding as they galloped on to the beach, killing any survivors they could reach. Cuellar set off inland where he met two other survivors. They later returned to the beach to scavenge food washed ashore, then they met an Irishman who could speak a few words of Spanish. He told them to head for Ulster, where English control was looser than elsewhere in Ireland. The Irishman helped himself to Cueller's necklace by way of payment for the advice. He later was helped by a man he calls Senor de Ruerque, actually the chieftain O'Rorke, who pointed him toward Dunluce from where he was able to get a ship to Scotland. The lord of Dunluce, Sorleyboy McDonnell was a Catholic who longed for a Spanish invasion. King James VI of Scotland kept safe any Spaniards who reached his lands and arranged for them to be taken to the Netherlands to join Parma.

The *Rata Encoronada* was wrecked on the coast of County Mayo. The ship was in bad condition, but was intact long enough for De Leyva to get all his men ashore complete with their weapons, ammunition and money. He marched to Ballycroy Castle, which he captured and occupied. Another ship was driven ashore at nearby Inver. She was dismasted before she was seen and was driven helplessly on to the rocks – about 100 men got ashore. Learning from the locals about de Leyva, they marched to join him at Ballycroy.

Soon after, two large Armada ships put in near Ballycroy in a reasonably good condition. De Leyva loaded his men on board, himself boarding the *Duquesa Santa Ana* of the Andalusian squadron. The ships put to sea, but a storm got up and the *Duquesa Santa Ana* was wrecked at Loughroas Bay, Donegal. Again de Leyva got a sizeable force ashore, though his leg was broken in the process. He had a chair rigged up with handles in which his men could carry him in relays. Hearing that a large Spanish ship was 20 miles away at Killibegs, de Leyva marched his column of men there.

The ship in question was the galleass *Girona*, which had a broken rudder but was otherwise intact. With the men de Leyva brought, the ship had over 1,300 men on board. There was not enough food on board to reach Spain, so it was decided to head for Dunluce to buy food and water, then to head for Scotland. On 28 October the ship got within sight of Dunluce, but a strong westerly wind was blowing and without a rudder she could not be steered properly. The *Girona* ran on to a submerged rock, rolled over and sank. Only nine men managed to swim ashore. Some days later the ship must have broken up for wreckage and bodies began to be washed ashore.

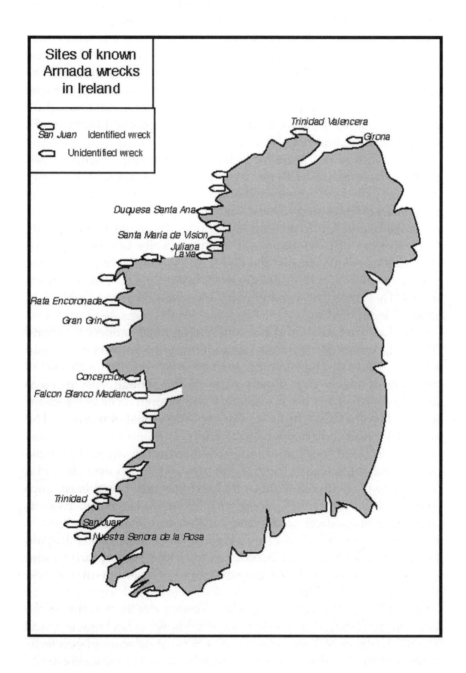

Sites of known
Armada wrecks
in Ireland

San Juan   Identified wreck
            Unidentified wreck

Trinidad Valencera
Girona
Duquesa Santa Ana
Santa Maria de Vision
Juliana
La via
Rata Encoronada
Gran Grin
Concepcion
Falcon Blanco Mediano
Trinidad
San Juan
Nuestra Senora de la Rosa

Among the bits and pieces were eight barrels of fine Spanish wine, which Sorleyboy McDonnell reportedly enjoyed hugely.

Don Alonso de Luzon got ashore with his men and arms near Ballygorman in Ulster from the *Trinidad Valencera*. The local O'Doherty clan did not recognise English rule and welcomed the Spanish soldiers. However, de Luzon had no intention of serving an uncouth Irish chieftain – he called him 'a savage' – and set off along the coast looking for a harbour where he could hire or steal a ship to take him and his 600 men home.

De Luzon had not gone far before he ran into a column of 400 English soldiers, half of them cavalry, led by a Captain John Kelly. De Luzon asked permission to continue to a nearby port, but Kelly refused and demanded instant surrender. The Spaniards retreated to a hillside and set up a camp surrounded by makeshift defences. After 36 hours of desultory skirmishing, Kelly offered a parley. This time he offered terms: the Spaniards would be fed, housed in a nearby village and their lives spared, but only if they surrendered at once. De Luzon knew many of his men were sick and that he had no food; he agreed.

Kelly had de Luzon and the senior officers marched off toward Drogheda where Sir William Fitzwilliam, Lord Deputy of Ireland was in residence. The remaining Spaniards were first stripped of anything of value, then hustled out of the village into an open field. Kelly lined up his musketeers and opened fire. Most of the Spaniards were killed, but over 100 got away. Most of them made it to Dunluce and so to Scotland and safety.

Rather luckier was Juan Gomez de Medina in the *Gran Grifon*. He was not able to reach Ireland and instead fetched up at Fair Isle. His ship was so knocked about that she was quite unable to reach Spain, so Medina landed, along with 500 men. He set up a camp, taking the precaution of digging earthen fortifications around it, and then set off to look for help. He found a fishing boat and paid the crew to take him to the Scottish mainland. There he hired a ship to go and fetch his men. The men eventually go home with the help of King James and Parma.

One of the most enigmatic and best known wrecks was that of the 'Tobermory Galleon', as she has become known. This large ship put into the harbour of Tobermory on the Scottish island of Mull early in September. According to the locals who were later questioned by men sent by King James, she was the *Florida*. The galleon anchored safely enough, but was in no condition to get out to sea again. The local clan chief wanted to use the Spanish soldiers to further his own interests, but the captain wanted to make contact with King James.

What happened next is unclear. According to one version the ship caught fire, some of the Spaniards being killed in the blaze and the rest marching off to reach King James. Another version has it that the fire set off a massive explosion of gunpowder that destroyed the ship and all but fifteen of her crew. A third version states that the explosion came first, having been set off by an Englishman who had been sent by Walsingham to find any Spanish ships that were lurking among the Hebrides.

Whatever the truth, the galleon did most certainly go down in Tobermory Bay. In 1607 divers working for King James arrived to recover the ship's guns and anything else of value. They left no record of what they did, but it was standard practice at the time to rip up each deck as it was emptied of things of value so that by the time divers had finished the ship was in pieces. There is not much left of the galleon these days, just a few timbers stuck in the mud and the odd artefact that is found from time to time.

Although the locals were adamant the ship was the *Florida*, there was no ship of that name in the Armada. The Scots decided that she must have been the *Florencia*, and that is how she is often described. However, that ship is known to have got back to Spain. Then a researcher turned up a reference in notes made by Marolin de Juan after talking to survivors of wrecks in Ireland who had got to Spain by way of Scotland. One of them said: 'The ship *San Juan* from Ragusa was burned in a Scottish port with Don Diego Manriquez on board.' The only ship known to have burned in Scotland was the Tobermory Galleon, so she would seem to have been this ship.

Meanwhile, the great galleass *Zuniga* had come into Liscannor Bay on 15 September. Her rudder was smashed and she could not steer properly. She stayed anchored off shore for eight days, then put out to sea again when a north-easterly wind got up and promised to blow the ship all the way to Spain. The galleass had got well down the Bay of Biscay when on 28 September a great gale sprang up and blew them back toward Ireland. The currents swept the ship around Brittany and into the English Channel. When the wind died down, the ship found itself off Le Havre, so she put in. As the *Zuniga* limped into the French port she passed the badly battered *Santa Ana* of the Squadron of Biscay. She had crept up the coast from La Hogue in an attempt to reach a port held by Parma. She had been attacked by English warships off Le Havre, been badly damaged and put in for repairs. Don Pedro de Igueldo, her commander, recorded the arrival of the *Zuniga*.

> I found that the galleass Zuniga, storm beaten with the rudder and spars broken and the ship in a sinking state, had brought up at the anchorage before the town. As she was in great danger, we got her into the port, not without trouble and risk, as she grounded at the entrance to the harbour and was within an inch of sinking. She arrived without food or a drop of water; a day later and they would all have perished of famine. I have brought bread, cider and other necessities and am distributing the rations. They need it badly, so emaciated are they.

Igueldo was actually the purser of the *Santa Ana*, all the more senior officers having been killed. His own ship was beyond repair, so it was decided to strip her of anything of value and sell it to raise funds to repair the *Zuniga*. The French first insisted that any galley slaves who were French had to be released. Several others got away from their chains by pretending to be French and stuttering out a few words of the language.

On 26 December a Scottish ship put into Le Havre. On board were 32 Italians who had survived shipwreck on the northern Irish coast and had managed to get to Scotland. They brought news of many wrecks and tales of survival and woe.

In April 1589 the *Zuniga* put out from Le Havre, but was caught in a storm and had to return. She left again later that summer and finally got home. She was the last of the Spanish ships to get home to Spain, but not the last of the Spaniards. In 1596 a Spanish ship called at Ulster to pass arms to the anti-English Irish clans. She found eight survivors of the *Juliana*, wrecked on the Streedagh Strand, working as mercenaries. They asked to be taken home.

In all some 34 ships or so are known to have been wrecked on the Irish coast. Others went down off Scotland and one on Fair Isle. The distance between the wrecks was over 1,200 miles. They were still foundering in October. Other ships must have gone down far out to sea with nobody to watch, for several Armada ships have no known end.

But for a few the struggle to reach Spain was still continuing. Having escaped the rocky shores of Scotland and Ireland, they were pushing south with tattered sails, shattered hulls and sick crews. And nobody was sicker than the Duke of Medina Sidonia.

XV

The Return Home

The Duke of Medina Sidonia fell ill on 3 September and two days later took to his cot. He had been stricken down by dysentery and spent the next fortnight slipping in and out of delirium. He had recovered enough to sit at his desk by 23 September when the coast of Spain finally came into sight.

A brisk westerly wind was blowing as the *San Martin* tried but failed to get into Corunna. The winds and current blew her on toward Santander, heading toward a ridge of jagged rocks. The ship fired a gun as a signal of distress, then another. Fishing boats put out from Santander to take the crippled ship in tow. A second smaller ship came over the horizon, she was equally battered but managed to get into port by herself.

As the fishing boats pulled alongside and passed up towing lines, one of them was asked to take a sick man ashore. It was Medina Sidonia. He staggered ashore and, as soon as it was realised who he was, took up lodgings. There he again took to his bed. But if his body was sick, his mind seems to have recovered itself. He called for secretaries, paper and messengers. Medina Sidonia would sometimes be so weak he could not sign his name and some days slept almost all day, but he spent the next few weeks working to care for his command. He wrote again and again to King Philip asking for doctors, food and medicines. He cajoled and begged local noblemen to send supplies down to the ports as the ships came in.

The ships and men on them needed all the help they could get. On the *San Martin* alone 180 men had died of wounds and disease during the return journey. Another ship ran aground at Laredo because none of her crew was fit enough to go up to take in the sails that drove her onto the beach. Of the ships that got home to Spain about half never put to sea again. They were so badly riddled by shot and shaken by storms that they were fit only to be broken up for spare parts. They were the lucky ones, at least 50 ships had been lost in the campaign. Half the men who had set out from Corunna were dead. The Armada had not just been defeated, it had been crushed out of existence.

On 1 October Medina Sidonia was loaded into a horse litter, hung around with heavy curtains. The care of the wounded was handed over to Garcia de Villejo, a competent bureaucrat who did his best for the thousands of sick and wounded in the weeks to come. Medina Sidonia, meanwhile, was carried south over the hills toward his home. He did not call at any noble houses on the way, as he would have done in happier times, nor did he stay in any towns or cities. His litter rested overnight in villages and country inns. He reached home in late October, but was not fit to ride a horse until the spring. Those who knew him said that he was never the same again.

In England the fleet was kept at sea long after the Armada had gone for fear that Parma had some secret store of flyboats and might yet come out into the North Sea. Fever broke out on several ships and deaths from disease began to rise. When the news from Ireland made it clear that the Armada was finished, and word from the Dutch showed Parma was busy elsewhere, the ships were finally brought home.

Many of the private ships had already returned. They crews were paid off and the ships put into dock for repairs and, in many cases, reconverted to merchant use. The royal ships were mostly also paid off and sent for repair. A copy of the repair bill survives and shows remarkably little battle damage, most of the work necessary was simply down to wear and tear. The crews suffered because there was a lack of money to pay their wages. Dover and Rochester suffered particularly from men having no money to pay for lodgings or food. Howard and Hawkins paid wages out of their own pockets and were still chasing the government for funds the following spring. Drake took his ships back to Devon where the crews were at least among friends and family while they awaited pay.

The English casualties in the campaign have long been a source of dispute. No ships were lost, that is certain, but there were certainly losses in men. Estimates of men killed in battle have ranged from 100 to 500, and the truth probably lay somewhere between the two. How many succumbed to the diseases that broke out after the fighting was over is hard to say. Contemporary accounts emphasise the distress of the sick men and particularly of those short of money, but little mention is made of actual deaths. There must have been perhaps a few hundred, but it is impossible to be certain.

The defeat of the Armada had been a great escape for England rather than a magnificent victory. The fighting had vindicated the long range gun fighting tactics of the English, but had also shown its limitations. The strict discipline and formation of the Armada had frustrated English attempts to use their guns to best effect. Shipbuilders learned the lessons and by the 1630s were producing ships specialised for gun fighting that were more powerful than anything Drake or Hawkins had even dreamed off. The basic pattern of sea fighting would not change significantly until iron warships carrying gun turrets entered service in the late nineteenth century.

Although England had escaped invasion, and would not come so close to it again for generations, the campaign had not changed the fundamentals of the international scene. Spain remained the richest and most powerful state in the world. England remained a relatively small nation off the coast of Europe earning a living by trade and playing only a minor role in the affairs of the world. Her rise to greatness was yet to come.

The war between England and Spain would drag on until both Philip and Elizabeth were dead and ended in an untidy stalemate that left neither side content. Yet the campaign had an importance far beyond its immediate impact. English mariners looked back on the Armada campaign with pride and hope. In later generations it was viewed as a great victory, the names of Drake and the others were held in high regard.

It could be said in some fairness that in the smoke and thunder of battle during the Armada campaign, England came to believe in herself and to shake off the medieval mindset that still had so many in its grip. England was prepared for greatness, and went on to take full advantage.

What Happened Next

Lord Burghley remained the leading figure in the government of Queen Elizabeth until his death in 1598. His family remained active in politics and government for generations, acquiring such titles as Earl of Exeter, Viscount Chelwood, Earl of Salisbury and Baron Wimbledon. The most recent member of the family to serve in government retired in 1957.

Captain Francisco Cuellar survived his shipwreck in Ireland to travel home to Spain by way of Scotland and the Netherlands. So far as is known he did not go to sea again.

Sir Francis Drake saw his prestige and fame rise even higher than before as a result of the Armada campaign. In 1589 he led an English naval expedition to Portugal. In 1596 he died while on a raiding expedition to the West Indies. He was buried at sea in Nombre Dios Bay.

Elizabeth I remained Queen of England to her death in 1603. Her later years were blighted by famines due to crop failures and by financial problems brought on by the costs of the war with Spain, as she had foreseen.

Sir Martin Frobisher was killed in 1594 at the Siege of Crozon.

John Hawkins briefly returned to his desk after the Armada campaign, but then returned to sea to raid Spanish possessions and ships. He died of disease in 1595 at Puerto Rico.

Lord Howard of Effingham continued his Naval career by sacking Cadiz in 1596. He thereafter returned to court and in 1603 held the hand of Queen Elizabeth as she died. He remained popular with the new monarch, King James of Scotland, but retired from public service around 1610 and died in 1624.

Robert Dudley, the Earl of Leicester, died suddenly on 14 September 1588 just days after supervising the disbandment of the army at Tilbury. Poison was suspected at the time, but never proved.

Don Alonso de Leyva died in the wreck of the Gironda.

Duke of Medina Sidonia returned to royal service in 1590 but never again held a major command or senior appointment. He died in 1619.

Miguel de Oquendo died of disease within days of returning to Spain in 1588.

The Duke of Parma continued to command the Spanish forces in the Netherlands. He was pulled back from a successful offensive in 1589 on the orders of King Philip of Spain to lead an invasion of France after the assassination of King Henry III. He died in 1592 following a long illness brought on by a wound received at Rouen in 1591.

Philip II continued as King of Spain. The later years of his reign were marred by revolts in various dominions, even within Spain itself. In 1596 he was forced to declare Spain bankrupt and plunged his empire into a financial crisis from which it arguably never recovered. He died in 1598.

Sir Walter Raleigh fell from favour with Queen Elizabeth in 1592 when he secretly married one of her maids of honour, Bessie Throckmorton. In 1595 he led a voyage of exploration to South America, sailing some way up the Orinoco. He served with Lord Howard of Effingham at the sack of Cadiz in 1596 and was then appointed Governor of Jersey. In 1603 he opposed the succession of James of Scotland and was imprisoned. In prison he wrote works on the theory of warfare and constitutional studies as well as several poems and began a *History of the World*. He was executed by King James in 1618.

Juan Martinez de Recalde died soon after returning to Spain in the autumn of 1588.

Don Pedro de Valdes spent several comfortable months in England living with Richard Drake, brother of Sir Francis, at Esher in Surrey. He was eventually released along with his men after Parma paid a ransom.

Sir Francis Walsingham retired from active government service in the winter of 1588 to devote himself to religious contemplation. He died in 1590.

Index